EDUCATION PO

Evidence of equity and e

Stephen Gorard

First published in Great Britain in 2018 by

Policy Press
University of Bristol
1-9 Old Park Hill
Bristol
BS2 8BB
UK
t: +44 (0)117 954 5940
pp-info@bristol.ac.uk
www.policypress.co.uk

North America office:
Policy Press
c/o The University of Chicago Press
1427 East 60th Street
Chicago, IL 60637, USA
t: +1 773 702 7700
f: +1 773-702-9756
sales@press.uchicago.edu
www.press.uchicago.edu

© Policy Press 2018

British Library Cataloguing in Publication Data
A catalogue record for this book is available from the British Library

Library of Congress Cataloging-in-Publication Data
A catalog record for this book has been requested

978-1-4473-4214-4 hardback
978-1-4473-4215-1 paperback
978-1-4473-4216-8 ePdf
978-1-4473-4218-2 ePub
978-1-4473-4219-9 Mobi

Cover design by Robin Hawes
Front cover image: istock
Printed and bound in Great Britain by CMP, Poole
Policy Press uses environmentally responsible print partners

This book is dedicated to the memory
of my sister Heather

Contents

List of figures and tables

Figures

Tables

List of abbreviations

AERA	American Educational Research Association
ASC	Annual Schools Census, the official dataset of all schools in England including school intakes
CA	contextualised admissions, a way of taking disadvantage into account when admitting students to university
CU	Children's University
CSE	Certificate of Secondary Education, a qualification that stopped in the 1980s
CVA	contextualised value-added, a measure of student progress based on prior attainment and background
DfE	Department for Education, the main government department dealing with education in England; also known as DCSF (Department for Children, Schools and Families), DfEE (Department for Education and Employment) and DfES (Department for Education and Skills) during the period covered in this book
EAL	English as an additional (or second) language
EEF	Educational Endowment Foundation
EMA	Education Maintenance Allowance (now only a policy in Scotland)
ES	'effect' size, or standardised difference/pattern involving two or more groups; includes here Hedge's g (difference between means) and Pearson's R (correlation)
ESRC	Economic and Social Research Council
EverFSM6	an indicator representing that the pupil had been eligible for free school meals for at least one of the prior six years
FE	further education, similar to Key Stage 5, a phase of education between Key Stage 4 and higher education
FSM	free school meals; eligibility for FSM is used as a legal indicator of family poverty
GCE	General Certificate of Education, a qualification that stopped in the 1980s
GCSE	General Certificate of Secondary Education, standard qualification for those aged 16
GS	Gorard segregation index

HE	higher education, in university or college
HEI	Higher Education Institution, a university or college of higher education
HESA	Higher Education Statistics Agency, holds records of all applicants and intakes to higher education
IDACI	income deprivation affecting children index
IT	information technology
ITT	initial teacher training
KS	Key Stage of education until recently, ending with standard attainment measure for all state-funded pupils; includes Key Stage 1 up to second year of primary, Key Stage 2 at end of primary, Key Stage 3 in first years of secondary, Key Stage 4 up to age 16 and Key Stage 5 up to age 18
$M|D|$	mean absolute deviation (also known as MAD)
NNTD	number of counterfactual cases needed to disturb a finding
NPD	National Pupil Database, a record of the characteristics, schools and attainment of all pupils at school in England
NQT	newly qualified teacher
OECD	Organisation for Economic Co-operation and Development, also host of PISA
P4C	Philosophy for Children
PISA	Programme for International Student Assessment
PTR	pupil-to-teacher ratio
R	Pearson's R, an estimate of the correlation between two or more variables, also used in regression
RCT	randomised control trial, which I prefer to the term 'randomised controlled trial'
RQ	research question
SCITT	school-based initial teacher training
SEN	special educational needs or additional needs including disadvantage; the terms used change over time, but SEN is the current Department for Education term used in official datasets
SES	socio-economic status
SD	standard deviation
SR	segregation ratio
STEM	science, technology, engineering and mathematics
TVAAS	Tennessee Value-Added Assessment System

UCAS   Universities and Colleges Admissions Service, handles UK-wide undergraduate applications to higher education

UTC   university technical college

VA   value-added, a measure of student progress based on prior attainment

VC   voluntary-controlled schools, usually of Roman Catholic faith

WAG   Welsh Assembly Government, or now more usually the Welsh Government, devolved from England in terms of most education policy since 2001

YU   Youth United

About the author

Stephen Gorard is Professor of Education and Public Policy at Durham University. He is a member of the UK DfE Associate Pool, the British Academy grants panel, the ESRC commissioning panel for Strategic Networks, and Fellow of the Academy of Social Sciences.

He regularly gives advice to governments and other policy-makers, and is a widely read and cited methodologist, involved in international and regional capacity-building activities, and used as an adviser on the design of rigorous evaluations by central and local governments, NGOs and charities.

Preface

This book is partly based on my inaugural lecture at Durham University in 2015, and for the most part, on my most recent research, especially the two Economic and Social Research Council (ESRC) studies listed below. It therefore covers 20 years of ongoing policy-related research, around £20 million of charitable and research council funding, published in around 1,000 papers, chapters, books, other articles and invited plenary presentations. I have worked and published on pre-school to the third age, using ideas and techniques from economics, geography, family and childhood, sociology, psychology and philosophy. I have given advice to policy-makers of all persuasions, advice that has been both acted on and ignored in equal measure.

Despite this range, many people see me as that person who writes about methods, for example, or who is solely concerned with widening participation, or the supply of scientists, or who focuses on school intakes, or who criticises school effectiveness work, and so on. In fact, I do all of these and more, and felt that it was time to put all of this material together with the newest findings into one book, although there is not enough space to cover my work on randomised control trials (RCTs) of attainment in maths and English, in crime prevention or health promotion, most of my work on the use of technology in education, or on research methods.

Each substantive chapter of this book represents part of a theme or strand of my research, covering education from early life to later adulthood. The book looks at recent, current and likely future policies in the UK in particular (it has to focus on somewhere, because actual laws are context-specific), with reference to related developments internationally. The research is both large-scale and in-depth, based on evidence from the home countries of the UK, and on work in all EU28 countries, as well as the US, Pakistan and Japan. It deals with worldwide themes such as school choice and school improvement. Underlying each theme is a series of systematic reviews funded by the Department for Education (DfE), Joseph Rowntree Foundation, Nuffield, European Union (EU), Brookings Institute and ESRC, considering over 100,000 research reports in aggregate. The research includes consideration of population data for all students since 1976, large-scale international surveys, focus groups with children and thousands of household interviews with individual learners. There are few, if any, books dealing with such a wide range of empirical material, or such a range of material about the wider and societal outcomes of education lifelong.

All of the issues, from selective education or contextualised admission to university and the supply of teachers, are hot topics in the UK and further afield. This book distinguishes between the possible causes of poor opportunities in education that are largely fixed for individuals – such as their sex, health record or family background – and those that are more modifiable – such as the school attended, area of residence or their motivation for learning. It is the latter that are the most important, because these can be of most use to anyone wishing to improve the educational chances of the most disadvantaged in society.

The book is as non-technical as possible, intended for education policy-makers, their advisers, those who teach about education policy, and, of course, for all students and researchers in this area.

Acknowledgements

The ESRC funded some of the newest work included (ES/N012046/1, ES/N01166X/1). Special thanks go to the fantastic colleagues I have worked with over the years – including, but not limited to, Nadia Siddiqui, Beng Huat See, Vikki Boliver, Neil Selwyn, Patrick White, Emma Smith, Chris Taylor, John Fitz, Gareth Rees, John Furlong, Ralph Fevre and Jane Salisbury. Thanks also to all of the policy-makers, staff, students and families who took part in the various studies.

Part 1: Introduction

ONE

Introduction: themes of the book

The policy evidence cycle

A cosy idea for many of those working in an area of public policy such as education is that policy-making is evidence-informed. Policy-makers and their advisers come up with ideas for changes in policy, which may or may not be based on solid research evidence. Some of these ideas are implemented and can be evaluated in terms of their policy objectives. Policy-makers and their advisers then react to this newer evidence, and the improving cycle of policy continues.

In reality, of course, the cycle is nothing like this. In education, new policies and interventions are rarely based on good prior evidence of effectiveness and of their side effects. Many policy areas are evidence-resistant, and examples of these are discussed in this book. Evidence-resistant here means that the policies are proposed and implemented, even though the clear weight of evidence is against them. Of the rest, too many policies are still not evaluated robustly at all. This means we can have no good idea whether they work as intended and whether they have damaging side effects. Of the few that are robustly evaluated, as far as this is possible with live policy issues, many are then found to have been ineffective or even harmful. But their ineffectiveness does not lead to them being improved or cancelled. The policy cycle does not seem to permit policy-makers to backtrack like this. Rather, policies are seemingly just left to wither or until they are formally reversed by a change of government. Again, examples are described in the book. This leads to at least three kinds of damage to society.

First and most obviously there is the cost. Large amounts of public and other money are spent around the world on educational initiatives that have no basis in evidence and little chance of working, and are continued overlong once their ineffectiveness has been revealed. Second, there is the possibility of harm from untested interventions for those learners in every generation who have only their one chance to get it right. There is *always* a kind of opportunity cost, given that every unwarranted policy uses time, effort and resources that could have been used for a genuine improvement. And finally, this chaotic approach inhibits the search for good policy – of a kind that would justify the costs and lead to real improvements in the future.

The problems uncovered in this book include exaggerating supposed 'crises' such as high failure rates at schools, the increasing student sex gap and cultures of laddishness, the unfairness of university admissions processes, poor social mobility and problems in the supply of teachers and scientists in particular. There are also equally exaggerated accounts of the success and power of new types of schools such as academies, older types such as grammar schools, approaches such as learning styles or enhanced feedback, improved leadership, the use of technology and setting targets in education. Because these areas are so commonly misunderstood, even if a good policy were available it would probably be deployed to address the wrong problem (or wrong interpretation of the problem). This misdiagnosis or failure to specify more carefully the precise issue or pattern to be addressed by policy is one of the biggest causes of money and opportunities being wasted, endangering the progress of learners. The new political arithmetic approach (see Gorard, with Taylor 2004) utilised in this book shows a way to help overcome this.

Of course, evidence cannot and should not determine education policy. It should simply help to inform policy-making, so that where a policy-maker has a clear objective, the best evidence can help to achieve that objective safely and efficiently, but the evidence itself should be largely neutral about the objective. For example, the most secure evidence might suggest that a particular education policy would increase the average attainment of students but also increase the average difference between high and low attainers. So how this evidence should be used depends on the policy objectives. If raising average attainment is paramount, the policy could be deemed a success. But if making the system fairer is a priority, the policy may be a failure (although, as this book shows throughout, raising attainment overall and reducing attainment gaps are not necessarily in tension).

Evidence must be 'multiplied' by the values of any policy objectives to reach an appropriate decision. The values themselves are not evidence-based in the same way, and it is possible to argue against a policy both because it has what appear to be incorrect values or, accepting its objective, because it will not work in the way it has been implemented. This book is mostly about the·latter issues.

Although my work has been concerned with improving the quality and provision of education of all kinds, where this leads to a tension with fairness (as in the hypothetical example above) I have tended to favour concern for fairness or equity over average outcomes. Partly this depends on a consideration of what education is for. Education prepares people for the world of work (see Chapters 11 and 12), or for more education (Chapter 10). It socialises them into society or gives them skills for life (Chapter 9). It provides them with a general knowledge about the world. And it keeps young children secure and engaged while their parents work. However, one of the main reasons that initial education is free, compulsory, universal and state-regulated in most countries is so that what, and how much, children learn is not just determined by their family circumstances. Education up to a certain level is one of the guaranteed rights for all children and young people in a civilised society.

These issues are revisited in Chapter 13 after consideration of the kind of evidence available in a wide range of education policy areas.

Structure of the book

The book is in three main parts. Following this introductory chapter, Chapter 2 illustrates what I have learned about the conduct of education research, some methodological innovations that I have proposed and used, and an outline of the methods used in the substantive Chapters 3 to 12. Chapter 3 then sets out the patterns of attainment and participation in education from early to later life – patterns based on geography, era, income, family background and personal characteristics such as age or ethnic origin. Chapters 4 to 12 examine possible explanations for, and solutions to, these patterns, starting with who one goes to school with and ending with the kind of occupation one is involved in. These chapters generally move towards consideration of older learners and later phases of formal education, and also towards more non-cognitive outcomes of education and learning beyond institutions such as schools and universities. Chapter 13 summarises what has been learned over 20 years, and what this might mean for researchers, research funders, policy-makers and educational systems worldwide.

TWO

The nature of
the evidence assembled

This chapter is in two parts. The first describes my approach to the conduct of research, and some of the innovations I have adopted or invented over 20 years. The second describes the kinds of designs, data and methods of analysis used in the substantive Chapters 3 to 12. There is no space for full details of the methods of each study, but all are referenced for readers to follow as they wish. If readers find this chapter hard to start with, it can be skipped and picked up again at the end.

My approach to research

One strand of my research work over 20 years, since 1997 (Gorard, 1997a), has been writing about the conduct of research itself, based on my own experiences, observation of the work of others and reading copious research reports for reviews of evidence. Part of this writing has been about the role of funders and research organisations (Gorard, 2002a, 2004a; Gorard and Cook, 2007). Much has been capacity-building and development work intended to benefit new researchers (Gorard, 2017a, b), including on combining methods (Gorard, 2002b; Gorard, with Taylor 2004), perhaps through design experiments (Sloane and Gorard, 2003; Gorard et al, 2004a). In retrospect, it is clear that much of the writing has been about simplifying the process of research for others, including showing that supposed divisions, such as the widespread 'qualitative':'quantitative' schism, are unfounded in any way, including philosophically (Gorard, 2002b, 2004b; Gorard and Smith, 2006; Symonds and Gorard, 2010). In the end, there *is* only research (Gorard and Siddiqui, 2018a).

Using large-scale data at an aggregated level tends to emphasise the role of structure and even predictability in people's lifelong education trajectories. The same factors rarely appear in individuals' own in-depth accounts of their lives, which tend to emphasise choice, the role of others and serendipity. Using only one of these forms of data in research would be likely to impoverish and even bias the findings, and any practical conclusions drawn from them. Therefore, both have a role in studying any research area. I apply this simple holistic idea to teaching, research capacity-building, knowledge transfer and all of my research. It makes the work simpler, the communication of findings easier to wide audiences and reviews of evidence more secure and less biased.

The current push in the UK and elsewhere towards more 'quantitative' work and more complex methods of analysis is therefore misguided (Gorard, 2003a, 2007a; Gorard et al, 2004b). There is a special problem with the abuse of inferential statistics (Gorard, 2010a, 2014a, 2015a, 2017c; White and Gorard, 2017). Working with numbers, as a matter of course, as part of any research study does not have to involve significance tests and related concepts, and it can and should be simple (Gorard, 2001, 2006a, b, 2010b, 2017d). At present, we need greater emphasis on initial research design, independent of subsequent methods of data collection, where the design permits a simple and intuitive approach to analysis (Gorard, 2010c, 2013a).

The research process, as revealed by conducting the projects described in this book, seems to me to be both more sophisticated and less inhibiting than is commonly portrayed. There is a clear spiral of research within programmes, fields or topics of study, moving from consideration of what we already know (as in Phase 1 in Figure 2.1) to developing ideas and artefacts, then to providing robust evidence, and eventually monitoring the results as they are used in policy (Phase 7).

Different kinds of research questions would be suitably addressed in successive phases, from the descriptive such as 'What do we know about this issue?' in Phase 1 to the causal 'Does this approach work to improve this issue?' in Phase 6. Each question in each phase requires different research designs (Gorard, 2013a). A comparative design might be suitable for descriptive work, a longitudinal approach could be used to identify risk factors for an undesirable educational outcome, and a quasi-experimental approach to try and modify those risk factors. None of these designs is related to specific methods of data collection or analysis. A longitudinal study is longitudinal whether it involves collecting observations, survey responses or physical measurements, or all three at once. And it doesn't matter whether, for example, those survey responses are collected face-to-face, using Skype, by mail or online. Some methods may turn out to be more useful or more frequent in some phases than others, but generally, data from several sources is collected and used in parallel in any phase – and this is illustrated throughout the book in my own work.

Figure 2.1: The full research cycle/spiral

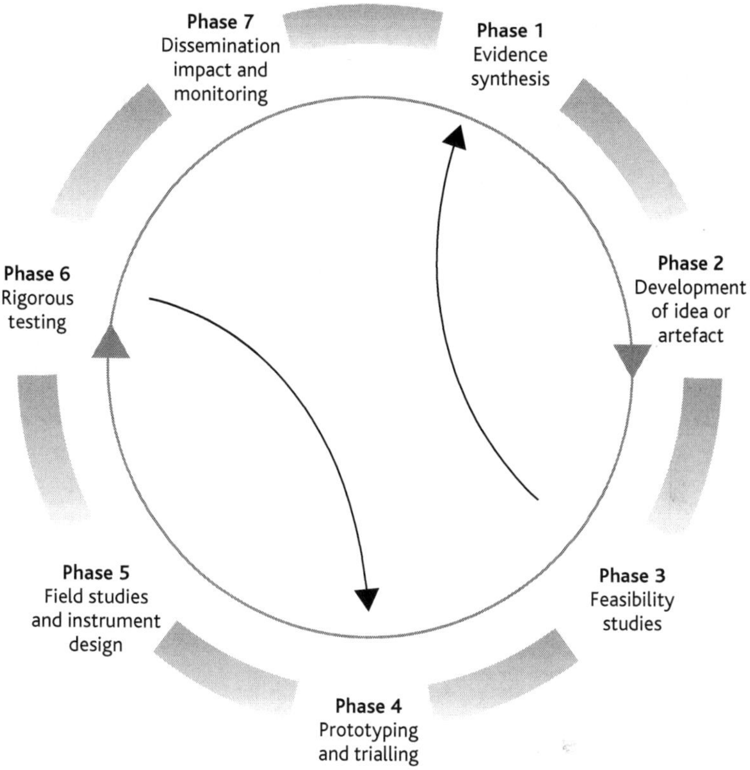

Examples of my other innovations

Over and above this general approach to making research as simple as possible, I have proposed and used a number of specific innovations in methods of research, which are used in the subsequent chapters of this book. The first two are about how we can judge whether to trust the findings of a piece of research.

The sieve

In order to help research readers to assess the security of the findings for any study, I have suggested the following procedure (Gorard et al, 2017a). We can judge the quality of each research report and therefore the trustworthiness of its findings based on its design, scale (sample size), attrition (missing data), outcome measurements (standardised, pre-specified), appropriateness, fidelity and validity. The ensuing five possible levels of quality are summarised in Table 2.1. Each study is

Table 2.1: A 'sieve' to assist in the estimation of trustworthiness of any research study

Design	Scale	Dropout	Data quality	Threats	Rating
Strong design for research question	Large number of cases (per comparison group)	Minimal attrition, no evidence of impact on findings	Standardised, pre-specified, independent	No evidence of diffusion, demand or other threat	4
Good design for research question	Medium number of cases (per comparison group)	Some attrition (or initial imbalance)	Pre-specified, not standardised or not independent	Little evidence of diffusion, demand or other threat	3
Weak design for research question	Small number of cases (per comparison group)	Moderate attrition (or initial imbalance)	Not pre-specified but valid in context	Evidence of diffusion, demand or other threat	2
Very weak design for research question	Very small number of cases (per comparison group)	High attrition (or initial imbalance)	Issues of validity or appropriateness	Strong indication of diffusion, demand or other threat	1
No consideration of design	A trivial scale of study or N is unclear	Attrition huge or not reported	Poor reliability, too many outcomes, weak measures	No consideration of threats to validity	0

given a rating representing its lowest row description for any of the first five columns. This approach is used throughout the book to assess the quality of research – my own and that of others.

The first step is to identify the information on each of these issues from the report of the research being assessed. If the report does not include important information, or is written in such a way that the reader cannot understand it, the research must be rated as having no security and is not to be trusted. A good report will usually have a section detailing the limitations of the study. While this can be a valuable shortcut to assessing its value, beware where this section is cursory and so tries to reassure the reader without really considering all of the issues in this sieve.

Many studies do not have a clear design, and this is a weakness. If the research question (RQ) is about changes over time, then a longitudinal design is required. If the RQ compares outcomes for two or more groups, this should involve a comparative design. If the RQ is causal, a stronger design such as a randomised control trial (RCT) or regression discontinuity should be deployed.

A large study is more believable than a small study, given that all other factors are the same (same design, dropout and so on). And this is true whatever the design or methods of data collection and analysis. When I began life as an academic many studies did not even report the number of cases. Most studies nowadays do report the number of cases, but care still needs to be taken. The strength of any study rests on the size of the smallest group in any comparison. And the number of cases can mean the number eligible to take part, contacted, taking part, analysed or a range of other things.

Perhaps the biggest problem with the reporting of most research is lack of clarity about missing data. All missing data from a planned study is a source of bias in the results, because there will be a reason why the data is missing (it is not random). And data can be missing at many stages and levels and for many reasons. All missing data reduces the trustworthiness of evidence. The sieve, including the other columns in it, is described fully in Gorard et al (2017a).

Number of counterfactual cases needed to disturb a finding (NNTD)

A simple way to encapsulate how trustworthy any study is according to several of the factors above involves converting the finding or 'effect' size (ES) into a number representing how different any missing cases or data would have to be in order for the ES to become zero (Gorard et al, 2017a). For example, in a comparison between two groups their average scores might differ, and this can be presented as an ES by subtracting one mean from the other and dividing the answer by the overall standard deviation (SD). But it is not always clear how substantial this difference really is. The number of counterfactual cases needed to disturb the finding (NNTD) involves creating a counterfactual score, such as one SD (of the mean of the larger group) away from the mean of the smaller group in the opposite direction to the ES. The number of these counterfactual scores (running against the finding) that can be added to the smallest group in the comparison before the ES disappears is a standard measure of the strength of the 'effect'. NNTD is a useful measure of the sensitivity of the scale of the *findings* (and their variability as represented by the SD used to compute the ES), taking into account the scale of the *study*.

This number can be more easily calculated as the ES multiplied by the number of cases in the smallest group. Then the number of initial cases missing data (attrition) can be subtracted from the NNTD. If the result is still above zero, it means that even in the unlikely situation that all missing data were in the opposite direction to the main finding (counterfactual), the ES would still be non-zero. This would suggest a strong finding. The larger the NNTD is, after attrition has been subtracted, the stronger the finding.

Based on a large number of studies (Gorard et al, 2016a), NNTD of 50 can be considered a very strong and secure finding, given how tough this definition is. Using this as a working assumption, Figure 2.2 shows the number of cases needed in each group (assuming equal size) for any ES from 0.1 to 0.5, in order to obtain NNTD=50 with no attrition. As expected, the number of cases needed decreases exponentially as the projected ES increases. For a typical education intervention or comparison, with an expected ES of 0.25, the number of cases needed per comparison group is 200. This applies however the data is collected and whatever form it is in, but most work in education is of nothing like this scale.

Reviewing and synthesising evidence

I have used the sieve, NNTD and other related ideas in major reviews of prior research evidence. As discussed later, in Chapter 7, huge meta-analyses of prior research can be very misleading because they confuse different kinds of studies and take no account of research quality. On the other hand, some systematic reviews simply exclude studies that do not meet any arbitrary standard, such as a minimum of 10 cases.

Figure 2.2: Projected 'effect' size (ES) and number of cases, for NNTD=50

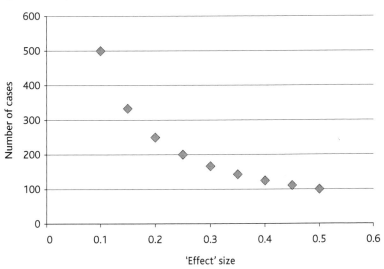

And this can be equally misleading because 10 studies of 10 cases each must be at least as important as one study with 100 cases.

Instead of these approaches I have retained and cited as many studies as possible in any review, but graded each study singly using the sieve, NNTD and other factors. Only then have I tried to summarise the evidence, as in the hypothetical example of Table 2.2. This intervention has 19 studies relevant to it, after widespread searching (see below). There may have been more studies discussing this intervention but not evaluating its impact, and so these would have been ignored for the impact summary here (but perhaps used in setting out the background to the review). Using the sieve, the studies are classified into quality bands, and divided into those that suggest the intervention worked, and the rest. The ensuing distribution is typical of any area of education research. The small and weak studies will tend to suggest positive (and exciting) outcomes. This is usually due to publication or other bias. The larger, more robust studies will tend to be more mixed. Table 2.2 suggests that, on current evidence and using my approach to reviewing, this hypothetical intervention does not work. However, vote counting or meta-analysis of all studies without suitable weighting for quality might easily suggest completely the opposite conclusion.

Mean absolute deviation (M|D|)

The next three innovations discussed here are indices used to help encapsulate the strength of a pattern or trend.

Around 100 years ago, the 'standard' deviation became the usual way of summarising the variation in a set of figures. Many people imagine that SD is the average deviation (that is, the average amount by which any figure differs from the average for all figures in the set). Of course, it is not; it is more complicated than that and involves squaring and square-rooting figures. This makes the kinds of statistics based on SD more complex as well. The simpler average deviation itself is termed the mean absolute deviation (or $M|D|$). It is calculated as the average of the distance of all figures from the average of all figures, ignoring the direction of the difference. No squaring is involved, and so it is

Table 2.2: Quality and impact summary: 'hypothetical policy intervention'

	Effective	Ineffective or harmful
Higher quality – 3 or better	0	2
Medium quality – 2	0	1
Lower quality – 0 or 1	13	3

simpler to comprehend and compute, and there is no distortion of outlying figures.

My paper proposing reverting to the use of the mean absolute deviation has now been cited as a basis for using it in almost every area of research, from astronomy through to health to the finance industry (Gorard, 2005a). It is simpler and easier to understand than the SD, and leads to the simplification of all that follows from it.

Mean absolute deviation effect size

One thing that follows from the M|D| is the M|D| effect size (Gorard, 2013b, 2015b). This is based on the difference between the means of two groups divided by their overall M|D|. The numerator is the same as in more traditional effect sizes such as Cohen or Hedges' – it is the difference between two means. The denominator is simply the M|D| rather than being a variant of the SD. This gives a fairer and less distorted assessment of the difference between means.

And the M|D| is also increasingly being used in correlation and regression and other statistics, in order to simplify these approaches as well, and so create a more intuitive kind of statistics altogether.

Gorard segregation index (GS)

When first considering the issue of the segregation of school intakes in terms of any measure of disadvantage (see Chapter 4 later), I devised an index of segregation, now termed the Gorard segregation index, or GS. GS is the proportion of potentially disadvantaged students in a school system who would have to exchange schools with another (non-disadvantaged) student for there to be no segregation by disadvantage between schools in that school system (or the area under consideration). However, GS is effectively the same thing as the much earlier Hoover index (Hoover, 1941), the Delta index (Duncan et al, 1961), the Women in Employment index, the Robin Hood Index, and the Student Change index (Glenn, 2011). Each school's residual for GS is the absolute value of the result of subtracting the population proportion of all students in each school from the population proportion of potentially disadvantaged students (such as those living in poverty) in each school.

As with the M|D| and its derivatives, there are more complex alternatives used as indices of segregation, most of which involve squaring and square-rooting, and so distort what is being measured by giving more emphasis to extreme scores. GS is simpler, more intuitive and easier to calculate.

Since first publication, other commentators have tried to suggest that GS is deficient in one or more respects, which led to considerable debate in academic journals (see, for example, Gorard, 2000a, 2004c, 2007b, 2011a; Taylor et al, 2003; Gorard and Fitz, 2006). It is now clear to most, if not all, that GS is a valid index yielding the same substantive results as the dissimilarity index and many others, when there is no abrupt change in the level of the underlying indicators (Gorard, 2009a). When there is an abrupt change in the relevant measures, it is the GS index that is most strongly invariant to composition (Gorard and Taylor, 2002a).

Attempting to capture non-cognitive outcomes

As shown later in Chapter 9, I have long been interested in the wider outcomes from education such as students' sense of justice and responsibility. Over time and with assistance from others, I have developed a number of single-item questions to assess a range of non-cognitive responses from students. The questionnaire items come from previously validated or standard instruments, provided by the Office for National Statistics (ONS), the Cabinet Office, literature reviews, prior studies by the evaluators, and professional and scholarly advice. The items selected were considered measurable and malleable in individuals by their authors, and deemed important by stakeholders either in their own right or because they are linked to behavioural outcomes including participation at school. All have clear audit trails leading to their derivation. The items have been piloted and tested with many thousands of students aged 8 to 16 across the world.

The core is now a set of 11 single-item Likert-style questions on a range of wider outcomes covering concepts including teamwork, communication, motivation, self-esteem, confidence, resilience and civic mindedness. Some of these items are reverse-coded to try and encourage pupils to focus on the meaning of each one. A further set of items consists of short stories (vignettes) in which the socially desirable responses are not immediately obvious. These questions were specifically developed to assess ideas such as social responsibility and generosity. There is also a question group about pupils' career aspirations and educational intentions.

Taking errors seriously

In most studies I have conducted I have been concerned with missing data (Gorard, 2013c). Taking this seriously can lead to key and useful findings. For example, in all datasets there is always missing data, even in official datasets such as the National Pupil Database (NPD) in England. When the 2015 Key Stage 4 (KS4) cohort started schooling in England, about 9 per cent of them had unknown status about their eligibility for free school meals (FSM). FSM-eligibility in England is a long-standing indicator of family poverty for any student. The 15 per cent or so FSM-eligible students nationally have lower levels of attainment at school, on average, and are less likely than their peers to make progress over time in terms of attainment (DfE, 2017), continue to post-compulsory education or training, and to attend higher education (HE) (Gorard and See, 2013). But pupils with missing values for FSM are even more often living in state care than non-FSM pupils, and more likely to have moved schools recently and at a non-traditional time in the year (see Table 2.3). So, they are both more disadvantaged and more mobile than their peers. Those pupils without FSM scores are more likely to be from a minority ethnic group in England, and also have lower attainment than even those known to be FSM-eligible.

At present, such pupils with missing values for FSM are assumed to be non-FSM (that is, not disadvantaged) by the Department for Education (DfE). This means that all schools with any of these pupils will not receive the additional pupil premium funding for them, or have their disadvantaged intake taken into account in school performance figures (Gorard, 2012a).

Therefore, ignoring cases with missing data when deciding which pupils are disadvantaged would be unjust because some of the most deprived and so most deserving of assistance would be put aside in favour of others. However, using the fact of missing data as an indicator in itself would also be unjust and would offer assistance to some of the least deprived pupils (who may simply have transferred from another

Table 2.3: Percentage of each FSM category by other characteristics, maintained schools, England, 2015

	Not FSM-eligible	FSM-eligible	Missing FSM code
Black African origin	1	5	9
Student joined in last two years	2	3	13
Student joined mid-year	5	11	29
In care while at this school	1	1	3

home country of the UK but are not part of the NPD). It would also provide an incentive for families not to provide clear data to schools and universities. Similar problems arise with almost all variables in any education dataset.

However, the problem of missing data does not end there, and I seem to be alone among education researchers in being concerned about the propagation of initial errors during ensuing calculations (Gorard, 2006a). When numbers such as education measurements and frequencies are used in calculations, any initial errors in those numbers propagate through the calculation. For example, subtracting two similar size numbers, each with errors caused by missing data or anything else, can yield a small answer that is almost entirely composed of the error parts from the original numbers. This can influence the results of an evaluation such as an RCT, and is a major problem in studies of school effectiveness or similar (see Chapter 6).

Ethics

About 15 years ago I proposed a second principle of research ethics in addition to the usual one about not harming the participants in research (Gorard, 2002c). It drew attention to the importance of considering the non-participants in research – effectively, everyone else who either pays for the research to be conducted or who could be affected by the results. From their perspective the most important thing is that research is done well, and that if the results have any real-life impact, then those results must be trustworthy (see above). This principle demands that funders and researchers put a much greater emphasis on trustworthiness than at present. My second principle of ethics is now cited and used in a number of guidelines and resources, including *An EU code of ethics for socio-economic research* (Dench et al, 2004) and *Ethics guidelines* (SRA, 2003).

Methods used in this book

The last part of this chapter outlines the further methods used to generate the evidence illustrated in Chapters 3 to 12.

Systematic reviews

Systematic reviews are, or should be, part of Phase 1 (see Figure 2.1 above) of any investigation. In most of the areas covered in this book I have conducted systematic reviews of the pre-existing literature, amounting to a total of around 100,000 distinct reports. This involved searching a range of electronic databases, although these are increasingly linked to each other and to more generic search engines such as Google Scholar. The databases included Web of Science (Science Citation Index; Social Sciences Citation Index; Arts and Humanities Citation Index; Conference Proceedings Science Citation Index; Conference Proceedings Social Science and Humanities Citation Index; Book Citation Index – Science, Social Science and Humanities, Emerging Sources Citation Index), EBSCOhost (American doctoral dissertations, British Educational Index, Child development and adolescent studies, eBook collection, Educational abstracts, Educational admin abstracts, ERIC, Library, information science and technology abstracts, MathSciNet via EBSCOhost, MEDLINE, PsyArticles, PsycINFO), ASSIA, Australian Education Index, Research papers in Economics (RePEc), Social services abstracts and Sociological abstracts. These were supplemented by hand-searching of recent journal articles, existing knowledge and following up references in any previous reviews uncovered by the searches.

Each search was based on a list of search terms, specific to each review, and linked together by Boolean operators. For example, the basic syntax used in Gorard et al (2016a), a study of primary school pedagogy with a focus on evaluations, was:

'Pedagog★' or 'teaching effectiveness' or 'teacher effectiveness' or 'classroom practi★' or 'classroom strategy★' or 'teaching strategy★' or 'teaching approach★' or 'teaching style' or 'effective instruction' or 'teach★ practi★' or 'teacher knowledge' or 'teach★ skill★' or 'whole class teaching'

AND

'Primary' or 'elementary' or 'middle school' or 'Key Stage 1' or 'Key Stage 2' or 'K-12' or 'Grade★' or 'infant school' or 'junior school' or 'mobile children' or 'migrant★'

'School outcomes' or 'learning outcomes' or 'academic performance' or 'standardi★ tests' or 'exam★' or 'key stage' or 'Grades' or 'assessments' or 'attainment' or 'Grade retention' or 'Grade point average'

AND

'Trial' or 'experiment' or 'intervention' or 'randomi★ control★ trial' or 'RCT' or 'regression discontinuity' or 'causal evidence'

A key purpose of any such search was to gather 'grey' unpublished literature as well as published work, as far as possible, in order to reduce the possibility of publication bias. I was generally looking for reports of research available in English over the past 20 years. This led to thousands of possible reports for each review, even after duplicates and a few obvious errors had been deleted. The next stage was to use the titles and abstracts to delete further reports now found not to meet the search criteria in practice. The remaining pieces were summarised in terms of the study design, scale, attrition and reviewers' calculation of effect sizes (if enough details were provided), plus judgements about the clarity of reporting (evidence of biased reporting, threats to validity) and the quality of the evidence (using the sieve described above, see Table 2.1). Further reports were deleted at this stage where the quality of reporting was so poor or deficient in detail that the research itself was impossible to judge in terms of design, scale and so on.

The results of such a review cannot be considered complete or definitive. However, the main conclusions of any such large unbiased review are unlikely to be changed substantially by the uncovering of research that was missed. Summary results for each are presented in ensuing chapters.

Secondary data

Using existing datasets to investigate a field before venturing further is another key element of Phase 1 of the research cycle. Like systematic reviews, the use of such secondary data can answer some research questions on its own. In fact, Phase 2 onwards in the research cycle really only applies if the prior existing evidence of all kinds is insufficient (Gorard, 2012b).

In different studies over 20 years I have used official figures and databases such as Edubase, the Annual Schools Census, Census of Population, Electoral Register, Labour Force Survey, Longitudinal Study of Young People in England, results of statutory assessments provided by the Welsh Joint Education Committee (WJEC), National Institute for Adult and Continuing Education (NIACE) survey of adult learners, the NPD, Universities and Colleges Admissions Service (UCAS) and Higher Education Statistics Agency (HESA) datasets, including the graduate destination survey. Other datasets include individual student data for those on initial teacher training (ITT) courses in England, supplied by the Teacher Training Agency (as it then was), a DfE national survey of newly qualified teachers (NQTs), Ofsted inspection results for teacher training courses and Ofsted inspection reports on schools. International data includes the Organisation for Economic Co-operation and Development's (OECD) Programme for International Student Assessment (PISA) over several years. Sometimes the datasets were linked, such as the NPD linked to HESA datasets by individual student number. The work also involved analysis of tape transcripts of oral interviews held in the South Wales Coalfield Archive.

Such datasets were used to draw samples of individual students, parents and teachers or institutions for new studies. More frequently they were used for substantive results themselves, such as those in Chapter 3. The national datasets have been examined by region, local area, school or other institution, or in terms of specific sub-groups such as students from poorer families. They contain individual data on students' subjects studied, attainment and participation from an early age, type of school/university attended, absences, family background, individual characteristics and their area of residence, among others.

Surveys and in-depth data

Where existing data was not available or was not detailed or recent enough, I conducted my own surveys and fuller interviews to collect in-depth data. For example, in Chapter 9 the study of enjoyment involved a survey of 4,900 school students, and interviews with school principals, chairs of governors, school governors, local employers, young people disengaged from education or training, young people with learning difficulties, Year 11 learners and some of their parents. In total there were 798 student and 295 adult interviews. Each school or college involved provided organisation strategic plans, achievement, retention and progression data, prospectuses, policies and information on advice and guidance, staff numbers/structure and curriculum range. As another example also from Chapter 9, the study of fairness in schools involved 20,000 Year 10 students in seven EU countries plus Japan, including a survey of all students and in-depth interviews with around 200.

For the results in Chapter 11, colleagues and myself conducted over 2,100 household interviews in South Wales and the West of England, around 50 interviews with post-compulsory education and training providers in the same areas, and 12 longitudinal in-depth case studies (Selwyn at el, 2006).

Kinds of analyses conducted

Most analyses are based on relatively simple descriptions of content, themes, patterns, correlations and differences. I present counts, frequencies, percentages, means and standard deviations (or absolute mean deviations where possible, see above). Real numbers are compared to categories by comparing means, categorical variables are cross-tabulated with each other, and pairs of real number variables are correlated using Pearson's R.

Differences between means where the SD is known are presented as 'effect' sizes, with the difference between means divided by the overall SD. Achievement gaps, such as those between males and females in Chapter 5, are used where the SD is unknown. Achievement gaps are defined as the difference between scores divided by their sum (Gorard, 2000b).

Segregation of student intakes between schools, as discussed in Chapter 4, is assessed via the GS (see above).

Individual education and training biographies from interviews are converted into a sequence of episodes (an educational programme, new job, etc) in which participation in education and training did or did not occur (see Chapter 12).

The more complex explanatory models used throughout the book are of two main types. Where an outcome variable can be construed as a real number such as the points scored in an exam, and most of the possible predictor and background variables are real numbers, multiple linear regression is used. When an outcome variable is categorical, such as whether to continue with education or not, logistic regression is used. In either kind of model, the main interest lies in the 'effect' sizes represented by R or the percentage of variation explained by each step of the model. Variables are entered into the models in steps representing the order in which the variables could be known, such as in the life order of an individual.

For example, the relative effectiveness of schools in the North East of England in Chapter 5 is assessed via a multiple linear regression model. The outcome variable to be explained is the KS4 attainment score for each pupil in England. The predictors at the first stage include their prior attainment and background characteristics. Then a variable is entered for attending a school in the North East or not. In this way, the amount of variation explained at each stage, and the coefficients for the explanatory variables, provide an estimate of the impact of attending a school in the North East, or not, shorn of the known differences in the intakes to each type of school. If variables add nothing to the explanation, they are ignored. Each explanatory variable that is retained has a calculated coefficient that gives an idea of its relative importance to the model. As with all such models, they do not represent any kind of definitive test but are a way of filtering the results to see potential patterns. For comparison purposes, the same variables were also used to 'predict' an entirely random outcome, with the same split, to assess the dangers of fitting any such model *post hoc*. These random models barely improved from the baseline figures quoted for each model, and this provided strong reassurance that the results of the models in this book are unlikely to be spurious.

Robust evaluations

I conducted a large number of robust evaluations of education policy and practice, partly because of the growth of the Educational Endowment Foundation (EEF) in England, which is similar to the US Institute of Education Sciences (IES). But such evaluations have also been funded by the Peter Sowerby Foundation, Nuffield Foundation, National Literacy Trust, and many others.

The evaluations have ranged from pilot to effectiveness trials, although the majority have been large efficacy trials (Gorard et al, 2017a). The purpose of these efficacy trials was to assess whether an intervention (programme, process, artefact or theory) works in the sense of improving one or more outcomes, to check that in doing so it has no undesirable unintended consequences, to estimate the extent of the improvement and its costs, identify possible barriers and facilitators to implementation, and provide formative advice on the intervention and any training that goes with it. This work is classified as being in Phase 6 of the full research cycle. As can already be glimpsed from its purposes, an efficacy trial has a wide range of research questions and leads to a wide range of data being collected, analysed and synthesised. And despite differences in emphasis, this is also true of pilot and effectiveness trials.

For example, each trial had an integrated process evaluation to monitor progress, observe testing and assess fidelity to intervention. This aspect of evaluation does not necessarily reflect the final results of the impact evaluation itself. The information achieved through the process evaluation, from observation of training and operation and interviews with staff, pupils and parents, helps in understanding how the intervention is received and any barriers to its implementation.

Conclusion

As shown by this brief summary of the methods used, the substantive chapters in this book are based on reviews of about 100,000 distinct research studies, consideration of datasets involving all students in all schools and universities in England covering decades back to 1976, teachers at the start of training, and NQTs in their first posts, fieldwork collecting in-depth data via survey and interviews from around 40,000 individuals worldwide, documentary and archival analysis back to the 1890s, and around 40 new RCTs and evaluation outcomes. It is unlikely that any other book in the social sciences has been based on so much primary evidence. All of the work is clearly referenced throughout, but only a small part of the results can be described in any detail in the following chapters. The book has very little on my work about the conduct of research itself, and on the link between information technology (IT) and education, for example.

THREE

Differential outcomes
at school and beyond

For over 20 years I have examined apparent differences in attainment by various social groups, girls and boys, types of schools, regions and countries. I have looked at patterns of participation in education and attainment after the age of 16, in HE, and throughout adult learners' lives. All of these and more are illustrated in this chapter and those that follow. This chapter presents the simple patterns, and successive chapters present more detail and possible explanations for these patterns. The key message of this chapter is that educational outcomes are clearly stratified by a number of important factors.

Differences linked to family income

One of the best established findings of education research is that students' social class and their attainment at school are linked. This is a worldwide phenomenon. Students from more prestigious social class backgrounds or higher-income families tend to obtain higher marks and examination grades, and are then more likely to stay on in any education system across the world that celebrates qualifications over equity. Students from lower socio-economic backgrounds are more likely to drop out of education (Fernandez-Mellizo and Martinez-Garcia, 2017).

This is evidenced to some extent by consideration of school pupils in England who are known to be eligible for free school meals (FSM). In practice, FSM has referred to any family entitled to Income Support, income-based Jobseeker's Allowance, Child Tax Credit, the first four weeks of Working Tax Credit following unemployment, the guaranteed element of state Pension Credit, Employment and Support Allowance, and/or where Part VI of the Immigration and Asylum Act 1999 applies. FSM-eligibility is widely used in policy and practice in the UK. In England, it influences the level of generic funding for many schools, and forms the main basis on which additional pupil premium funding is allocated to schools. It is also used to compute a pupil premium attainment gap by which school performance is monitored. It is already an important contextual variable used by the school inspection regime Ofsted when conducting statutory inspections of schools. FSM may be the best single indicator of relative disadvantage in education, despite a small number of cases having missing values, as discussed earlier, in Chapter 2.

FSM-eligible pupils have lower attainment than non-eligible pupils at all stages of schooling, and make less progress between Key Stages (see Table 3.1). This can influence the options and subject choices available to them, and the kind of education they receive.

Young people from poor backgrounds are therefore less likely to continue with formal education after the age of 16 (see Table 3.2). They are increasingly less likely to attain any specified level of qualification at KS5, being less than one-third as likely as non-FSM students to gain the equivalent of grades ABB or better at A level. And because KS5 qualifications are often the key to admission to HE, FSM students will then tend to be even fewer in the most selective universities.

In England since 2015, young people can stay on in formal full-time education at age 16 or leave for other training or do at least 20 hours per week working or volunteering while undertaking part-time education or training. They must continue in one of these paths until the age of 18. It is too early to say what the long-term impact of this will be. In the other home countries of the UK, young people can simply leave school at age 16, or not.

Other than poverty, pupils eligible for FSM at any stage of schooling are potentially more disadvantaged on average in most other respects

Table 3.1: Mean attainment scores of pupils in each FSM category, KS4 cohort, England, 2015

	Not FSM-eligible	FSM-eligible
KS1 average points (early primary)	16	13
KS2 total points (end of primary)	41	35
KS4 capped points (age 16)	319	243

Note: N=560,735 pupils with full data (and for the rest of the tables using this dataset).

Table 3.2: Percentage of pupils continuing with post-16 education by FSM, KS5 cohort, England, 2008

	Not FSM-eligible	FSM-eligible
Continued post-16	56	31
Achieved EE+ at KS5 (sixth form)	48	25
Achieved CCC+ at KS5	33	13
Achieved ABB+ at KS5	25	8

as well (see Table 3.3). They are more likely to be recent arrivals in their schools, with English as an additional language (EAL), and having special educational needs (SEN). They are also more often from certain minority ethnic groups.

Eligibility for FSM is a binary classification with a clear legal definition, and whether a pupil is currently or has ever been eligible is used in policy for many purposes, including the distribution of extra funding to schools. However, eligibility can change over time, and I propose instead using a measure of how long a pupil has been known to be FSM-eligible. This makes the pattern of stratification even clearer (see Figure 3.1). There is a substantial gap between those

Table 3.3: Percentage of pupils with specified characteristics by FSM category, KS4 cohort, England, 2015

	Not FSM-eligible	FSM-eligible
Non-white	19	31
EAL	14	22
SEN	15	32

Figure 3.1: Attainment by number of years FSM, KS4 cohort, England, 2015

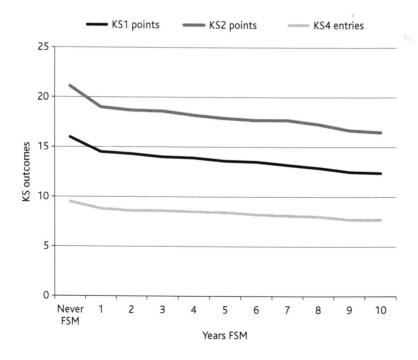

who have never been eligible for FSM and the rest. But then the longer a pupil has been known to be FSM-eligible by age 16, the lower their attainment at every age and stage, including entry to KS4 examinations. Some pupils spend their entire childhood in poverty, while for others poverty is only a temporary state, and this is linked to their relative progress from then on.

The same gap appears in KS4 results and beyond. The only group with positive value-added (VA) (making positive progress) scores on average at KS4 are those never eligible for FSM, and otherwise the VA scores decline in a clear progression with every year of eligibility. This is terrible because it is no longer about absolute attainment but progress. Poorer children already start school with lower attainment than their peers, and then continue to lose ground over time, and the poorer they are, the more they fall behind. They are also more likely to be clustered in schools with others who are also poor (a point taken up in full later, in Chapter 4).

Many characteristics, such as having EAL and mobility between schools, are largely unrelated to the number of years a pupil has been FSM-eligible. The key is simply whether a pupil has ever been eligible or not. However, the longer-term poorer pupils are, for example, far more likely to have a SEN, be from certain minority ethnic groups and also much less likely to be in a selective grammar school (see Figure 3.2). There are clear differences within the characteristics of FSM students as well as between them and the majority. These differences are currently being missed or ignored by policy in England.

Differences linked to special educational needs (SEN)

'Special educational needs' is a legal term used to describe 'children who have a difficulty or disability which makes learning harder for them which calls for SEN provision to be made available' (Section 20, Children and Families Act 2014). In order to have a statement of SEN, the specific challenge and ensuing provision is agreed by a combination of the school, local authority, social services, doctor and/or educational psychologist. Alternatively, SEN without a statement can be agreed by a smaller group including, perhaps, the school and parents. Not surprisingly, pupils with SEN or disabilities have lower than average attainment and make less progress between phases of education (see Table 3.4). This is especially so for pupils with statements of SEN.

SEN pupils are also much less likely than average to continue in education post-16, and even less likely to obtain the sort of qualifications permitting entry to university under the current system

Figure 3.2: Percentage of pupils with specified characteristics by number of years FSM, England, 2015

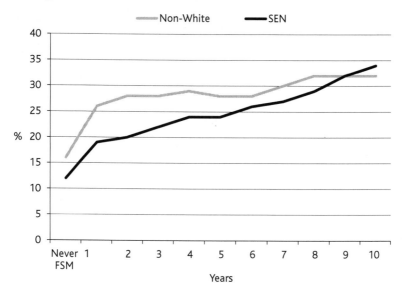

(see Table 3.5). SEN students are less than one-fifth as likely as non-SEN students to gain the equivalent of ABB or better at A level in KS5. Whatever provision for help being labelled as SEN puts in place, it is clearly not enough to allow easy access to HE.

These differences in attainment are linked to above-average levels of poverty (see Table 3.6). Pupils with any SEN are clearly more disadvantaged than those without, on most available indicators, and

Table 3.4: Mean attainment scores of pupils by SEN category, KS4 cohort, England, 2015

	Not SEN	SEN with no statement	SEN with statement
KS1 average points	16	12	8
KS2 average points	21	17	11
KS4 capped points	330	225	114

Table 3.5: Proportion of pupils continuing with post-16 education by SEN, England, 2008

	Not SEN	SEN
Continued post-16	60	19
Achieved EE+	52	15
Achieved CCC+	36	8
Achieved ABB+	26	5

Table 3.6: Percentage of pupils with specified characteristics by SEN category, England, 2015

	Not SEN	SEN with no statement	SEN with statement
FSM-eligible	12	25	31
EAL	15	13	10
Non-White	21	19	18

again this is especially so for pupils with statements. They are much more likely to be FSM-eligible, from a minority ethnic group, to speak a first language other than English (EAL), and to have recently arrived at their current school.

As with FSM-eligibility, the length of time a pupil is known to have SEN is linked both to their other indicators of disadvantage and to their attainment (see Figure 3.3). The longer a pupil is known to have SEN, the worse their average attainment, the more likely they are to be known to be FSM-eligible as well. However, pupils with chronic SEN are actually less likely to be from a minority ethnic group and to speak EAL. It is possible that EAL is being partly misdiagnosed or treated as SEN in the pupil's early school years in England, but that once English fluency is attained, this no longer occurs.

Figure 3.3: Percentage of pupils with specified characteristics by number of years SEN, England, 2015

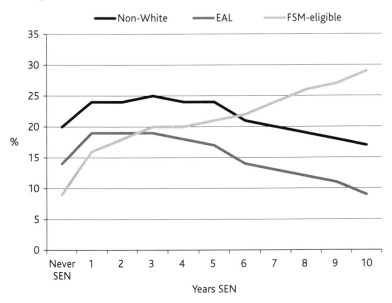

Differences linked to precise age-in-year

Age is a legally protected characteristic in the UK, but is not usually considered an indication of disadvantage at school. It is discussed here because the age of a child in their year or cohort at school is clearly linked to their success or otherwise in education, and because it is strangely linked to some indicators of socio-economic and other disadvantage (Gorard, 2015c).

In England, children generally attend school with an age cohort of whom the oldest was born on 1 September of one year and the youngest born almost a year later on 31 August the following year. The precise age of a child within their school year has been shown to be strongly linked to attainment, later life outcomes and wider personal development. In England, 49 per cent of summer-born children who start school in September having just turned four achieve a 'good level of development' in their first year compared with 71 per cent of autumn-born pupils, who are aged nearly five when they start. In 2016, 60 per cent of pupils born in September reached the expected KS2 standard in reading, writing and maths compared to only 46 per cent of those born in August (DfE, 2016). Figure 3.4 shows that younger pupils have lower attainment, on average, throughout their schooling, and that their attainment declines with every month that they are younger than the oldest in their year.

Figure 3.4: Attainment by age-in-year, KS4 cohort, England, 2015

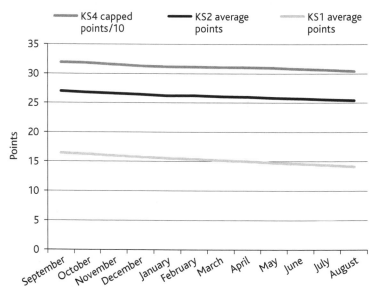

The younger children in any cohort are less likely to pass the entrance test for a grammar school, be entered for any public examinations, and are 10 per cent less likely go to university. By the age of 18, they have had 12 or more years as the youngest, least mature and maybe the smallest person in their year. The summer-born pupils are less likely to be picked for competitive sports, more likely to be bullied, are less happy at school, have lower self-esteem and are rated as lower ability both by teachers and in tests (Crawford et al, 2011). This is an international phenomenon (Ballatore et al, 2016; Melkonian and Areepattamannil, 2017), and up to and beyond HE (Abel et al, 2008). In England, it is worsened by any attempt to select or band pupils by ability, as is done in grammar schools at the young age of 10 or 11 when their age-in-year matters more (Campbell, 2014).

These differences in outcomes cannot be explained by most other characteristics of the children. Younger children are no more likely to be boys, or come from less educated families, specific ethnic groups or poorer areas, for example, all of which are also factors related to differences in attainment. They *are* more likely to be labelled as having SEN. Figure 3.5 shows that labelling of students as having SEN is clearly related to their age-in-year (and the same happens to a lesser extent with labelling as not having English as a first language). SEN

Figure 3.5: SEN reporting by age-in-year, KS4 cohort, England, 2015

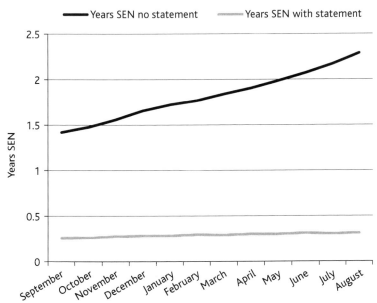

labelling without a statement is over 60 per cent more common for the youngest pupils than for the oldest in any year.

There is no reason to believe that genuine SEN should be distributed like this. Therefore, the differences in attainment are most likely to be just an artefact of the key dates in the education system. It is probable that children with lower results at school tend to be considered for SEN labelling more often, and that their precise age-in-year is not being taken into account sufficiently. This explanation is reinforced by the fact that the distortion by age is worse when schools make the decision to label as SEN (without statement), and better when a doctor or educational psychologist is involved. Younger children in any cohort will tend to struggle more on average, and so become visible as apparent 'under-achievers'. SEN or EAL then provides a mistaken reason for this. Even more seriously, these younger children are leaving school with worse qualifications for no apparent reason other than being younger.

Changing the cut-off date for entry to school would not solve this problem. For example, using 1 January would simply convert the problem into one concerning autumn-born children (the new youngest in their year). Having two or more age cohorts per year, with one starting in September and one in February, might reduce the impact of age slightly, but the problem itself would remain, and this approach would be expensive and disruptive. Allowing parents to delay starting school for their child might help those individuals but would penalise all others to the same extent. If a child who would have been the youngest delays for a year, they now become the oldest and another child becomes the youngest in their year. The situation is zero-sum for the school system and for society, and would probably lead to many parents delaying school for their child just to be safe (hence making the delay pointless).

The simplest way to deal with some of this would be to routinely age-standardise all attainment scores, or to do this better than currently (Gorard, 2015c). This could mean pupils still sitting annual tests at the same time, but with the results adjusted for their precise age-in-year. The adjusted results would form the official record for educational decisions by schools, universities, employers, individuals and families. Age-in-year could become an indicator for contextualised admissions to university, and used as a variable when assessing progress at school by Ofsted and others. Some assessments are already age-standardised, but perhaps not accurately enough, and later examination results are not age-standardised at all. Age would then be an easy-to-handle variable that would reduce unfairness for summer-born children (but perhaps not eliminate it entirely because of the enduring impact of early experiences).

Teachers and other practitioners need more initial training and professional development to recognise the problem and how to handle its consequences other than for formal assessments. And more activities in schools, including sports, can use vertical and other cohort definitions to reduce the impact of always being the youngest. Such solutions and interventions need to be robustly evaluated to check that they do, indeed, reduce the summer-born penalty.

Differences linked to ethnicity

In England, the majority of the population is described as White in terms of their ethnic origin, but there are some sizeable minority ethnic groups, some of which tend to be disadvantaged educationally. There are relatively stable differences in the average attainment outcomes for different ethnic groups – stable both in terms of annual snapshots and over individuals' school careers. Chinese-origin pupils have the highest average attainment at KS1, KS2 and KS4 (see Table 3.7). The majority White pupils obviously have scores close to, but just above, average until KS4. Asian, mixed and other groups have scores below average until KS4 (although this obscures the above-average attainment of Indian-origin pupils). The only group with consistently lower average scores at school is pupils identified as Black – although the highest level of attainment by Black pupils is higher than that of Chinese pupils (Gorard et al, 2017b). These relative attainment figures are, of course, only averages, and there are high attainers in every sub-group. There are also variations between the average scores for Black African and Black Caribbean-origin pupils.

Unlike the indicators considered so far, participation post-16 by ethnicity does not follow the KS4 results. Although Chinese students are much more likely, on average, to continue to KS5, White students are much less likely than average (see Table 3.8). Black and especially Asian students continue to KS5 in greater proportions. The same patterns are then reflected in the numbers gaining EE or better at

Table 3.7: Mean attainment scores of pupils by ethnicity, England, 2015

	White	Asian	Black	Chinese	Mixed	Any other
KS1 average points	15	14	14	16	15	14
KS2 average points	21	18	19	22	20	19
KS4 capped points	306	324	303	373	311	313

Table 3.8: Percentages of pupils continuing with post-16 education by ethnicity, England, 2008

	White	Asian	Black	Chinese	Mixed	Any other
Continued post-16	51	67	58	84	55	61
Achieved EE+ at KS5	44	57	48	77	47	51
Achieved CCC+ at KS5	30	37	27	62	32	34
Achieved ABB+ at KS5	22	25	16	50	23	23

the end of KS5. However, Black students are less likely to obtain ABB+, the kind of qualification that offers access to the most selective universities.

To a large extent, these differences in attainment reflect and can be explained by differences in poverty, and to some extent SEN (see Table 3.9). Chinese pupils are far less likely to come from families living in poverty (FSM), while Black pupils are far more likely to. What appears as an ethnic difference in Table 3.8 is most likely an economic one. Similar issues arise in other countries, including the US (Morgan and Farkas, 2016). This does not make ethnic origin, in itself, a good indicator of disadvantage.

Table 3.9: Percentage of pupils with specified characteristics by ethnicity, England, 2015

	White	Asian	Black	Chinese	Mixed	Any other
FSM-eligible	12	19	26	7	20	27
EAL	5	76	43	75	15	80
SEN (any)	17	13	19	8	18	16

Differences linked to first language

Teaching in England is mainly via the English language (and the equivalent situation arises in most countries), and so pupils for whom English is not their first language may be at a disadvantage, at least temporarily. In the 2015 KS4 cohort, 15 per cent of pupils were recorded as having EAL. At the start of schooling, pupils whose first language is not English have lower attainment, but make considerably more progress. By KS4 there is little overall difference between the two main language groups in terms of attainment, and those with the most years of being considered EAL have the highest attainment, suggesting that for most pupils, having EAL is not a (permanent) indicator of disadvantage (see Table 3.10). Pupils recorded as having

Table 3.10: Mean attainment scores of pupils by first language, England, 2015

	Not English language	English language
KS1 average points	14	15
KS2 average points	18	20
KS4 capped points	309	308

EAL tend to be from poorer families and minority ethnic groups, and to have recently arrived in their current school, but are less likely to be recorded as having SEN. It is possible that EAL is somehow used as a label that stands as a substitute for SEN for some pupils. If so, this would bring the validity of both labels further into question, to some extent.

By KS5 and beyond, students not originally having English as their first language have the clear advantage. They are more likely to continue to KS5 and obtain KS5 qualifications than first-language English-speaking students (Table 3.11). So, as with ethnicity, EAL is not a good long-term indicator of disadvantage.

Table 3.11: Proportion of pupils continuing with post-16 education by first language, England, 2008

	Not English language	English language
Continued post-16	63	52
Achieved EE+	54	44
Achieved CCC+	34	30
Achieved ABB+	22	22

Differences linked to recorded sex

The NPD and other official databases still record students as either male or female, and this is the operational definition used here and in later chapters. Male and female students are, as would be expected, very similar in most known respects – including levels of poverty, ethnic origin, first language, age-in-year and school mobility. However, males are much more likely than females to be labelled as having SEN (21 versus 13%), and have markedly lower average attainment results by KS4 (see Table 3.12).

Substantially fewer male than female students continue in formal education post-16, and fewer again attain any A level or equivalent qualifications at KS5 (see Table 3.13). The attainment gap at ABB+ is 16.5, while it is 10.2 at EE+, and the post-16 participation gap is only

Table 3.12: Mean attainment scores of pupils by reported sex, England, 2015

	Female	Male
KS1 average points	16	15
KS2 average points	26	26
KS4 capped points	323	294

Table 3.13: Proportion of pupils continuing with post-16 education by sex, all pupils in England, 2008

	Female	Male
Continued post-16	57	48
Achieved EE+ at KS5	50	41
Achieved CCC+ at KS5	35	26
Achieved ABB+ at KS5	26	19

8.5. This is one of the few gaps that worsens during and after post-16 education, because the gap is worse among higher attainers. Despite this, little policy is directed at overcoming this clear difference that is routinely misunderstood (see Chapter 5).

Participation in higher education (HE)

So far, this chapter has been based on data from the NPD for England. This is useful because it contains records throughout their schooling for all students in state-funded schools or colleges up to the age of 18. Records concerning HE or university, however, only contain data on those attending HE. This can lead to confusion and bias for unwary commentators. Here, the HESA records are linked to the full corresponding NPD cohorts in order to help maintain the fuller context. However, many of the ensuing tables are only about students in HE.

Just like those entering KS5, students entering HE are predictably higher qualified than average, having started out with higher test scores at KS4 and earlier, and having made more progress at school on average (see Table 3.14). And those leaving university with a 2.1 degree or better after four years (where such classifications are used) have higher prior qualifications again.

Table 3.15 shows even more clearly that the vast majority of students not entering HE do not enter KS5 beforehand. The stratification of HE is not principally a problem of the admissions process for universities (see Chapter 10). For example, only 31 per cent of FSM-

Table 3.14: Mean prior attainment scores for pupils at each stage of post-16 education to higher education (HE), KS4 cohort, England, 2006

	Entered KS5	Achieved EE+ or equivalent	Entered HE	2:1 or first degree
KS4 capped points	358	364	372	393
KS5 total points	660	752	762	889

Note: 2006 NPD KS4 cohort has been linked to the HESA dataset.

Table 3.15: Percentage of pupil characteristics at each stage of post-16 education to higher education (HE), KS4 cohort, England, 2006

	Entered KS5	Achieved EE+ or equivalent	Entered HE	2:1 or first
SEN with statement	11	8	6	2
Living in care	16	11	10	2
SEN	19	15	11	3
FSM-eligible	31	25	20	5
Male	48	41	31	12
Unclassified ethnicity	48	41	30	13
White ethnicity	51	44	31	15
Not EAL	51	45	31	15
Not living in care	53	46	38	15
Mixed ethnicity	55	47	40	15
Not FSM-eligible	56	49	36	17
Female	57	50	38	18
Black ethnicity	57	49	48	11
Not SEN	60	52	39	18
Other ethnicity	61	52	51	15
EAL	62	54	52	16
Asian ethnicity	67	59	57	19
Chinese ethnicity	84	78	72	35
Overall	52	46	34	15

eligible students continue to KS5 at the age of 16, and 65 per cent of these enter university. Overall, 52 per cent of all students enter KS5 and 65 per cent of these enter university (exactly the same proportion as those living in poverty). For FSM students the key problem doesn't lie in KS5 or the qualifications gained there, or even applications and admissions to HE; the problem lies in whatever determines their decisions to leave formal academic education disproportionately at the earliest opportunity, and, as the previous section has shown, this is strongly linked to qualifications gained during compulsory schooling. The same applies to most or even all indicators.

Table 3.16 shows the same figures, but this time the percentages in each column are of the figures in the previous column. For example, 80 per cent of FSM students who entered KS5 attained EE+ and 80 per cent of those entered HE. The bulk of all students entering KS5 attained EE+ and the bulk of those entered HE, with over 40 per cent of entrants gaining a 2.1 degree or better. There are variations, but the big gaps are in entry to KS5 for many indicators such as SEN, living in care, FSM and some ethnicities. Black students, for example, are more likely than average to continue to KS5, and 98 per cent of those obtaining minimum qualifications enter university (but are then less likely to obtain a 2.1). Male students are slightly less likely than average to continue to KS5, and then less likely to get to each successive stage.

For only those students who end up in HE there is a clear pattern of occupational class differentiation in terms of KS5 attainment – precisely the qualifications needed for entry to HE (see Table 3.17). This clearly does not affect their entry to HE, since these students are in the HESA dataset, but it could easily influence which kind of university they attend and so the social composition of different sectors

Table 3.16: Percentage of remaining pupil characteristics at each stage of post-16 education to higher education (HE), KS4 cohort, England, 2006

	Entered KS5	Achieved EE+ or equivalent	Entered HE	2:1 or first
SEN with statement	11	73	75	33
Living in care	16	69	91	20
SEN	19	79	73	27
FSM-eligible	31	80	80	25
Male	48	85	76	38
Unclassified ethnicity	48	85	73	43
White ethnicity	51	86	70	48
Not EAL	51	88	69	48
Not living in care	53	87	83	39
Mixed ethnicity	55	85	85	38
Not FSM-eligible	56	88	73	47
Female	57	87	76	47
Black ethnicity	57	86	98	23
Not SEN	60	87	75	46
Other ethnicity	61	85	98	29
EAL	62	87	96	31
Asian ethnicity	67	88	97	33
Chinese ethnicity	84	93	92	49
Overall	52	88	74	44

Table 3.17: Parent occupational class characteristics and prior attainment of students in higher education (HE), KS4 cohort, England, 2006

	Prior KS5 points
Higher managerial	885
Lower managerial	834
Intermediate	827
Small employers	781
Lower supervisory	795
Semi-routine	774
Routine	763

of HE (see below). The patterns are likely to be stronger (worse) if they could be calculated for all students, including those dropping out at KS4 or KS5 (the NPD doesn't include this social class data).

The same is true of whether students in HE have parents who also had degrees (see Table 3.18). Students disadvantaged in terms of FSM and EAL are less likely to have parents in managerial occupations or who attended HE. However, as with many such indicators, it is the students whose parental occupation and education is unknown who appear the most disadvantaged (see Chapter 2 earlier).

The above figures begin to suggest why current widening participation policy in the UK is so misguided (see Chapter 10 later).

Table 3.18: Parental education and prior attainment of students in higher education (HE), KS4 cohort, England, 2006

	Parental HE	Not parental HE
Prior KS5 points	857	787

Adult participation in education and training

In considering participation in learning opportunities as adults, I have to change datasets again. This section is based on the large-scale household surveys described in Chapter 2 (and in more detail in Gorard and Rees, 2002, and Selwyn et al, 2006).

Only around 40 per cent of adults have historically continued with any form of formal learning directly after reaching compulsory school-leaving age. And less than 50 per cent of adults report any formal learning other than directly after reaching compulsory school-leaving age. The most common pattern is a report of no formal education or training since reaching compulsory school-leaving age – the non-participants (see Table 3.19). Non-participants in lifelong learning

Table 3.19: Frequencies of lifelong learning 'trajectories'

Trajectory	Frequency	%
Non-participant	710	35
Transitional	399	19
Delayed	390	19
Lifelong	562	27

Note: N=2,061.

are those who reported no extension of their education immediately after ending compulsory schooling, and then no return to education, no continuing education in adult life, no participation in government training schemes and no substantive work-based training. Of course, some of these will be informal learners not wishing or needing to participate in formal episodes or to gain qualifications (see Chapter 8).

The transitional learners reported only the continuation of full-time education or a period of initial work-based training immediately after completing compulsory schooling. Once this initial education was over they reported no further formal education (FE) or training at all. Those on the delayed 'trajectory' have a gap in participation between leaving school at the earliest opportunity followed by a minimum of one substantive episode of education or training after the age of 21. The optimistically termed 'lifelong' learners reported at least one episode of both transitional participation and a later episode of education and training. The nature of these later episodes of lifetime learning varied widely, from routine health and safety training at work to long-term academic study.

The scale of non-participation and trivial participation after compulsory schooling is considerable and shows that much education policy, predicated on those in education and training, is missing its key constituency. And as all of the foregoing in this chapter should presage, the task is made harder by the clear socio-economic stratification of these learning trajectories. Participation is patterned by sex, age, ethnicity, disability, caring responsibilities, educational background, employment and local deprivation.

Non-participation in post-compulsory education in the UK is strongly patterned by social and economic background, and has been for as long as records exist (Pettigrew et al, 1989; NIACE, 2003). The patterns are based on indicators including 'pre-adult' social, geographic and historical factors such as socio-economic status (SES), year of birth and type of school attended (Marsh and Blackburn, 1992; Sargant and Aldridge, 2002). Individuals from families with less prestigious occupational backgrounds, with lower incomes, unemployed or economically inactive people, older people, people with severe disabilities and ex-offenders with lower literacy skills or with negative attitudes to institutional learning are all less likely than average to have participated in any episodes of formal education or training after the age of 16.

For example, participation is lower among older people despite the longer time they have had (see Table 3.20). Younger people are more likely to stay on after compulsory school leaving age but not to study or train later in life in proportion to that. Over time, non-participation has declined, and has largely been replaced by transitional rather than lifelong learning.

There is also a clear relationship between participation and the characteristics of parents (Gorard et al, 1999a; San-Segundo and Valiente, 2003). Adults born to service and non-manual class parents are more likely to be lifelong learners, and much less likely to be non-participants (see Table 3.21). The children (now adults aged 40+ themselves) of part- and unskilled parents are much more likely to be non-participants as adults.

Post-compulsory participation is further stratified by the higher age of leaving education for the mothers and fathers of transitional and lifelong learners (see Table 3.22). Education in England, the UK and worldwide tends to be strongly patterned by family background, from first steps to the third age.

Table 3.20: Percentage in each trajectory, by age range

Trajectory	Age 21-40	Age 41-60	Age 61+
Non-participant	26	27	54
Transitional	22	17	12
Delayed	23	29	25
Lifelong	28	27	22

Table 3.21: Percentage in each trajectory, by father's social class

Trajectory	Service	Non-manual	Skilled	Part-skilled	Other
Non-participant	5	13	24	49	55
Transitional	40	27	20	12	18
Delayed	18	22	29	26	18
Lifelong	37	39	28	14	8

Table 3.22: Average age of parent leaving school, by trajectory

Trajectory	Age father left school	Age mother left school
Non-participant	14.2	14.3
Transitional	16.3	16.0
Delayed	14.5	14.6
Lifelong	16.4	16.1

Conclusion

There are many other ways of representing disadvantage and inequality in educational outcomes. Some indicators are as important as those portrayed here, but may be either not as easily available or high quality, or only affect small groups. For example, students living in state care have lower average attainment than others at every stage of education, are less likely to continue in education, are more likely to be poor, from a minority ethnic group and to have EAL. They are also much more likely to have SEN (60% compared to 18% of their peers). However, even from the simple summary figures in this chapter it is clear that attainment and subsequent participation in education lifelong is strongly patterned by the background of students from as soon as they enter the school system. And this is true for all countries I have looked at (EGREES, 2005).

Similar analyses to those above have been conducted with the school-age datasets from 2005, 2006, 2008, 2012, 2014, 2015 and 2016, but not all are presented here. In all important respects the results are the same. Of course many of the indicators presented separately in this chapter are interrelated and I have always considered them in combination. FSM-eligible pupils are more likely to be labelled SEN and vice versa, for example. The relevance of age or student sex may vary with social class, and so on. These are chronic patterns of difference in educational outcomes linked to personal characteristics and disadvantage. The remainder of the book looks at each in more detail, considering why they arise and what policy-makers may do to reduce them.

Part 2:
Possible explanations

FOUR

The clustering of access to schools

Chapter 3 illustrated the clear patterns in educational participation and outcomes linked to the characteristics and backgrounds of learners. The indicators of possible educational disadvantage may vary over time and place, but these kinds of patterns are clear in all such studies worldwide. How do they arise and what can be done about them? This chapter starts looking at the possible reasons and solutions by considering who goes to school with whom.

My concern with school intakes started in the 1990s when I looked at issues of school choice (Gorard, 1997a, 1998a, 1999), including the choice to use fee-paying schools (Gorard, 1996, 1997b), and the operation of a 'market' or quasi-market in education (Gorard, 1998b). This chapter is chiefly about a theme that developed from this – the extent to which children of similar social and economic backgrounds are then clustered within the same schools, the reasons this happens, the impact on attainment and the wider damage this causes. This kind of clustering is referred to here as 'segregation' between schools. I have looked at levels of segregation, the causes and results of segregation and its links to attainment (Gorard and Taylor, 2002b; Gorard, 2006c).

Although all state-funded schools in England are 'choice' schools in the sense that any family is entitled to express a preference to attend any of them, this does not mean that all preferences are met. Schools have a planned fixed number of places. A small number of these schools are selective, taking only those children scoring above a certain level on an entrance test or in terms of aptitude. Many more schools continue to have a faith basis, and can restrict the number of children accepted who come from families apparently without that faith. Even more commonly, popular schools or their admissions authorities use over-subscription criteria such as the proximity of home to school to decide who gets contested places. Because of the segregated nature of housing in parts of England, due to differences in cost and availability, children can then turn out to be clustered by their family backgrounds into particular schools. This is measurable in terms of a range of characteristics including low attainment, poverty, ethnic origin, immigrant status, disability or learning difficulties.

Such problems are not unique to England (EGREES, 2005). Some developing countries do not even have full participation of young children in school, some developed countries have universal tracks that divide children by ability from an early age, and many others have higher levels of clustering by faith (Siddiqui and Gorard, 2017). In all of these countries the problem of socio-economic segregation between schools is worse than in England (Gorard and Smith, 2004), with stronger links between child background and school outcomes (OECD, 2014).

Why this clustering of pupils matters

The disproportionate clustering of students within schools in terms of their personal characteristics is a matter of concern worldwide for many reasons (Logan et al, 2012; Belfi et al, 2014). For students not speaking the language of their country of residence, the most important factor in successful learning is exposure to native speakers (Lee and Madyun, 2008), thus requiring a mixed intake to schools. Integrated and unsegregated school systems seem to lead to the desirable outcome that a pupil's achievement depends less on their social and cultural background, whereas more between-school stratification leads to attainment more strongly linked to student SES (Parker et al, 2016).

All other things being equal, school systems with unequal distribution of resources and the stratification of students between schools by their parental income or immigrant status have been linked to lower overall attainment wherever this has been assessed (Danhier and Martin, 2014; Mendolia et al, 2016; Yeung and Phuong Nguyen-Hoang, 2016). The segregation of students is also linked to lowered patterns of high school graduation and college enrolment in the US, even after controlling for individual and other school factors (Palardy, 2013). People growing up in segregated settings may then be less prepared for the academic challenges of subsequent education.

There are many possible reasons for these unfair outcomes (Roew and Lubienski, 2017). Lower achievers and poorer students may have less experienced or less qualified teachers (Kalogrides and Loeb, 2013), leading to worse teaching and opportunities to learn (Schmidt et al, 2015). In the 2008 economic recession, when teachers were made redundant in the US, this occurred disproportionately in already disadvantaged areas (Knight and Strunk, 2016). The school mix of students by SES even seems to influence how students are treated or diagnosed within each school (McCoy et al, 2012), teachers' expectations (Parker et al, 2016) and relationships between pupils and teachers, and between pupil peers, leading to poorer social skills (Gottfried, 2014). Classes in poorer areas have different patterns of teacher–student interaction, more like those of younger classes in more affluent areas (Harris, 2012).

One of the most obvious reasons why similar children go to schools together is because they live close together and then go to local schools (Gorard et al, 2003a; Camina and Iannone, 2013). Residential segregation itself is linked to life outcomes such as income mobility, probably via school-level segregation in a reinforcing vicious cycle (Chetty et al, 2014). Parental preference for local neighbourhood schools is often greater among disadvantaged and minority ethnic families, which exacerbates the kinds of segregation found in urban areas (Jacobs, 2013). Any system of allocating school places, especially contested places in over-subscribed schools, which uses catchments, distance from home or ease of travel, will tend to reinforce patterns of pre-existing residential segregation (Frankenberg, 2013). In turn, these rules for allocating school places can then influence where people choose to live (Liebowitz, 2014), and housing becomes more expensive near highly advantaged schools.

The mix of peers in schools is also linked to wider non–cognitive student outcomes such as emotional and behavioural problems (Muller and Hofmann, 2014), students' sense of justice (Gorard and See, 2013), civic knowledge (Collado et al, 2015) and subsequent civic engagement (Hoskins et al, 2014). This, in turn, relates to how students see society, their sense of belonging (Gorard and Smith, 2010), and the levels of SES, ethnic and other cohesion in that society (Mickelson and Nkomo, 2012). School segregation may polarise information about future opportunities by removing role models or influencing aspiration (Burgess et al, 2005), and assist in the creation of wider social ills, such as ill health and delinquency (Clotfelter, 2001). Mainstream schooling for lower attainers is reported to have a generally positive effect on the aspirations and self-concept of pupils with learning difficulties (Casey et al, 2006).

The segregation of pupils of different types between schools is therefore not merely a question of who goes to school with whom. Segregation whether racially or by religion or social class can have alarming and dangerous consequences for the school system and for society more widely and in the longer term. The potential impact on attainment is discussed further in Chapter 6, and the more solid impact on wider outcomes is covered in Chapter 9.

The number of years any student has been known to be eligible for FSM was introduced in Chapter 3. Here it is used as one explanatory variable in a regression model, looking at the possible impact of school intakes on pupil attainment. Table 4.1 includes three estimates of the level of disadvantage in the school attended by each student – its GS intake segregation levels for 2005 (their first school) and 2015 (their KS4 school), plus the average number of years all pupils in that school have been eligible for FSM. There are generally noticeable but far from perfect correlations between each measure of individual and school-level clustering of disadvantage. Pupils in more disadvantaged schools have lower attainment and make less progress between Key Stages. This is, of course, zero-sum, and so there is no advantage in such pupil clustering. Segregation only worsens the pre-existing poverty and attainment gaps a little bit further.

In general, the strongest correlations between individual and school-level variables involve the average number of years FSM (of the order of 0.40), and this is the justification for using years FSM in the rest of the book. It explains more of the patterning in Chapter 3 than current eligibility for FSM or whether a student has ever been eligible.

Table 4.1: Correlations between school-level disadvantage and individuals, KS4 cohort, England, 2015

Individual indicator	Segregation 2005	Segregation 2015	Mean years-FSM
FSM 2005	0.40	0.09	0.07
FSM 2015	0.27	0.29	0.30
Years-FSM by KS4	0.41	0.34	0.39
Years-FSM missing	0.01	0.09	0.07
KS1 average points	−0.22	−0.23	−0.31
KS2 average points	−0.14	−0.16	−0.18
N GCSE equivalent entries	−0.15	−0.16	−0.26
Total GCSE capped points	−0.19	−0.21	−0.30
Best 8 value-added score	−0.12	−0.11	−0.17

Note: Value-added or progress scores are described in Chapter 6.

Figures for England over time and place

I have published figures for the level of between-school segregation, first in Wales and then in England, with an increasing number of available indicators every year (Gorard and Fitz, 1998a,b, 2000a,b; Gorard, 2002d, 2015d,e; Gorard and Cheng, 2011; Gorard et al, 2013a). These have shown that segregation between schools by poverty is generally lower in Wales than in England, that segregation by take-up of, and eligibility for, FSM is substantially the same, and that the same trends over time appear in primary schools as in secondary schools (the remainder of this chapter focuses more on secondary schools). Because mainstream state-funded schools are the most common, it makes little difference to the overall figures whether independent and special schools are included as well or not. This prior work has also shown that the scale and trend over time of segregation for each actual indicator of disadvantage, such as poverty or ethnicity, is different.

Figure 4.1 provides a summary of results for between-school segregation at the national level for a sample of four indicators – eligibility for FSM, statements of SEN, non-White ethnicity, and having EAL. Each has a different level of segregation and a specific pattern of change over time. The overall trend for how clustered children are in schools by SEN, ethnicity and language is generally down over time, and the reasons for this are examined in the next section. The overall long-term trend for segregation by poverty (FSM) is also down, but the pattern is more cyclical. Figure 4.1 illustrates that, in addition to the changes over time, the actual levels of segregation vary considerably, with children without English as their first language much more segregated in the system than those with statements of SEN, for example. Therefore, whatever is producing these figures, we need to explain both their level and their trends independently.

The laws concerning allocating places in over-subscribed schools were amended and tidied up in 1998, 2003 and 2007. There is no consistent, abrupt or delayed change in the patterns for the following

Figure 4.1: Segregation indices for four indicators, state secondary schools, England, 1989–2015

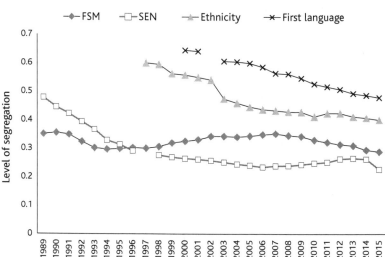

years. The rules were already largely fair for most pupils (White et al, 2001; Fitz et al, 2002). Whatever benefits such changes in policy made for a minority, it seems to have been marginal in comparison to the other determinants of segregation. However, in other countries, national-level policies have made a considerable difference. When New Zealand abolished zoning in 1990, so that school places did not depend on where students lived, the levels of SES and ethnic segregation plummeted. They then went back up again once proximity was re-introduced as a factor the following year. Something similar may have happened with SES segregation in England from 1990 to 1995 (Gorard et al, 2003a). This was the period in which all schools filled with students who had arrived since the onset of the Education Reform Act 1988. It is likely that increased parental choice as provided by this Act had a brief role in driving down FSM segregation between schools. This is so because families in the neighbourhood of desirable schools had no reason to look elsewhere, whereas families in disadvantaged areas now had the right at least to request a place outside their area.

Some other indications of why segregation varies over time and by indicator come from consideration of more local figures – here for local authority (government) areas in England. Table 4.2 shows the average level of FSM segregation for local authorities depending on their population density. In general, rural and less densely populated areas have higher segregation, presumably because there are fewer schools within reach of each household.

Such factors are explored in more detail by looking at each of the 149 local authorities in England individually (apart from the City of London and the Scilly Isles, which have too few schools). These have been sorted into ascending order of segregation (based on years FSM). The 20 least segregated areas in Table 4.3 have this in common – they are mostly in large urban areas such as London and Manchester and none have pupils in selective schools. Otherwise they have a range of school types, with between 0 and 40 per cent of pupils attending private schools. But the kinds of state-maintained schools in each area may matter (see below). These areas have high levels of long-term

Table 4.2: Levels of segregation by FSM and years FSM, by local geography, England, 2015

Type of area	Segregation FSM	Segregation years FSM
Urban	0.23	0.21
Village	0.23	0.21
Town and fringe	0.21	0.21
Hamlet and isolated dwelling	0.26	0.25

Table 4.3: FSM years segregation, by local authority characteristics, low segregation, England, 2015

Local authority	Segregation years FSM	Mean years FSM	N pupils	Selective schools	Private schools	Voluntary-controlled schools	Community schools	Academy schools	Area type
Tower Hamlets	5	5.09	2,446	0	20	11	5	58	Urban
Islington	5	4.61	1,350	0	37	13	6	44	Urban
Newham	6	3.24	3,576	0	2	11	6	56	Urban
St Helens	7	1.94	1,832	0	2	25	8	25	Urban
Camden	7	3.80	1,430	0	–	8	8	67	Urban
Barking and Dagenham	9	2.56	2,139	0	1	10	0	70	Urban
Lewisham	9	2.71	2,119	0	2	6	6	50	Urban
Greenwich	9	2.86	2,165	0	14	14	0	29	Urban
Hackney	10	3.74	1,974	0	12	7	0	36	Urban
Wandsworth	11	2.71	1,803	0	12	6	0	44	Urban
Sandwell	11	2.32	3,504	0	0	5	11	16	Urban
Manchester	11	3.45	4,758	0	14	14	6	29	Urban
Cornwall	12	1.20	5,545	0	4	3	33	14	Town
Waltham Forest	13	2.41	2,527	0	8	5	5	48	Urban
Knowsley	13	3.67	1,218	0	0	22	0	33	Hamlet
Westminster	13	3.8	1,469	0	29	0	0	17	Urban
Isle of Wight	14	1.68	1,362	0	8	0	25	13	Town
Hounslow	14	1.98	2,606	0	5	6	0	19	Urban
Lambeth	14	3.45	1,892	0	33	11	11	38	Urban
Rutland	14	0.41	489	0	66	0	0	0	Village

Note: Voluntary-controlled (VC) schools are generally Roman Catholic faith-based. Church of England voluntary-aided (VA) schools are not related to segregation, and the number of schools of other faiths is too small to matter at present.

53

poverty, as evidenced by the average number of years pupils are known to be eligible for FSM. Having more FSM pupils locally seems to create a better mix of such pupils between schools, as long as schools are relatively close to each other, which they are in dense urban areas.

The simple number of people resident in any local authority is linked to lower and reduced segregation in terms of FSM, ethnicity and SEN (Gorard, 2015d). More populous areas have reduced all forms of segregation faster than other areas. Areas with high unemployment or indicators of multiple deprivation have lower levels of FSM (and ethnic) segregation. As with the number of local residents, the number of students in any area is linked to reduced segregation, perhaps for the same reasons. However, areas with greater growth of student numbers have higher segregation, at least temporarily. It may be that accommodating more students creates a short-term imbalance in school intakes. The prevalence of any indicator of disadvantage is linked to lower segregation, but any increase in that prevalence is linked to a temporary increase in segregation. Again, this could be a short-term phenomenon, as schools struggle to find local places for the growing population.

Segregation is lowest in London where houses and schools are closer together, and so easier to walk to, and neighbourhoods with both rich and poor housing adjacent, so reducing the impact of residential segregation. Public transport is better in London than elsewhere, again making mixing of intakes more feasible than in rural areas. Big cities may also have higher levels of disadvantage. All of these factors would tend to favour the existence of relatively mixed school intakes. Of course, there are exceptions. Big cities like Birmingham could have been like London in many ways, but Birmingham has no underground transport service, only a weak radial rail service and more 'ghettoisation' of poverty and ethnicity. It also runs a selective grammar school system. All of these factors would tend to favour school intakes segregated by poverty and ethnicity. Islington and other central London boroughs may also have lower segregation because the users of local schools are more homogeneous than expected, with a high proportion using fee-paying schools or schools in neighbouring boroughs. This leaves a rump with apparently high levels of FSM, and so low segregation in terms of FSM.

In contrast, the Isle of Wight and similar areas have low population densities, but segregation remains relatively low. The driver of low segregation here could be uniformity among the local permanent population – where nearly everyone is deprived or no one is from a minority ethnic group – then segregation in terms of those characteristics must be low. North East England also has much lower population density than London but similar levels of segregation. This could be because the levels of disadvantage there are both higher and more uniformly distributed. There are parts of Middlesbrough in the North East, for example, where no school has less than 50 per cent of students eligible for FSM.

The 20 areas in the middle of the full 149 local authorities in terms of segregation appear in Table 4.4. These are all outside the big cities, but most are not rural (smaller towns or mixed areas), confirming that high population density tends to be linked to low segregation. They have higher levels of long-term poverty than areas in Table 4.3. There is little or no selection, and a mixture of other school types.

The 20 areas with the worst problem of social segregation between schools have, on average, lower population density and are more rural. Most notably, they are much more likely to have high levels of selection in their schools (see Table 4.5). The worst segregated 10 areas are all selective in nature. They also have a reasonably large local private sector, but a mixture of other types of schools. The key here appears to be selection. Areas like Bexley, Reading and Barnet have relatively high population densities like those in Table 4.3, but are in Table 4.5 just because they are selective. This shows the danger for social cohesion of having such divisive schools in an otherwise relatively comprehensive school system.

The economic cycle and local events such as changes in employment may be linked to changes in segregation. Areas can become more or less attractive to live in, students can move in and out of state-funded benefits like eligibility for FSM, and parents can find fee-paying schools more or less affordable. Immigration can increase the number of children from minority ethnic groups or with EAL. Nationally, the figures for the level of segregation using each indicator are not related to the proportion of students educated in the private sector (around 7% in England), nor with changes in the tiny proportion educated in hospitals or Pupil Referral Units. However, the segregation level for each indicator is strongly linked to the simple prevalence of that indicator in the national school system. As the number of pupils in any category grows, the dispersal of students with that characteristic tends to be more evenly spread between schools (see Table 4.6).

Given the scale of correlations in Table 4.6, it is not necessary to look much further for the determinants of segregation by SEN, ethnic origin or first language. The prevalence of any indicator of disadvantage can change because of a change in population for the mainstream school system, such as those caused by increased

Table 4.4: FSM years segregation, by local authority characteristics, medium segregation, England, 2015

Local authority	Segregation years FSM	Mean years FSM	N pupils	Selective schools	Private schools	Voluntary-controlled schools	Community schools	Academy schools	Area type
Durham	20	1.99	5,091	0	5	5	5	49	Town
Herefordshire	20	0.79	1,845	0	7	5	0	21	Town
Wiltshire	20	0.77	5,083	0.05	13	3	11	20	Urban
Salford	20	2.46	2,155	0	8	18	0	47	Urban
Central Bedfordshire	21	0.85	2,709	0	1	0	7	13	Town
Wokingham	21	0.60	1,613	0	11	0	0	60	Hamlet
Cambridgeshire	21	0.93	5,772	0	16	0	0	24	Urban
Bolton	21	1.79	3,392	0	10	15	5	30	Urban
Bath and NE Somerset	21	0.92	2,014	0	24	6	6	0	Urban
Worcestershire	21	1.06	5,673	0	16	3	3	16	Hamlet
Enfield	21	2.44	3,624	0.05	2	9	4	52	Urban
Derbyshire	21	1.30	8,020	0	5	4	7	54	Town
Blackburn with Darwen	21	2.01	1,749	0	12	14	14	14	Urban
Suffolk	21	1.13	7,402	0	11	2	4	20	Hamlet
Dorset	21	0.68	4,143	0	16	0	19	27	Urban
Medway	21	1.29	3,114	0.28	3	5	0	10	Urban
Coventry	22	1.96	3,399	0	7	12	16	16	Urban
Bournemouth	22	1.25	1,660	0.19	8	0	0	7	Urban
Norfolk	22	1.28	8,240	0	8	0	22	19	Hamlet
East Sussex	22	1.27	5,159	0	14	3	3	43	Urban

Table 4.5: FSM years segregation, by local authority characteristics, high segregation, England, 2015

Local authority	Segregation years FSM	Mean years FSM	N pupils	Selective schools	Private schools	Voluntary-controlled schools	Community schools	Academy schools	Area type
Sutton	28	0.98	2,675	0.29	4	12	0	6	Urban
Cumbria	28	1.11	5,294	0.02	6	9	7	34	Urban
Hertfordshire	29	0.83	12,690	0	16	2	6	29	Urban
Solihull	29	1.29	3,055	0	5	5	5	26	Town
North East Lincolnshire	29	1.82	1,816	0	1	0	0	0	Urban
Reading	29	1.66	1,132	0.19	31	10	20	0	Urban
Bromley	30	1.04	3,240	0.08	11	0	5	14	Urban
Cheshire West and Chester	30	1.28	3,571	0	11	7	18	33	Hamlet
Sefton	30	1.57	3,136	0	8	24	12	28	Urban
Warrington	30	1.02	2,437	0	0	14	0	29	Hamlet
Plymouth	30	1.46	2,722	0.15	4	0	0	35	Urban
Kent	30	1.15	16,012	0.29	10	2	22	17	Town
Gloucestershire	30	0.89	6,508	0.13	12	0	10	18	Urban
Bexley	31	1.28	3,280	0.23	0	0	0	16	Urban
Lincolnshire	32	0.87	8,125	0.22	4	0	7	21	Urban
Southend-on-Sea	33	1.34	2,114	0.28	2	0	19	19	Urban
Poole	34	0.72	1,530	0.23	9	0	10	10	Urban
Buckinghamshire	36	0.59	5,683	0.38	10	2	7	25	Hamlet
Barnet	37	1.67	3,526	0.10	13	17	0	13	Urban
Trafford	38	1.12	2,850	0.38	3	8	13	21	Urban

Table 4.6: Correlation (R) between level of segregation for any indicator and the prevalence of that indicator in any year, secondary schools, England, 1989-2013

Indicator of possible disadvantage	Number of pupils, SEN statement	Number of pupils, SEN no statement	Number of non-White pupils	Number of EAL pupils	Number of FSM pupils
Correlation with level of segregation by the same indicator	−0.94	−0.90	−0.93	−0.96	−0.80

immigration (affecting the number of non-White UK children and those with EAL). This means that schools in some areas are taking in a slightly different profile of students. The prevalence can also change due to an improvement or modification in reporting, such as greater sensitivity in spotting SEN or in classifying minority ethnic status. Here it is not clear that students are actually moving schools; rather, the suggestion is that students are being identified differently in their existing schools. The impact on segregation would look the same (that is, it does not matter here whether a FSM-eligible pupil exchanged into a new school or whether an existing pupil became FSM-eligible due to a change of circumstances). Similarly in England, there is an ongoing policy of integrating children with SEN into mainstream schooling, and a parallel increase in the number of children diagnosed as having a SEN of any kind (Tomlinson, 2012). Schools are also closed or merged, and new schools spring up in areas of high demand. Factors such as these can affect the prevalence of any indicator of disadvantage and/or the distribution of such indicators between schools.

Changes in segregation over time are therefore linked to changes in the level of that indicator in the state-funded school system as a whole. When indicators of disadvantage grow in frequency, their dispersal across schools also tends to grow (creating lower levels of calculated segregation), and for FSM this is clearly linked to the economic cycle (Cheng and Gorard, 2010). For example, the level of segregation for FSM take-up 1989 to 2013 is correlated with the percentage of FSM students, at −0.80. When the economy is good, segregation tends to be higher, perhaps partly because fewer families live in poverty. When the economy falters, there is more 'equality of poverty' and levels of FSM students rise and appear more evenly spread between schools (Gorard et al, 2003a). A similar picture has emerged from the US, where greater income segregation between schools is linked to increased disparity in income (Owens et al, 2016). However, there is more to FSM segregation than the other indicators because the correlation with prevalence is lower (R of 0.8 means that about 36% of the variation in segregation is yet to be explained).

Local school types

Most of the factors discussed so far are largely fixed in the sense that education policy is unlikely to have any impact on them. To make a difference to populations, areas of residence for recent immigrants, transport and housing would take a long time to have an impact on the local intakes to schools. The most malleable factors identified as associated with SES segregation between schools relate to the types of schools in each area, and the ways in which school places are allocated.

The problem of segregation seems to arise partly from school diversity, giving families a reason, often perhaps a spurious reason, for choosing a school other than its quality or proximity (Taylor et al, 2005). In the US, newer types of school include a range of charter schools (Gleason et al, 2010; Ni, 2012), similar to the Swedish model of 'free' schools. Both have been emulated in England by academies and free schools since 2000, and more recently by university technical colleges (UTCs) and studio schools (Gorard, 2014b). In addition, any school that selects its intake in terms of religion will tend to increase segregation by ethnic origin (Harris, 2012), parental income and education (Allen and West, 2011) and social class (Shepherd and Rogers, 2012). Any school that selects students by prior attainment will inadvertently increase segregation by social class because of the well-established association between social background and attainment (see Chapter 3 earlier).

Some of the strongest associations are between segregation and the types of local schools (see Table 4.7). The proportion of local schools that are controlled by the local authority, comprehensive or at least not selective (here labelled 'community schools') is strongly linked to lower levels of, and reduction over time in, all types of segregation (−0.7 R for FSM). This is a crucial finding. Diversity of schooling, and giving families any reason to choose schools by their type rather than perceived quality or convenience, is linked to increased clustering of types of pupils, with all of the dangers that this entails (see above).

The remaining special schools in any area drive up both SEN and FSM segregation because of the link between FSM and SEN (see Chapter 3). Foundation schools and city technology colleges are partly or overtly selective, and this drives segregation because of the link between early attainment and disadvantage. The more surprising result,

Table 4.7: Correlation between local school characteristics and local authority segregation figures, England, 2015 (%)

	FSM-eligible segregation	SEN statement segregation	Non-White ethnicity segregation
Community schools	−0.7	−0.3	
Foundation schools	0.3		
Special schools	0.3		
City technology colleges	0.3		0.3
Academy converters	0.5	0.3	0.2
Selective schools	0.6	0.3	

Note: Blank cells represent correlations of less than 0.2 in absolute value.

to some extent, is raised segregation in areas with more converter academies (see also Chapter 6).

Originally, academies were set up both to stop the spiral of decline in existing schools and to improve student results in heavily disadvantaged areas. The schools selected to participate at the outset were among the most disadvantaged, and so where new academies ended up taking a smaller share of local FSM-eligible students than previously, this meant that neighbouring schools had to take more, and so the local clustering of poorer children into specific schools actually reduced.

However, the academies programme has, more recently, been driven by a purported school improvement agenda, and the social justice element is now largely ignored, meaning that almost any school is eligible to convert. Private fee-paying schools, ex-grammar schools, foundation schools and many others (including primary) have become academies. And the even newer free schools have been set up as academies from fresh. All of these are clearly nothing like the most disadvantaged schools in their area, and were not in anything like a spiral of decline beforehand. This raises the very real danger of increased local SES segregation between schools, especially where the new academies also begin to take a smaller share of FSM-eligible students like the early ones did (Gorard, 2009b). Over time and across political administrations, their number has grown quickly to become the majority school type at secondary level.

The newer converter academies generally take far less than their fair share of FSM pupils, while the original sponsor-led academies generally take more than their share. They have very different profiles. For example, 51 per cent of converter academies take less than half their 'fair share' of FSM pupils, whereas only 3 per cent of sponsor-led academies do. The difference between converter and sponsor-led academies then manifests itself in their association with local levels of

SES segregation between schools (see Table 4.8). Whereas, in 2012, the existence of converter academies in any local education authority (LEA) was strongly positively linked to local levels of SES segregation between schools (Pearson's R or around +0.41), the existence of sponsor-led academies was weakly but negatively linked to SES segregation (R of around –0.14). However, LEAs with both types of academies were linked to higher levels of segregation than LEAs with a higher proportion of community schools. In terms of mixed intakes, having state-maintained community schools is clearly preferable.

Internationally, it is quite clear that the extent to which pupils are clustered together with others like them socially and ethnically as well as in terms of ability is much higher in countries with selective systems (Jenkins et al, 2008; OECD, 2014). Segregation tends to be high in countries with tracking or selection at a young age such as Germany, Austria, Belgium and Hungary. Such 'segregation' is lower in developed countries with little or no diversity of schooling such as those in Scandinavia, linked to low achievement gaps, higher average attainment and also the highest percentage of very skilled students (Alegre and Ferrer, 2010).

In England, in areas that have grammar schools, those students living in the most disadvantaged parts are less likely to attend a grammar school even where they have high prior attainment scores (Cribb et al, 2013). Grammar schools are fully selective by attainment testing at age 11, and take only 28 per cent of their 'fair' share of poorer children (DfE, 2017). And even where those attending grammar schools are denoted FSM-eligible, they will have been so for fewer years. Of course, some of these differences could be due to the kind of pupil populations in areas where the minority of 163 grammar schools remain, which could differ from the rest of the country. To assess this, Tables 4.9 and 4.10 compare those attending grammar schools with only those pupils in areas with grammar schools. These make it clear that the differences are not produced by the geography of where grammar schools still exist. In fact, pupils in grammar schools are even less representative of their local areas than they are of pupils in England as a whole. Those attending grammar schools live in less deprived IDACI (income deprivation affecting children index) districts within

Table 4.8: Correlation between percentage of each type of local school with local level of segregation, England, 2012

LEA-level segregation GS FSM	Percentage of sponsor-led academies	Percentage of converter academies
2012	–0.14	+0.41

Table 4.9: Characteristics of grammar school pupils compared to pupils in selective areas, 2015

	Grammar	Not grammar
Mean IDACI score	0.1	0.2
FSM years by KS4, all pupils	0.3	1.6
FSM years by KS4, FSM pupils	5.1	6.8

Table 4.10: Characteristics of grammar school pupils compared to pupils in selective areas, 2015 (%)

	Grammar	Not grammar
Non-White UK	25	18
EAL students	11	13
SEN students with statement	0	4
SEN students no statement	5	13

each local authority. In particular, even the few FSM-eligible pupils in grammar schools have been eligible for noticeably fewer years than in the rest of the school system.

Grammar schools admit negligible numbers of students with statements of SEN (biased towards dyslexia), and take more Pakistani and Chinese-origin students than represented by the local population.

Conclusion

All of the above factors can and do influence whether children go to schools with others like them, and so to the changes over time shown in Figure 4.1. In England, around 30 per cent of students would have to exchange their schools if SES and related segregation between schools were to be eliminated. Evidence from around the world shows that such segregation is unnecessary, and harmful to students. It is associated with greater unfairness in practice, worse opportunities for the most disadvantaged, lowered aspirations and lower participation rates in later education. And all of these risks are run by the system for no clear gain (see Chapter 6).

The clustering of students with similar characteristics in particular schools is partly determined by factors outside education, indeed, often outside immediate government control. The economic cycle, the nature of regional populations, residential segregation within regions, local population density, quality of public transport (especially in rural areas) and patterns of recent immigration are all determinants of either the level or trend in SES segregation between schools. Other determinants are quite clearly within education and within government control. The policy of inclusion for children with disabilities and learning challenges and the growth of diagnoses for non-visible disabilities has led to a general decline in segregation by SEN. The allocation of over-subscribed school places in terms of catchment, distance or feeder schools exacerbates or at least retains the impact of existing residential segregation (Taylor et al, 2003). Policy solutions include area-wide bussing, banding or local authority lotteries, combined with free travel, for those entitled, to any feasible school rather than simply to the nearest available. However, the biggest single controllable factor is the diversity of national school provision.

The quality of education available in a national school system should not depend on where a student lives or which school they attend. Therefore, new school types or schemes for only *some* pupils are not the way forward. The poverty gap in education will more likely be reduced by reducing differences between schools, opportunities and treatments than by celebrating them. There should therefore be no state-funded diversity of schooling, with the state wilfully continuing to provide what they claim (by implication) is an inferior experience for some. For example, if grammar schools were clearly better schools, then their advocates are effectively arguing that the 80 per cent in secondary modern schools should be condemned to an inferior education by the state. In fact, it is not clear that any type of school is better than any other, and so the money invested in them could have been used more fruitfully elsewhere. All young people should be included in mainstream institutions as far as possible. Controlling the school mix like this is one of the most important educational tasks for central and local governments – but it is one that they routinely evade (or worse).

FIVE

Differential attainment at school

This chapter looks in more detail at some of the patterns of attainment in Chapter 3, such as by sex and area of residence. I have assessed how these patterns change over time, over the lifetime of an individual and how they vary by level of education (Gorard, 2000c, 2001b). All of these factors give further clues as to why the patterns themselves exist and, as discussed in later chapters, what might usefully be done to improve attainment.

Background

There is a range of possible explanations for why individuals reach different levels of attainment at school. They include physical or physiological explanations such as differing maturity or diet, family and background characteristics such as variation in the stability of home life or the ability of parents to assist with education, differences in the quality of schools and teachers, and other reasons including chance. It is also possible that the differential attainment of boys and girls at school is linked to differences in their rate of maturation. While this book considers the role of poverty and other challenges in detail throughout, Chapter 6 focuses on the role of schools and teachers and Chapter 9 on the impact of parental involvement in their child's education, along with further factors influencing attainment that lie outside the control of schools. However, explanations such as the physiological one are mostly beyond the scope of this book.

There is a high correlation between the results of early cognitive ability tests and later social class, and between social class and qualification, and, of course, between qualification and HE participation (Bond and Saunders, 1999). Traditionally, studies based on twins and fostering have emphasised the role of inherited 'talent' in the reproduction of family educational attainment (Herrnstein and Murray, 1994). Children from high-SES families appear better at solving problems from a very young age, even though children from all families seem to use the same approaches to solving problems (Ginsburg and Pappas, 2004). But all such studies acknowledge that talent flourishes more in certain environmental conditions. Very early differences and progress in learning might be more to do with hereditary general ability and physiological growth or not, but as children grow older, the role of early ability appears to lessen (Gottfredson, 2004). Or it may be that IQ (or similar) is key to progress in higher-income families, whereas the home and community environment is key for lower-income families (Turkheimer et al, 2003). Indeed, IQ might improve with education, which is a more hopeful thesis (Ritchie and Tucker-Drob, 2017).

Of course, all such studies suggest that physical *and* social background are relevant, but that their importance varies with age and levels of disadvantage. A more recent study suggested a clear but relatively weak link between genetics and educational outcomes, such as explaining only 9 per cent of variation in achievement at age 16 (Selzam et al, 2016). Genetics is also linked to eventual family SES by about the same amount, meaning that it may play both a direct and indirect part in reproducing education outcomes over generations. Capron and Duyme (1989) found that children born to high-SES parents scored higher than children born to low-SES parents in general, but that children adopted by high-SES parents scored higher than children adopted by low-SES parents. This is, as might be expected, evidence that both sets of factors matter – perhaps poor early diet affects early development, for example, and poor diet will appear more often in families living in poverty (Wallace, 2005). As in Hebb's rectangle, it probably makes little sense to ask which side contributes more to the area.

Therefore, when the remainder of this book focuses on background, social conditions, schooling, and so on, this is not because early or even innate differences between individuals do not exist. They probably do. But these are not the subject of my research, and are not something that we can easily do anything about directly via education. It is better to focus on the more easily malleable explanations such as poverty or schools because interventions in these areas can be used where needed to ensure that everyone reaches the standard of education to which they should be entitled.

The fact that some individuals do better in education than others is therefore a given, whether due to luck, talent, effort or family background. The remainder of this chapter looks at the extent to which high and low achievers are clustered geographically or in terms of their apparently unrelated characteristics such as sex (the issue of age-in-year was covered in Chapter 3).

Differences between countries and regions

One theme of my work has been responding to claims by others that schools in a different country or region are especially effective in producing attainment outcomes. These claims have included the supposed superiority of schools in England compared to Wales (Gorard, 1998c,d), schools in the Pacific Rim compared to the UK (Gorard, 2001b), and schools in the South of England compared to the North, especially the North East (Gorard, 2016a).

Comparisons between the educational processes and outcomes in different countries or between regions within one country are popular among policy-makers and commentators. Indeed, they have become a kind of annual 'education Olympics' for some. Such evidence allows policy-makers and others to compare changes in countries in which a new policy is introduced, with changes in a country unaffected by the new policy. However, it is very difficult to draw practical answers from international comparisons within education because of the huge variations in age ranges, curricula, motivation and forms and times of assessment. All geographical comparisons need to take into account local social and economic factors if they are not to be misleading.

England and Wales

Some of my earliest work in this field involved comparisons of school outcomes in England and Wales. This was done in reaction to claims made by some senior academics, politicians and the press that students in Wales were 'schooled to fail' because Welsh schools under-perform, and the schools should be looking to their more successful neighbour schools in England as models for their own improvement (Jones, 1996). The supposedly poor Welsh school effect was based simply on the fact that schools in Wales had (and still have) lower average school outcome measures than the average for England. For example, in 1995 around 67 per cent of pupils in England gained five or more GCSEs grade A★-C (the Foundation Stage target for 16-year-olds at that time) compared to only 62 per cent in Wales. And this level of percentage point difference was maintained until 2016 (the last year in which England used A★-C grades). The same relative position applies to the level of qualification more generally across the population of Wales, the publication of 'league tables' of school examination results and school inspection reports. On almost any score of educational achievement that can be devised, the results in Wales were and remain inferior to those in England.

Such comparisons have had important implications for Welsh education policies. The relative ineffectiveness of schools in Wales has been the basis for politicians' improvement strategies and targets across Labour and Conservative administrations (Welsh Office, 1997). It was linked to the creation of targets for schools (see Chapter 12). And the comparisons became part of the push for more Welsh-medium schools, or *ysgolion Cymraeg*, deemed to be more effective than their English-medium counterparts in Wales, again because of their higher average examination outcomes (see Chapter 6).

However, these policy implications were not appropriate because the comparisons are not valid. Raw-score comparisons take no account of the underlying differences between Wales and parts of England. Wales has a lower population density, flatter occupational class profile, older population and more long-term sick and registered unemployed residents than England, on average. These problems of remoteness, relative poverty and economic inactivity may be sufficient by themselves to explain the lower levels of attainment in schools in Wales compared to England. The raw-score comparisons also take no account of prior attainment (see Chapter 6). This all makes the comparisons intrinsically unfair in a way that should have been obvious to the academics peddling them and the policy-makers believing and acting on them.

Without presenting the details here, I created a regression model with the KS4 examination outcomes for individual schools as the predicted variable, and the local level of FSM segregation (as in Chapter 4) as predictor. I created equivalent models for the local authorities in Wales and an equal number of authorities in England that were their closest match in terms of population density, social class figures and adults with HE qualifications, based on the national census. There was no difference between the scores for the two countries once these background factors had been taken into account. Looked at another way, I also used all schools in England to create a regression model linking the percentage of pupils gaining 5+ GCSEs grade A★-C in England to these same background factors. The ensuing model was then used to 'predict' the scores for schools in Wales, and this suggested that, if anything, schools in Wales may have been producing slightly better results than equivalent schools in England. The policy-makers, media commentators and others were wrong and the policy was not misguided. The policy effort was needed elsewhere, so this red herring created a needless opportunity cost (Gorard et al, 1998c,d).

North–South comparisons for England

Most recently I have been concerned with comparisons between education outcomes in the North and South of England, and I will cover this issue in a bit more detail here. It has the same approach, results and implications as the earlier work for Wales, and in any such comparison that I have ever seen (Gorard, 2000c). Since at least the 1990s it has been relatively common for policy-makers, commentators and even academics to use differences in school-level attainment between economic regions of England to claim that the lower-attaining region is somehow under-performing. No allowance is made for differences in school intakes, levels of relative poverty or usually even the prior attainment of students. When these differences are factored in, or a comparison is made with similar regions in terms of school intakes, the differences will reduce or even disappear (Gorard and See, 2013). But the pattern of abusing raw-score regional figures continues. This can be distressing for schools, staff, pupils and families. It can lead to wasteful or even harmful attempted solutions. For example, there might be claims that it is somehow the students' fault because they are not aspirational enough despite clear evidence that high aspirations are relatively common and un-stratified in schools (Gorard, 2012c). Perhaps such attitudinal causes are proposed because they would then have cheap solutions. But these solutions do not work. It is not, like the X Factor programme on television, simply a question of wanting 'it' more. Despite policy often being directed at local level, the region, authority or district attended has little or no relevance for student attainment in the UK (Henderson, 2008).

A recent example of such a policy issue concerns the apparent North–South divide in attainment in England. Many commentators agreed with the former Chancellor George Osborne, that 'There is now overwhelming evidence that attainment at 16 is too low in the north, leaving us lagging behind UK and international competitors' (quoted in Halliday, 2017). The then Chief Inspector of Schools in England said that in northern England, 'children have less of a chance of educational success than children south of the Wash' (quoted in Adams and Weale, 2016). According to Ofsted, there are more than twice as many secondary schools judged 'inadequate' in the North and Midlands compared with the South and East. And these views influence policy in and beyond education, such as whether to fund transport links and improve the rail network in the north (*Financial Times*, 2016). According to the CBI after 'an analysis of official statistics', ensuring that pupils get good GCSE or equivalent qualifications would be the most effective way of tackling productivity differences across the UK rather than prioritising faster road and rail links in the Midlands and North of England, as the government had planned. Educationally, schools in the North East of England are being asked to improve their results in a North East Challenge akin to the supposedly successful London Challenge (Hutchings et al, 2012), but with the difference that the North East would not receive the extra funding that the London schools did. The London Challenge schools were already receiving more funding per pupil than those in the North East, and started their 'challenge' with already higher attainment and a lower poverty gap. It remains unclear how successful the London Challenge really was.

The North and South of England are similar in many ways and there are high-attaining pupils everywhere, but there are bigger pockets of long-standing disadvantage in the North, of a kind that is well known to be linked with lower average attainment at school. In the same way, two schools may be similar in some respects according to official data, such as the percentage of pupils eligible for FSM. But they could be very different in reality, with one school having mostly pupils FSM-eligible for that year only and the other having pupils who had been officially classified as poor for their entire school career (a distinction shown to be important in Chapters 3 and 4). Even the otherwise excellent pupil premium funding that follows disadvantaged pupils to their schools is 'unfairly' distributed between rich and poor areas (Gorard, 2016b). It must be recalled that any student ever eligible for FSM will attract pupil premium funding and be taken into account in official performance figures. But such students are likely to have been recorded as poor for over six times as long in Middlesbrough (in the North East) as Wokingham (in the South East), for example (see Table 5.1). This suggests that official accounts of failure in the North East could be at least partly due to such a big difference in real levels of poverty.

Table 5.1: Mean number of years FSM by local authority, England

Local authority	Mean years FSM by KS4
Wokingham	0.5
Buckinghamshire	0.6
West Sussex	0.7
Middlesbrough	3.1
Manchester	3.4

The difference that this could make to the pupil premium attainment gap as used in policy is illustrated using two local authority areas. Kensington and Chelsea, and Middlesbrough, are both urban areas and have around the same proportion of pupils who have never been eligible for FSM, which means that they each receive comparable pupil premium payments based on the number of pupils who had ever been eligible for FSM (47% for both areas in Table 5.2). However, Kensington and Chelsea in the South is a relatively rich area of London, while Middlesbrough is a very deprived area in the North East with high unemployment. They therefore differ considerably in terms of the proportions of the kind of FSM-eligible pupils they contain.

In Kensington and Chelsea, the clear majority of pupils who have ever been FSM-eligible are not now. These include, therefore, a proportion that are near the threshold of FSM rather than among the very poorest in the country. This could affect the level of qualifications obtained. In fact, over 36 per cent of pupils in Kensington and Chelsea are missing any data on FSM eligibility, confirming that a large number of residents use private fee-paying schools. This will remove some of the highest-attaining or richest pupils from attendance at local state-maintained schools. Because of the well-established correlation between SES and attainment, this would then tend to reduce the overall level of attainment in local state-funded schools. But it would also reduce the likely gap between the poorest and the majority of those pupils remaining in state-funded schools. This is the kind of factor never considered by those promoting the apparent success of the London Challenge. Therefore, as well getting as much extra pupil premium funding as Middlesbrough, the schools in Kensington and Chelsea are more likely to be praised by Ofsted and rewarded in pupil premium awards for having a low poverty gradient. This is unfair.

The situation in the deprived authority of Middlesbrough is very different. Here only 4.7 per cent of pupils are missing data on FSM eligibility, which is around the same as the national average. This confirms that few pupils attend private fee-paying schools. Almost all

Table 5.2: Percentage of each FSM group in Middlesbrough, and Kensington and Chelsea

FSM group	Middlesbrough	Kensington and Chelsea
Never FSM	53	53
FSM previously	14	27
FSM now	33	19

pupils are in the state-funded system and so contributing to the pupil premium attainment gap there. Unlike in Kensington and Chelsea, the clear majority of pupils who have ever been FSM-eligible still are. They are likely to include many of those from families permanently receiving other benefits or on low incomes. And it should be expected that these two factors would both tend to increase the pupil premium attainment gap (irrespective of what actually goes on in schools or how the pupil premium is used). Not taking account of the duration or level of poverty may be badly misleading both policy and school funding in England.

A regression model is one way to assess the relevance of this for attainment outcomes in the North East (where Middlesbrough is). I used capped GCSE or equivalent point scores as the outcome variable for each of the 600,000 pupils in England in 2015. The predictors were pupil background variables such as sex, FSM status, first language, ethnicity, precise age-in-year and prior attainment at KS1 (when they were aged 7). I then added whether the pupil was at school in one of the 10 local authorities in the North East of England or not. Putting all of the background variables in the first step of the model explains or predicts around 67 per cent of the variation in KS4 outcomes (see Table 5.3). However, then adding knowledge of whether a pupil was at school in the North East of England or not added nothing to the explanatory power of this model. This strongly suggests that any surface differences between the North East and other regions disappear once the differences in school intakes are taken into account. There is greater poverty and lower early attainment in the North East, but there is no additional educational problem in terms of school or teacher quality for policy to address. As with Wales, policy is being misled by raw scores.

Table 5.4 lists the coefficients from the model. As would be expected, prior attainment at KS2 is the best single predictor of attainment at KS4. Aside from prior attainment, the most important predictor is the number of years any student has been eligible for FSM (here negative, as FSM pupils have worse average outcomes than others). Adding context, and using this more refined measure of poverty, leads to a different substantive finding to that of the CBI and others

Table 5.3: 'Effect' sizes (R) from multi-stage regression models predicting total capped KS4 points

Background predictors	0.82 (or R-squared of 0.67)
Whether in North East	0.82

Table 5.4: Standardised coefficients from multi-stage regression models predicting capped KS4 points

KS2 average points (prior attainment)	0.57
KS1 average points (prior attainment)	0.10
Sex of pupil	0.08
Month in year (summer-born)	0.04
Number of years known to be FSM-eligible	−0.10
IDACI scores (deprivation)	−0.05
SEN	−0.10
Mean number of years FSM-eligible, school	−0.05
Joined school in last two years (mobility)	−0.08
EAL	0.08
Non-White UK (minority ethnic group)	0.06
Schooled in North East	0.01

(above). In fact, as with Wales, the coefficient for the North East yields a negligibly small benefit for attending a school in the North East ('effect' size 0.01).

Of course, it is possible to argue that such value-added or pupil progress models do not work (see Chapter 6). If they work at all, it is with large numbers and where there is no attempt to deal with individual schools or teachers, as here. Given that a true experiment is not possible – whereby students from the North are taught in the South and vice versa – if this kind of progress model is not accepted, there is no way for all of those policy commentators (see above) to judge whether there are regional differences in school effectiveness. Is there evidence that schools and colleges in the North East of England perform worse with equivalent students? Either way, the answer has to be 'no', and any blame for the local schools, teachers, students or families by Ofsted or politicians is therefore invalid. And so the policy of improving transport and local infrastructure should probably have gone ahead, or at least should not have been prevented by the excuse of poor attainment.

Differences linked to student-reported sex

It has been shown in Chapter 3 and throughout the book that particular social and economic groups have lower attainment on average than their peers. In many cases this is easily understandable. For example, it is part of the current definition of SEN in the UK that children with SEN will find school more challenging. It is therefore no surprise that SEN children have lower average levels of attainment. The key is what can be done to assist them. I have also looked at differential attainment by family income, first language and recent immigrant status. In each of these examples there is at least a surface explanation for the patterns. But there are other student characteristics linked to lower attainment that are not so easily explained. The remainder of this chapter uses the example of students' reported sex.

In all OECD countries and almost all countries for which there is data, girls do better at school than boys. The dominant account of the student sex gap in attainment in the UK still tends to be that boys were once ahead, girls have overtaken them, the gap widened over time and the problem of boys' under-achievement is most marked at the lowest level of attainment (David et al, 1997). In the late 1990s it appeared that boys' under-achievement at school had reached 'crisis point'. These historical changes were explained by ideas such as there being an increase in 'laddishness' in modern society, the breakdown of the family, feminisation of the workforce reducing the gains from education for males, too many female primary teachers and even the prevalence of mixed-sex teaching.

What I showed then and subsequently is that, other than the fact that girls are doing better than boys at school, all of these claims are incorrect (Gorard et al, 1999b, 2001; Salisbury et al, 1999). And therefore, the supposed explanations such as the increasing poor behaviour of boys do not work either.

Using the figures for all students in Wales over several years, I computed both achievement and entry gaps for every level, grade and subject of examination, over several years. In maths at KS1 there was no difference between the proportion of boys and girls in the age cohort attaining at least the lowest level results (Level 1 in Table 5.5). This was a common finding. At every Key Stage including at A level, there was no gap between the results of boys and girls at the lowest level of qualification. Whatever the differential attainment is, and is caused by, it is not an issue for low achievers at all. There is a small gap in favour of girls at Level 2 of KS1 (the 'expected' level for this assessment), and a small gap in favour of boys at Level 3 (exceeding

Table 5.5: Achievement gap in favour of girls: KS1 maths, Wales

Year	Level 3	Level 2	Level 1
1995 task or test	−2	3	0
1996 task or test	−5	3	1
1997 task or test	−2	3	1

expectation). The figures for Level 3 are more volatile from year to year, as they represent such a small fraction of the cohort.

In the same years, there was no student sex gap in either entry or low achievement in maths at GCSE (see Table 5.6). There had not been an entry gap since 1992, although there had been an achievement gap in favour of boys at grades A and then A★. This gap has disappeared at all grades below A★, without there being a clear trend towards a gap in favour of girls. The gap at A★ is very volatile, being attained in 1997 by 25 more boys than girls from an examination cohort of 32,000. As with KS1 to KS3, maths at GCSE is close to neutral in student sex terms, and the differences, such as they are, tend to favour only boys at higher grades. Since 1994 there has been consistently no difference in the attainment of boys and girls at grade C and above (the key benchmark grade). The picture for science was the same.

In some respects the picture for English was like the other two core subjects at KS1. Approximately similar proportions of boys and girls attained Level 1 (see Table 5.7). Again, there are few indications that the gaps are growing over time. However, unlike in maths and science, there is a significant gap in favour of girls at Level 2 (the 'expected' outcome), and a very large gap at Level 3. Again, this is a common finding. The only level at which there are substantial gaps with girls ahead is at the highest levels of attainment. This is clearly not a situation that is likely to be explained by theories of school avoidance, bad behaviour or 'laddishness'.

Table 5.6: Achievement gap in favour of girls: GCSE maths, Wales

	Entry	A*	A	B	C	D	E	F	G
1995	−1	−2	−2	0	1	0	1	1	1
1996	0	−16	−5	2	1	1	1	0	0
1997	1	−11	0	3	1	1	1	1	1

Table 5.7: Achievement gap in favour of girls: KS1 English, Wales

Year	Level 3	Level 2	Level 1
1995 task or test reading	19	7	1
1996 task or test reading	20	8	2
1997 task or test reading	20	7	2
1995 task or test writing	34	8	2
1996 task or test writing	28	8	3
1997 task or test writing	39	7	3

At GCSE level there was a very small entry gap for English language in favour of girls, hovering since 1992 between 1 and 2 units, but there are large gaps in achievement at grade D and above (see Table 5.8). While this clear evidence of differential attainment may be alarming, it should be noted that apart from the accentuation at high grades caused by the introduction of the A★ grade in 1994 (which affected the student sex gap in all subjects), there is no evidence here of any increase in the gap, and some evidence of the reverse. Overall, 1997 was the most neutral year for English GCSEs and student sex since records began in 1992.

Other subjects have a pattern somewhere between the almost neutral science and maths, and the strongly unbalanced results in favour of girls in English. Those subjects involving essay writing such as history have gaps more like English, whereas more technical subjects are more like maths.

When the results of all subjects are combined to give an assessment of the examination system for each age group as a whole, the rather complex details above can be simplified somewhat. Table 5.9 shows the achievement gap in favour of girls at the benchmark or expected level for each assessment (Level 2 at KS1, Level 4 at KS2, Level 5 at KS3, grade C at GCSE and C at A level). Given that the entry gap at GCSE remains constant at around 3 units in favour of girls (taking

Table 5.8: Achievement gap in favour of girls: GCSE English, Wales

	Entry	A*	A	B	C	D	E	F	G
1992	2		27	23	16	10	5	1	0
1993	2		31	24	16	10	5	2	0
1994	3	43	34	27	18	11	5	1	0
1995	1	44	35	24	16	8	4	1	0
1996	1	43	36	25	16	9	4	1	0
1997	2	43	35	25	15	9	5	2	1

Table 5.9: Achievement gap in favour of girls for each Key Stage 'benchmark', Wales

Year	KS1	KS2	KS3	GCSE	A level
1992				7	1
1993				7	-1
1994				8	0
1995	4			8	2
1996	5	2	5	8	0
1997	4	0	5	8	2

more GCSEs) and 10 units at A level, it is clear that the differential attainment of boys and girls has not changed much over these six years. Indeed, on these figures, it would be impossible to 'extrapolate' to a time when the situation was much different. Girls in any year group were proportionately more likely to achieve any individual benchmark grade up to A level (taking into account entry gaps, which could themselves be the result of prior differential attainment).

Figure 5.1 shows the student sex gap in England for the five GCSEs grade A★-C or equivalent threshold for as far back as the DfE has records. There is no evidence of a period when the scores for boys were ahead of girls (Gorard, 2004d). Until 1987/88 the overall trend in the student sex gap was small and relatively static. Then, there was a sudden jump in the size of the gap over a two-year period until it stabilised again at a considerably higher level from 1988/89 onwards. A number of changes occurred at the same time as this sharp rise. The separate CSE and GCE examinations were merged into GCSEs, annual rises in qualifications began, there was a move from norm referencing to criterion referencing when judging exam standards and an increase in the proportion of coursework. All of these alterations provide a rich source of explanations for the sudden increase in the student sex gap. It is peculiarly naive to assume, as the DfE and some researchers in this field appeared to, that the assessment system is

Figure 5.1: Proportionate gap in favour of girls attaining 5+ GCSEs A*-C or equivalent

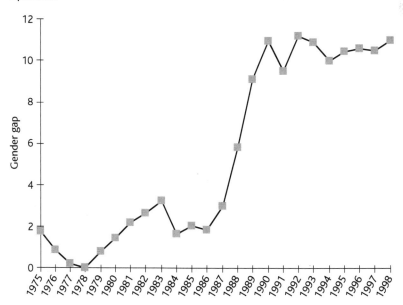

neutral by student sex and that any differential is related to genuine discrepancies in achievement or performance.

The dramatic shift from 1987-89 and relative stasis in the student sex gap both before and after this suggests that many potential explanations are untenable. Whatever is considered to have produced the change, it must be almost instant in impact, and one-off in nature. Any useful causal explanation should focus on attainment at all levels, not just at the lowest grade. One obvious conclusion would be that differential attainment by student sex is a product of the changed system and nature of assessments rather than any more general failing of boys, their ability, application or the competence of those who teach them. This pattern of change over time is unlikely to be the result of a cultural change in society, the direct outcome of new styles of teaching, seating arrangements in schools, mixed-sex classes, boys' laddishness or poor attendance at school. So again, the costly policy 'remedies' have been misdirected.

When examined using total subject entries it is clear that the examination system at KS1 to KS4 favours girls to some extent, and teacher assessment even more so. Girls tend to enter more, and more varied, subjects at GCSE, achieving higher grades. However, they do not achieve more than their proportionate share of any qualifications since there is effectively no student sex gap at grade G in any subject at GCSE (which, it must be recalled, is the original pass grade). When broken down into subject groups it is clear that different patterns occur in English from maths and science. Although there are no significant entry gaps, and no achievement gaps at the lowest levels of attainment in *any* subject, there are achievement gaps at higher levels of attainment in English (as well as languages and humanities at GCSE). In general, the data show little change from year to year, but where change occurs, it is generally towards a decrease in the gap at any level. This is most obviously the case in aggregate measures such as the proportion attaining five or more GCSEs. At grades G and C the figure for boys is getting closer to the figure for girls every year. At A level, entry gaps in subject groups tend to be larger, while the achievement gaps that exist tend to be smaller. Later adult participation in education or training is still heavily unbalanced in favour of males (see Chapter 12).

A problem for boys' literacy not only appears in every country for which there are figures, but also across all outcome groups. If anything, the gap is higher among the highest attainers and smallest among the lowest attainers. For example, there are 4 per cent more boys than girls in the PISA study attaining the lowest level of reading scores, and 5 per cent more girls than boys attaining the highest level. In

England, this pattern is even more marked with a gap of 2 per cent at the lowest level and of 5 per cent at the highest level. These findings, confirmed by my more detailed analysis of UK examination statistics (Gorard, 2000b), have several implications. If the differences between males and females are universal, they are unlikely to be the result of culturally specific, or even of pedagogic, changes. The differences occur in very different education systems with different ages of school entry, curricula, teaching styles, forms of assessment, methods of allocating school places and so on. Any plausible explanation for the apparent under-achievement of boys must therefore transcend all of these differences. This means, of course, that a lot of money, time and effort has been wasted in the UK by policies to overcome the attainment gap, which are based on an incorrect diagnosis of its causes.

Discussion

This chapter has looked at some of the evidence on what were 'moral panics' at the time, such as the failure of pupils in Wales and the increasing under-achievement of boys and of parts of the UK. None survive even superficial scrutiny in the form presented by the media and politicians, and each may have led to inappropriate and therefore wasteful policies.

This chapter has also suggested that using the more sensitive measure of the duration of poverty (years FSM) has much to recommend it. Using the number of years a student has been eligible for FSM, and how segregated a school system is by poverty and other indicators of disadvantage, it is possible to explain substantive differences such as the apparently superior attainment of schools in the South of England compared to the North. Any policies predicated on the surface difference are being misdirected. Improving schools in the North East may not be as effective as investment in infrastructure, for example.

The potential implications of the analysis by years FSM for policies and practices based on calculating a pupil premium attainment gap are also substantial. The findings mean that when policy-makers, advocates of the success of the London Challenge, Ofsted, awards committees and others use the pupil premium gap as a measure of success, they are probably and unwittingly being very unfair. There is a problem for all such pupil premium attainment gap calculations caused by missing data, and because they take no account of the proportion of local residents using private schools (both influencing the calculation by their absence). They are also unfair because they do not take account of the threshold nature of FSM eligibility. They are ignoring the variation *within* that category stratified by prior educational challenges like SEN and EAL, and then again, by the qualification outcomes used to calculate the gap. Almost as importantly, the analysis shows that different areas have different proportions of types of FSM pupils. Heavily disadvantaged areas are likely to have more of the always FSM-eligible pupils, and this makes any comparison with other areas based on the pupil premium gap intrinsically invalid. This is in no way an argument against the pupil premium policy itself, but it does suggest that the impact of the policy needs a rather more robust evaluation than simply measuring changes in the pupil premium attainment gap.

Currently extra resources are given to schools on the basis of the number of pupils in that school who have ever been eligible for FSM (for the previous six years). This means that schools not only miss out on the extra money when data is missing, but that those schools taking the most disadvantaged pupils (likely to attain the lowest at KS4) get the same *per capita* as those who take the pupils moving in and out of eligibility. Currently, until all else is resolved, it would make more sense to allocate the pupil premium primarily on the basis of pupils eligible for FSM at the time of allocation, and then to update this every year throughout their school career. This would mean money going to the schools of those most in need, while they are most in need.

SIX

Differential school effects

Chapters 3 to 5 have shown that different social and economic groups have different average learning outcomes, even from an early age. It follows that schools taking markedly different types of students will tend to get different average results. Despite this, too many commentators, policy-makers and even some academics mistake raw-score educational outcomes for evidence of differential school and teacher effectiveness. A simple example, or what should be a simple example, is selective grammar schools in England (or similar schools across the world). Where schools select the most able or highest-attaining students at age 11, and these young people then obtain good qualifications at age 16 or high levels of competitive entry to university, this shows that the schools have selected well. It does not, in itself, mean that the schools have been particularly effective in enhancing learning. These high-ability students might have done as well or better at non-grammar schools.

Since the 1990s I have been investigating and writing about the supposed differential effectiveness of schools, school types and teachers, in terms of attainment outcomes. One theme has been responding to claims by others that schools of a specific type are especially effective in producing attainment outcomes. These claims have included the supposed superiority of Welsh-medium schools in Wales (Gorard, 1998c), specialist schools in England (Gorard and Taylor, 2001a), academies (Gorard, 2005b, 2009b), and grammar schools and private schools in both Wales and Pakistan (Siddiqui and Gorard, 2017).

In general, these claims for superiority do not stand up to even superficial scrutiny because the nature of the student intake to each type of school differs by so much. It is very like the comparisons between countries and regions in Chapter 5. Once differences in pupil prior attainment or in characteristics such as chromic poverty are taken into account, the surface differences in attainment are usually adequately explained. Put another way, no type of school within the national school system has been found to be more effective than any other with equivalent students. This chapter explains why.

Progress and contextualised scores .

There is a number of valid possible reasons for wanting to judge the performance of schools. In most developed countries, the majority of schools are publicly funded, and so the custodians of public money want to assess how well that money is being used. Policy-makers will be interested in how well this public service is working, and what the impact of any recent reforms has been. Parents and students might want to use a measure of school quality when making school choices. Heads and teachers might want feedback on what is working well and what is in need of improvement at their own schools. There are also, of course, a number of differing ways of judging school performance. Schools could be evaluated in terms of financial efficiency, student attendance, enjoyment of education, future participation in education, aspiration, preparation for citizenship and so on. The most commonly used indicator of school success around the world is student scores in assessments intended to discover how much or how well students have learned what is taught in the school.

For any set of schools, if we were to rank them by their student scores in assessments of learning, we would find that schools at the high and low ends differed by more than their student assessments. Schools in areas with more expensive housing (or more local income in the US), schools that select their student intake by ability, aptitude or religion and schools requiring parents to pay for their child's attendance will be more prevalent among the high scores. Schools with high student mobility, in inner cities, taking high proportions of children living in poverty or with a different home language to the language of instruction will be more prevalent among the low scores. This is, or ought to be, well known, and means that raw-score indicators are not a fair test of school performance. However, commentators and policy-makers still mistake high raw-score results as evidence of superior school effectiveness. A recent example was the 17 supposed factors of what works, based on best practice from world-class schooling systems in terms of PISA results (Lewis, 2017). This kind of misleading use of evidence is hard to halt.

This is not to say that particular schools do not make a difference, but that a great deal of the difference between school outcomes is directly attributable to their pupil intakes. Where a school is sited, its specialism, organisation and precise methods of allocating places to pupils mean that there is considerable variation in school intakes, in terms of prior pupil learning and indicators of possible disadvantage (Chapter 4). Some early studies of school effectiveness in the US found very little or no difference at all in the outcomes of schools once differences in student intake had been taken into account (Coleman et al, 1966), and successive studies across the world have found the same (Gorard, 2000b). The differences in student outcomes between individual schools, and types and sectors of schools, can be largely explained by the differences in their student intakes. The larger the sample, the better the study, and the more reliable the measures involved, the higher percentage of raw-score difference between schools that can be explained (Tymms, 2003). Looked at in this way, it seems that which school a student attends makes little discernible difference to their learning (as assessed by these means).

However, a different series of studies have come to an almost opposite conclusion, based on pretty much the same evidence. Starting with Rutter et al (1979) in the UK, and earlier in the US, school effectiveness researchers have accepted that much of the variation in school outcomes is due to school intake characteristics. But they have claimed that the residual variation (any difference in raw scores unexplained by student intake) is evidence of differential school effectiveness (Nuttall et al, 1989; Kyriakides, 2008). Like the first set of studies, these have tended to become more sophisticated and more technical over time.

Using the promising value-added (VA) approach, such studies judge schools by the progress that their pupils make during attendance at the school, not their absolute levels of attainment. Data on all pupils in the relevant school population is used to predict as accurately as possible how well each pupil will score in a subsequent test of attainment. Any difference between the predicted and observed test result is then used as a residual. The averaged residuals for each school are termed the school's 'effect', and are intended to represent the average amount by which pupils in that school progress more or less when compared to equivalent pupils in all other schools. A school with an average residual of zero is estimated to be 'performing' about as well as can be expected, given its intake. A school with an average above zero is doing better than expected. This judgement about progress is intended to be independent of the raw-score figures, making it fairer than assessment by raw scores. Since this 'school effect' is deemed a characteristic of the school, not its specific cohort of pupils, it should be reasonably consistent over time where the staff, structures, curriculum, leadership and resources of the school remain similar over time.

In England, and almost everywhere else, this approach took firm hold in policy and practice, and the results are in widespread use. The DfE publishes national figures for all schools as 'School

Performance Tables'. Individual school results are used in setting targets, development plans, assisting the school inspectorate Ofsted to help judge the quality of schools, and by some parents to help select a school for their child (Evans, 2008). They have even been used to close schools down. Disaggregated results have been used to reward (or caution) individual teachers and departments. The results therefore matter, and the assumption has generally been that the method works well enough to form the basis for such life-changing decisions.

Problems with progress and contextualised scores

However, this plausible-sounding approach does not really work very well in practice for a number or reasons (Hoyle and Robinson, 2003). School effectiveness analyses are error-ridden (Gorard, 2010d), and very sensitive to assumptions about errors (Televantou et al, 2015). Their ensuing school 'effects' are small, volatile across years, inconsistent across different kinds of achievement (Marks, 2015), and heavily dependent on the model used (Darling-Hammond, 2015). Therefore, published school performance measures based on VA scores are likely to be profoundly misleading, particularly for those such as parents and policy-makers unfamiliar with the high level of uncertainty in the estimates for individual schools (Perry, 2016).

Perhaps the biggest single problem with a VA approach is that it could never do what it was designed to – to be independent of the raw-score results. Because the VA score is based on the difference between prior and subsequent attainment, the variation in VA scores is half derived from the variation in prior attainment scores and half derived from subsequent attainment. This means that the R-squared correlation between prior attainment and the VA for any set of schools will be at least 0.5 (or R of above 0.7). In fact, the observed correlations can be even higher than this. An example from Gorard (2006d) follows.

Figure 6.1 shows GCSE results in 2004 for the 124 schools with complete information in York, Leeds, East Riding of Yorkshire and North Yorkshire. The x-axis shows the percentage of students in each school gaining Level 2 at age 16 (five or more GCSEs or equivalent at grade C or above). The y-axis shows the official DfE VA scores (with 1,000 added so that 1,000 becomes the average score rather than zero). There is a near-linear relationship, yielding a correlation of +0.96. This means that purported VA and raw scores are here measuring what is effectively the same thing. VA is no more independent of subsequent attainment than prior attainment (also correlated with VA scores at

Figure 6.1: The relationship between value-added (VA) (y) and absolute attainment (x), North Yorkshire, 2004

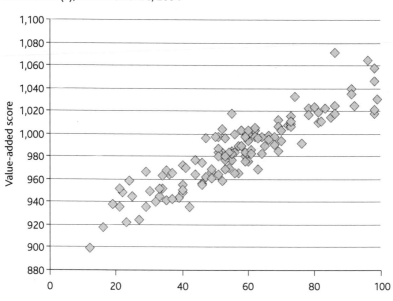

+0.96). VA is almost entirely predictable from the raw scores. But these raw-score values have been rightly rejected by alert commentators as not being a fair indicator of school performance. Therefore, VA must be rejected for the same reason. The same patterns appear for all schools in England every year, for both primary and secondary (Gorard, 2008a).

This makes such VA scores completely useless for their purpose – of judging progress rather than raw-score attainment. Worse than that, they are misleading because unwary commentators and users will assume that the VA scores are independent of the raw scores because of their seeming technical sophistication. This leads to unintended injustice, because the VA scores are no fairer than the heavily stratified raw scores presented in Chapter 3.

A second problem is illustrated in Figure 6.2, which shows the VA scores for all 2,897 schools in England with complete VA information for 2010. It is a cross-plot of the VA score (x-axis) and number of students in the school used to create that VA score (y-axis). It shows that all of the very large schools have VA at or near average (1,000), and that the most extreme VA scores are for schools with very few pupils. This suggests that many school VA results are a consequence of the volatility of small numbers.

Figure 6.2: Crossplot of value-added (VA) measures and the number of students in each school, England, 2010

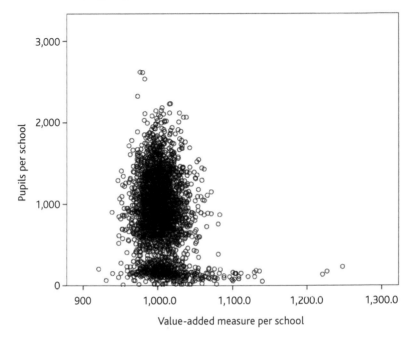

There is a similar correlation between the proportion of pupils in each school for whom measures are available (coverage) and VA score (Gorard and See, 2013). This means that there is a tendency for schools with less than 100 per cent of the data for their students to appear to have more divergent VA scores. Again, the variation in percentage of pupil data provided by different schools is not something that users of VA scores tend to consider.

VA scores are also much less stable than raw scores, and schools portray what are apparently dramatic swings in effectiveness every year (Kelly and Monczunski, 2007). A number of studies have found VA correlations of only around 0.5 over two successive years for the same schools (Gray et al, 2001). For example, McCaffrey et al (2009) found annual correlations for teacher VA scores of between 0.2 and 0.7. This means that less than half of the variation (and usually less than a quarter) is not common to successive years (Gorard, 2011b). This is confirmed in an analysis of all secondary schools in England over five years, by Gorard et al (2013b). Within two years the clear majority of variation in schools' VA is unrelated to their prior VA (see Table 6.1). Around 75 per cent is attributable to something else. This instability makes VA almost entirely useless for practical purposes because it is

Table 6.1: R-squared comparing VA scores over time, 2006 versus 2007-10, England

	VA 2007	VA 2008	VA 2009	VA 2010
VA 2006	0.62	0.26	0.31	0.21

Note: N=2,897 schools, because 1,118 of the total of 4,015 secondary school or college entries on the DfE School Performance website had significant amounts of relevant information missing for at least one year.

not a consistent characteristic of schools, and so may not even be a characteristic of schools at all.

This instability was illustrated by taking the VA measures of the 2,897 schools used in Table 6.1 and, assuming that these VA scores meant nothing, estimating how many schools would have five years of consistently positive or consistently negative VA scores. This is very generous to VA scores because consistency should mean more than simply consistently positive or negative, but also similar magnitude. But VA did not survive even this weaker test. In each year, almost exactly half of all schools will have positive VA because that is how VA is calculated. If the VA measure was really a fluke or otherwise not a consistent measure of the school to which it is attached, in each succeeding year almost exactly half of those with positive scores the previous year will have a positive score again. After two years, around 25 per cent of schools will have had two positive scores, 25 per cent will have had one positive followed by one negative, and so on. Thus, after five years, 2006 to 2010, 1/32 schools would be expected to have consistently positive scores each year. This would be 91 out of 2,897, and there would be a further 91 with consistently negative VA (total 182). Accepting that schools might have up to 5 per cent of data missing (95% minimum coverage), which is also a generous interpretation, I found only 173 out of all schools in England with a consistent direction of VA over five years. This again suggests that VA is completely meaningless.

The situation is actually even worse than this. The precise results of any VA calculation are heavily dependent on the quality and completeness of the data. In every VA calculation there can be pupils with final scores but no prior attainment recorded. For example, a child moving from a private school or from another country like Wales where there has been no KS2 testing will have no record of prior attainment in England. And there can be pupils moving in the opposite direction, with prior attainment but no final scores. In practice, the KS2 (primary) to KS4 (secondary) VA data has over 10 per cent such un-matched pupil records every year (Gorard, 2010d). This creates an initial error component (source of inaccuracy and bias) of at least 10 per cent in any VA calculation, and there is no way of adjusting for this statistically since the data just does not exist. It would be wrong to assume that the missing data was somehow a random subset of the data that does exist (Pugh and Mangan, 2003).

The situation is worse than this in three important ways. First, even where the scores exist they cannot be assumed to be totally accurate. Creating valid, comparable and reliable attainment scores is fraught with difficulty (Newton, 1997). Issues of comparability between forms and sources of assessment are widely known and international in nature (Lamprianou, 2009). Second, the system used in England from 2006 to 2010 factored pupil background characteristics into the calculations. This was done in order to improve the quality of the predictions and reduce the size of the residuals for disadvantaged groups of pupils (Evans, 2008). Again, this contextualised value-added (CVA) sounds a sensible and fair innovation. But it means that more data is needed on each pupil and this adds considerably to the level of missing data. At least 10 per cent of pupils are missing data every year on each key variable such as whether they are eligible for FSM, living in care, their ethnicity or additional educational needs. The overwhelming majority of student records had one or more key piece of information missing.

In practice, missing cases are usually just ignored, and missing values within cases are replaced with a default substitute – usually the mean score or modal category. So the DfE analysts have assumed that pupils without IDACI scores (usually because they have no postcode) live in average-income neighbourhoods. Anyone whose eligibility for FSM is not known is assumed not to be living in poverty, anyone without a KS2 or KS4 exam score is an average attainer, and so on. These kinds of assumptions have to be made in order not to lose the high number of cases with at least one missing value in a critical variable. But these are very questionable assumptions, and there is plenty of evidence from this book and elsewhere that pupils with complete and incomplete values in such datasets vary considerably (Amrein-Beardsley, 2008). Making these unjustified assumptions then means that a very high proportion of cases will have an incorrect value in at least one critical variable.

Third, and perhaps most importantly, all of these initial errors are compounded by the VA calculation itself to generate a far higher level of error in the residuals that result (see Chapter 2 earlier). Put simply, the 'residual' is the difference between the predicted and attained score for each pupil, and because the VA model is the best fitting one for each dataset, the residuals tend to be very small. They are small in comparison to the actual scores. But because the errors in the actual scores can be negative or positive, when the residuals are created their initial maximum errors are added. The outcome is a larger error component in a much smaller result. The maximum error can, and usually does, dwarf the residual by several orders of magnitude, perhaps being thousands of times bigger than initially (Gorard, 2010d). This makes the estimated results just about meaningless – as their volatility and the other issues above would suggest.

There is growing evidence, therefore, that for all of its appeal the VA method just does not work in identifying differential schools (Bradbury, 2011). One implication of this is that with no evidence that individual schools are differentially effective, in terms of test outcomes at least, it follows that there is no evidence that any specific types of schools are differentially effective.

Differences between schools and school types

In much the same way that unwarranted claims have been about the poor performance of some regions (see Chapter 5), claims have long been made that particular types of school are better or worse than others. For over 20 years I have examined such claims for a wide range of schools including fee-paying, foundation, faith-based, single-sex and Welsh-medium schools in Wales (Gorard and Siddiqui, 2018b). This chapter uses academies and grammar schools in England to establish the more general point. Within a state-funded, universal, quality-maintained school system such as in England and Wales there is no good evidence of systematic difference between the progress of students in any type of school. The claims for superiority are again based on a mistaken understanding of the differences between school intakes.

Policy-makers worldwide keep creating new kinds of schools that are similar to every other kind (that is, there is no fundamental dismantling or radical re-engineering of the concept of schools), claiming success for electoral or other reasons, and then not allowing these schools to be evaluated properly. Several studies based in the US have reported evidence that attainment can be affected by the type of school attended, such as the Promise Academy charter middle schools, Knowledge is Power Program (KIPP) middle schools (Tuttle et al, 2010) and more general charter schools (Gleason et al, 2010). Some studies suggest that attending a private school can lead to enhanced cognitive progress (Parsons et al, 2017). However, there are just as many studies or commentaries suggesting the opposite (Nelson, 2016).

The impact of charter schools in the US may be slightly negative (Clark et al, 2015), and the vaunted difference between faith-based and public schools in the Netherlands does not survive analysis that takes into account differences between student intakes (Driessen et al, 2016).

Academies

An example from England is the academies programme, started by one government in 2000, continued by the next government from 2010, and now extended to include 'free' and studio schools, and university technical colleges (UTCs). City academies were announced as a new form of secondary school for England in 2000, and the first three opened in 2002. They were independent of local authority control, like the prior city technology colleges (CTCs), and received preferential and recurrent per-pupil funding, like the prior specialist schools. These early academies were all replacements for existing schools deemed to be in spirals of decline, with low levels of pupil attainment, set in deprived inner-city areas, losing pupil numbers and taking more than their fair share of disadvantaged pupils. They were re-badged and often re-built, with new names, new governance and management, relaxation of National Curriculum requirements, and part-funded by sponsors from the private or third sectors. Advocates claimed they were better than their predecessor schools in terms of pupil performance, and as models of better schools for the future. Over time and across political administrations in the UK, their number has grown quickly. By the time of the Schools Census in 2012 there were 1,165 secondary academies – making up more than a third of all state-funded secondary schools in England (see Chapter 4 earlier).

The earliest three academies set up in 2002 were acclaimed as an almost immediate success for reportedly achieving better results than their predecessors with equivalent pupils. These claims by politicians and the media were modified when it was pointed out that these schools no longer had equivalent pupils, and all were recording weaker examination results than their predecessor schools had for at least one recent year (Gorard, 2005b). The same was true four years later (Gorard, 2009b), and subsequently.

For example, the predecessor school to the Bexley Business Academy had 24 per cent of pupils reaching Level 2 at GCSE in 1998 long before academisation in 2002, but the figure was only 21 per cent in 2003 after becoming an academy (see Table 6.2). And this was despite an increase in pupil exclusions, a decrease in FSM pupils and a national rise in GCSE results over time. Until recently, its Level 2 indicator

Table 6.2: Intake and outcomes for Bexley Business Academy, 1997-2008

	FSM (%)	Level 2 (%) KS4	Level 2 including English and maths	VA progress
1997	53	13	–	–
1998	49	24	–	–
1999	52	14	–	–
2000	50	10	–	–
2001	49	17	–	–
2002	46	–	–	–
2003	42	21	15	–
2004	37	34	13	984
2005	38	29	15	972
2006	39	32	17	1,004
2007	39	31	19	988
2008	30	50	29	1,012

Note: By 2008 all compulsory-age pupils in the school would have entered when it was an academy.

including English and maths was also low (in comparison to Level 2 without English and maths), suggesting that the school might have been 'playing' the system of qualification entries by entering pupils for less prestigious qualifications. In order to boost their apparent league table position, some schools at this time began entering students for dual and triple award qualifications (such as IT), deemed to be equivalent to GCSEs, but apparently considerably easier to pass. In 2005, the Academy recorded 15 per cent of pupils with the tougher Level 2 indicator, while all Bexley LEA schools recorded 46 per cent. In nine recorded years the VA measure of pupil progress for this school, as published by the DfE, has been just about as often negative as positive, and more strongly negative than positive (for example, 984 is 16 units away from the average of 1,000, whereas 1,012 is only 12 units away). If VA is trusted by the DfE, as it appears to be, this is not evidence of a superior kind of school any more than the poor raw scores are. And as is clear, the school has continuously reduced the proportion of its intake coming from families living in poverty (from 53 to 30%), meaning that the scores should have improved much more than the annual increase nationally. Equivalent and longer-term figures for all of the original academies appear in Gorard (2014b).

Overall, there is no clear evidence from these, or from the newer academies, that they have performed better (or worse) than the schools they replaced would have done. In fact, detailed analyses using as much data as possible have tended to show little or no substantive difference between the effectiveness of any types of schools within a national school system (Rutt and Styles, 2013), in England, the US or elsewhere. This issue is revisited later, in Chapter 13.

Grammar schools

A further example is provided by grammar schools. Historically, grammar schools were widespread in the UK, set up as part of a planned tri-partite system after 1944 that actually became a two-tier system of grammar schools and secondary moderns. Children took a series of tests at age 10/11 (the 11+), and a minority with high scores were selected to attend grammar schools, with the remainder going to secondary modern schools. In England, the number of grammar schools peaked at 1,298 in 1964, and then dropped to as low as 150 in 1989, before returning to the current level by 2004 (House of Commons Library, 2017). The 163 remaining schools are disproportionately academies, and single-sex with a sixth form, and their pupil intake has increased since 1980 (Bolton, 2016). These schools are over-subscribed and popular with many local parents (Lloyds Bank, 2016). The system has largely been abolished in Scotland and Wales for the same reasons as in England (they tended to segregate by excluding poorer children). The system was retained in Northern Ireland, where it was made even more segregated by having sectarian grammar schools for Catholic and protestant families (Gallagher and Smith, 2000).

In September 2016, the UK Prime Minister proposed removing the law banning state-funded schools in England (other than the 164 grammars in place in 1997) from using academic selection to allocate their pupil places. Instead, new schools such as free schools and academies would be able to become new grammar schools, and the existing grammar schools could expand further by opening satellite schools. The Prime Minister and the DfE describe this as a way to provide more good school places through 'schools that work for everyone' (see https://engage.number10.gov.uk/good-school-places). They see it as a responsibility of the state to provide especially for pupils who are gifted and talented, and feel that a comprehensive school environment cannot fully nurture the potential of such students. They claim that this will assist overall standards, reduce the poverty attainment gap and so aid social mobility.

Some VA studies comparing grammar schools with comprehensive or other types of school have suggested that the former have better pupil outcomes even once prior attainment is accounted for (Levačić and Marsh, 2007). However, these studies also suggest that the subsequent lower attainment of the much larger number of pupils in the associated secondary modern schools at least outweighs any such gains. The system of selection is zero-sum at best. Intriguingly, these same VA results appear if the model is still based on pupils attending grammar schools after age 11, but uses their KS1 results when aged 7 as a predictor, and their KS2 results when aged 11 as the outcome. This cannot be due to attending a grammar school because pupils only move after KS2, and so this odd result suggests that the purported grammar school effect is, in fact, a form of unmeasured pre-selection (Manning and Pischke, 2006). If the intakes to grammar schools really are already on a path to success based on their KS1 results, that subsequent success at KS4 at age 16 *must* not be mistakenly attributed to having attended a grammar school in the meantime. Grammar schools did not confer a real advantage in the past and in their prime (Halsey and Gardner, 1953), and do not appear to do so now (Coe et al, 2008; Sullivan et al, 2014). They do not increase social mobility in comparison to comprehensive schools, and do not assist working-class pupils with social class mobility (Boliver and Swift, 2011).

Children aged 10 or 11 are put forward and then tested for entry to grammar schools on the basis of their ability, prior attainment and motivation. However, this selection process indirectly also selects for a wide range of other characteristics, most of which should not be relevant. It is understandable that pupils with serious learning challenges will be less likely to pass an 11+ test of ability or attainment, even assuming it is a fair test in that respect. It is also understandable that children for whom English is not their first language might tend to do worse. But it is harder to see why family income, ethnic origin and precise area of residence should be so stratified. For the present, the key point is that those who go to grammar schools differ from the rest of the schools in England by far more than their talent as tested by the 11+. This is not like schools in the North and South happening to differ in terms of student disadvantage. This is now deliberate sorting by background since it has long been known that the extent to which pupils are clustered with others like them socially and ethnically is much higher in countries with selective systems (see Chapter 4 earlier), creating even further handicaps for the most disadvantaged students (Danhier, 2017).

Grammar schools and the areas they are in are also much more segregated by any of these indicators than the rest of England (see Chapter 4). However good grammar schools are (or not), this must be set against the real dangers from such a deliberate policy of socio-economic segregation between schools. Grammar schools use examinations to select children aged 10 or 11 who are predicted to do well in subsequent examinations at age 16. They select well, as evidenced by the high raw-score outcomes of these pupils five years later. This seems to confuse some commentators, members of the public and even policy-makers who assume that the good results are largely due to what happens in the school rather than the nature of the children selected. This is not a correct interpretation, and a counterfactual is needed to tell us what would have happened to these children if they had attended a different school. This is often attempted by looking not at raw-score outcomes but at the amount of progress made by each pupil while at the school (the 'value-added' model).

The differential effectiveness of grammar schools is estimated here via two regression models – one based on all schools, and the other only in areas that contain grammar schools (see Table 6.3). The R-value using all of the pupil background variables was 0.82 for both models (just the same as for the North East model in Chapter 5, of course). Additional background variables could improve this somewhat, but there will always be an error term due to missing data, measurement errors and so on (Gorard, 2010d). Each model is slightly better than it would be traditionally due to knowledge of exactly how many years each pupil has been FSM-eligible rather than using the traditional binary classification. If the model is run with 'current' FSM eligibility at KS4 as is standard rather than the number of years eligible, the R for the first model drops to 0.77. Although this difference is small, it does demonstrate that the new measure of chronic poverty (years FSM) is picking up variation that neither current FSM nor EverFSM6 does.

The first model including all pupils does not improve at all when knowledge is added of whether a pupil goes to school in a selective area or not. This means that if grammar schools are at all differentially effective, their effect is indeed zero-sum and wiped out by exactly equivalent harm done to the rest of the nearby school system. However, adding knowledge of whether a pupil goes to a grammar school also does not improve either model at all. With only 163 grammar schools,

Table 6.3: R from multi-stage regression models predicting capped KS4 points, England

	All pupils	Pupils in selective area
Background predictors	0.82	0.82
Whether in selective area	0.82	–
Whether in grammar school	0.82	0.82

it could be argued that they would not be expected to add much to the full model for all pupils in England. But they do not add anything to the smaller model restricted only to areas with grammar schools either. On this basis, grammar schools appear to be no more or less effective than other schools, once their clear difference in intake has been taken into account.

Table 6.4 shows the standardised coefficients for each variable in the models. Prior attainment at KS2 is by far the best predictor of KS4 outcomes, followed by prior attainment at KS1, the number of years eligible for FSM, and whether a pupil has any kind of special need. Among the least important variables are whether the school is in a selective area, and whether it is a grammar school – and these tend to cancel out because there are more students in selective areas than in the grammar schools. So, as with the international and regional comparisons, there is a small positive 'effect' size for grammar pupils, but a negative one for the larger number of all students in selective areas. The level of deprivation would increase in importance if FSM eligibility were not available because the two are correlated. Similarly, the month of birth in year appears less important than in reality because the prior attainment scores are acting as a proxy to a great extent (younger pupils do less well at KS1, KS2 *and* KS4).

As with academies, there is little evidence here that grammar schools have better results with equivalent pupils – a point taken up further in Chapter 13. More generally, it is hard to create consistently superior

Table 6.4: Standardised coefficients from multi-stage regression models predicting capped KS4 points, England

	All pupils	Pupils in selective area
KS2 average points (prior attainment) for individual	0.57	0.55
KS1 average points (prior attainment) for individual	0.10	0.11
Sex of individual	0.08	0.07
Month in year (summer-born) for individual	0.04	0.04
Number of years known to be FSM-eligible for individual	−0.10	−0.10
IDACI scores (deprivation) for individual area of residence	−0.05	−0.05
SEN for individual	−0.10	−0.10
Mean number of years FSM-eligible for school attended	−0.05	−0.07
Joined school in last two years (mobility)	−0.08	−0.07
EAL for individual	0.08	0.06
Non-White UK (minority ethnic group) for individual	0.06	0.05
Schooled in a selective area – individual	−0.01	–
Attends grammar school – individual	0.04	0.07

types of school within a national school system, and without creating more segregation.

Comprehensive, centralised, equitably funded school systems tend to produce both better outcomes overall and also smaller attainment gaps between rich and poor and high and low attainers (Burstein et al, 1980; Domovic and Godler, 2005; EGREES, 2005). Systems with early tracking of students by ability, or with high levels of fee-paying provision, or covert selection on the basis of faith or curricular specialism, or differential local funding arrangements tend to have stronger links between SES and attainment than egalitarian ones (Haahr et al, 2005). Therefore, poorer families will be helped more by the abolition of existing grammar schools than the creation of new ones, with inevitably a much larger number of schools around them that cannot be comprehensive in intake and that tend to receive less funding.

Differences between teachers

Despite the evidence so far, not only are VA models used to argue for the superiority of some schools or types of schools, they are used increasingly by policy-makers to judge the supposedly differential performance of teachers. Individual student experiences suggest that there are differences between teachers in their friendliness, empathy, efficiency and so on. There is also good evidence that the quality of the pupil–teacher interaction in schools is linked to pupils' sense of justice, trust in others and reports of citizenship activity (see Chapter 9). Perhaps this is the clearest difference that individual teachers make, through their daily behaviour and on the wider outcomes of schooling. In addition, there is indicative evidence, particularly from pupil reports, that there is considerable variation in the skills, even very basic skills, of teachers. This may be partly the result of variability in the process of admitting and qualifying trainee teachers (see Chapter 11).

Pupils report considerable variation in the quality of teaching, as they experience it (Gorard and See, 2011). They appreciate innovation and preparation in learning activities. Some said they enjoyed lessons that involved physical activities, like getting them to move around or acting out a scene. Others liked practical work, debates, dramatisations or just the unexpected – almost anything where there is variation in delivery and activity:

> 'We had to do this electrons thing and then the teacher got us all to stand round in a circle and we had to hold this rope, and we were the electrons and then we kind of

moved around, so they only move in one way the electrons. If like one falls, then the other can like push the other one.'

There are also pupil accounts of teacher behaviour in stark contrast. In fact, poor basic pedagogic skill and uninspiring teaching were the basis for most complaints from pupils. There were accounts of having to listen to a dull teacher for lengthy periods, passive copying, note taking and having to sit still:

'He just stands at the blackboard, or the whiteboard ... and just writing on the board....'

'[The teacher will] give you a sheet and you'll just go through each question and they might not even, unless you express a want to be told how to do it, they might not even, you know, support you in any way.'

'Teachers often go too fast, like you're saying; you don't end up knowing what's going on because you're trying to take notes, like, as fast as you can, and so you are not listening, so then your notes aren't completely there, so....'

''Cos, as soon as the teachers ask a question he doesn't, like, give anyone else a chance to think about it, he just shoot[s] off. Basically all of you just sit there, you're still thinking about the question and [expletive] gives the answers.'

However, it is not certain that students learn better or make more progress when taught by teachers that the students rate highly. In fact, there is almost no relationship between the two (Uttl et al, 2017). Is there a more accurate way to isolate the impact of good or bad teaching on student attainment?

There are systems in operation around the world that claim to be able to make that identification safely, and teachers are therefore rewarded and punished on that basis, such as in the long-running Tennessee Value-Added Assessment System (TVAAS) in the US. Since at least 1996, Sanders and others (Sanders and Rivers, 1996; Sanders and Horn, 1998; Sanders, 2000) have claimed to be able to estimate teacher effectiveness from pupil test scores. The claimed result is that 'Our research work ... clearly indicates that differences in teacher effectiveness is [sic] the single largest factor affecting academic growth of populations of pupils' (Sanders, 2000, p 334).

TVAAS has been claimed to be 'an efficient and effective method for determining individual teachers' influence on the rate of academic growth for pupil populations' (Sanders and Rivers, 1996, p 1). The system uses the academic test scores of pupils, tracked longitudinally, in a complex statistical analysis, to estimate the impact of teachers. There is a plausibility about their logic, which, coupled with a hunger for teacher accountability measures and a faith in technical solutions, has led some commentators to extol this approach. Barber and Mourshed (2007), for example, call the research by Sanders 'seminal' in showing how important effective teachers are, and how damaging poor teachers are, for pupil learning. This McKinsey report, and others like it, has been highly influential, and the research 'finding' about the importance of 'good teachers' is now reflected in some important policy documents, including those of the European Commission and the OECD (Coffield, 2012).

TVAAS defines teacher effectiveness in terms of progress made by their pupils while at school, as judged by changes in their test scores. It uses the 'scaled scores' of pupils over time (usually an average of three years) in each curriculum area to calculate gain scores, also referred to as a pupil's progress. Such a model of teacher effectiveness makes a number of important assumptions.

One key assumption is that differences in test scores can be attributed to the impact of teachers. As shown so far, most of the variation in test outcomes can be explained by pupil prior attainment and background. It is not clear that any residual variation in pupil gain scores can be safely attributed to teacher quality any more than to external determinants such as the continuing influence of differential family support, socio-economic trajectories and cultural and ethnic-related factors, or to school-level factors such as resources, curricula, timetabling and leadership, or educational factors beyond the school, such as district and area policies and funding arrangements. In addition, of course, the residual scores contain a substantial error component.

Sanders and Horn (1998, p 248) explain that they are dealing with 'fractured pupil records, which are always present in real-world pupil achievement data.' What they mean by this is that some pupil records will be missing or damaged, and some records that are present will contain missing data. They do not explain in any publication how large a problem this is. Estimating from the excellent NPD records for England discussed above, a very high proportion of the apparent gain scores for any pupil will actually be an error component deriving from the propagation of missing data, measurement errors and representational errors. All of the problems of school VA also exist for teacher effectiveness work, but are made worse by the fact that the number of pupils per calculation is so much smaller. It would be quite unwise to attribute the meaningless differences in these 'scores' to the influence of teachers. Teacher effectiveness will be even more volatile across years than VA scores for schools. In this context, it is intriguing to note the observation by Glass (2004) that one school directly on a county line was inadvertently attributed to both counties in the TVAAS, and so two VA measures were calculated. These two measures were completely different – probably because they did not really mean anything at all. Therefore, much of the variation in gain scores between pupils will be the result of error. There may be a small 'residual' of this residual that could be attributed to the impact of teachers (and of course to all other competing explanations, such as the continuing effect of pupil background), but it is hard to see how this might be identified separately, and then quantified in practice.

A further problem is that not all areas of teaching are routinely subject to statutory testing in Tennessee or elsewhere. Even in England, which has had a relatively prescriptive curriculum and programme of statutory testing at ages 7, 11 and 14, the focus is largely on maths, science and English. This means that some teachers cannot be included in any teacher effectiveness system, since their subject contributions are not tested for (most obviously, perhaps, sports and PE staff). It is also very rare for one pupil to come into contact with only one teacher, even for one subject. Team-teaching, teaching assistants, online and virtual participation and replacement and pupil teachers, among other factors, will confuse the issue further.

There is currently no way to demonstrate with convincing evidence that some teachers are more or less effective with equivalent pupils in terms of test outcomes. This is not necessarily because teachers are not differentially effective, but because the calculations involved are not possible. Teacher effectiveness research has all of the problems of school effectiveness research and more. And, of course, this is not to suggest that teachers in general do not make a difference – only that they are not obviously *differentially* effective.

Discussion

Going to school is an important formative experience for young people, and going to school is very different to not going to school. But this is not what VA assesses. VA is not yet a safe way of measuring progress for students, teachers or schools. Until its problems with such small units of analysis have been resolved by further development, it would be better not to use VA models in practice. Commentators, policy-makers, educators and families need to be warned. If VA scores are as meaningless as they appear to be, there is a serious ethical issue wherever they have been or continue to be used to reward and punish schools or to make policy decisions. VA is zero-sum, meaning that it is inherently competitive and schools can only improve their scores at the expense of others. When assessing the impact of teachers on pupil attainment, the propagation of initial errors and the stratified nature of the confounding variables are such that no teacher 'effect' can be safely attributed. The teacher effectiveness model does not work as intended, and should not be used for making policy.

Perhaps most crucially we need to clearer about what question VA is attempting to answer, and why we should be so concerned with differential effectiveness (Everson, 2017). When used at a national level for very large numbers of pupils, and no attempt is made to claim that different schools or types of schools are differentially effective, VA avoids several problems, including the volatility of small numbers. A more promising approach, however, although also not yet ready for policy use, is regression discontinuity design (Gorard, 2013a). Because children in England are assigned to school years by their birth date (see Chapter 3), it is possible to examine how much difference a year at school makes by comparing those who are just old enough to attend one year, and those who are just too young. The impact of going to school (as opposed to not going for that extra year) tends to decline with each year of age at school. Luyten et al (2017) estimate it at around 40 per cent difference per year in learning gains at primary age. This kind of approach could be used to assess progress per year for individual schools, clusters of schools or regions. And it could do so in comparison to the absolute scores for not going to school for one year, and therefore be free of the competitive element forced on the system by VA.

Why do so many analysts, policy-makers, users and practitioners seem to believe that school effectiveness yields useful and practical information? It is tempting to say that perhaps many of them have not really thought about the process and have simply bought into what appears to be a scientific and technical solution to judging school performance. The Schools Minister who introduced one form of VA in England admitted to me that he had not realised it was zero-sum. Schools are paying public funds to external bodies for VA analyses and breakdowns of their effectiveness data. Parents and pupils are being encouraged to use school effectiveness evidence (in league tables, for example) to judge potential schools, despite the fact that the VA scores of each school will be unrecognisable by the time their child completes schooling.

SEVEN

School improvement

School improvement has been a considerable part of my work over the past 10 years, reviewing and synthesising evidence on the best pedagogical and other approaches, and conducting trials and other robust evaluations of school improvement interventions. This book has a policy focus, and so most of these trials and reviews are not discussed in any detail here, but they are dealt with in detail in Gorard et al (2017a), and the most recent comprehensive review of evidence on school improvement appears in Gorard et al (2016a). This chapter looks at how evidence is synthesised, what such syntheses can tell us and what school leaders can do to use such evidence successfully.

Until recently, school improvement policies have either been created on little robust evidence at all, or have simply been based on the correlates of the kinds of school effectiveness studies described in Chapter 6. This is a very misleading approach because high- and low-attaining schools might differ in a range of ways that are unrelated to whether their results are better or worse. This includes their type (such as academy or community school), their location and even their décor (potted plants for example). School improvement policies have also been influenced by highly vocal single studies, and developers acting as agents selling their wares via conferences and similar. Teacher action research is widely used but is not really research let alone *action* research as originally devised (Gorard, 2013a). None of these is appropriate for advising national or local policy on improving schools.

'Hyper-analyses'

More recently, school decision-makers around the world have been increasingly influenced by 'hyper-analyses' of prior evidence. A systematic review of evidence is an attempt to summarise the findings of key studies in response to a specific research question (see Chapter 2 earlier). This is perfectly proper as long as full account is taken of the relative strength and clarity of each study. A meta-analysis is a particular kind of systematic review that combines the 'effect' sizes of all of the studies in the review to provide an aggregate 'effect' size, or an overall single answer to an effectiveness question. This, again, is perfectly proper as long as full account is taken of the relative strength and clarity of each study, and the studies being aggregated are fully commensurable – same interventions, age range, outcomes and so on. All studies for a meta-analysis also need to have key details reported in addition to the effect sizes, such as the attrition in each comparison group. Where the studies are not commensurable, or are included despite deficient reporting of details, or no account is taken of their quality, the results of the meta-analysis can be very misleading indeed.

Hyper-analysis is a term I use to denote studies that synthesise the results of many meta-analyses, such as those by Hattie (2008), described on its book cover as revealing 'teaching's Holy Grail'. The term also refers to the early versions of the Educational Endowment Foundation's (EET) Teaching and Learning Toolkit in England, and to many similar attempts around the world. As with VA models (see Chapter 6), it is easy to see why users and others want such appealing summaries of what works, and considerable progress has been made in developing better models over 10 years. However, again, as with VA, they remain fundamentally flawed and so could be misleading school improvement in important ways as much as the school effectiveness correlates have done in the past. I use the example of the impact of teachers using enhanced feedback, as listed by both Hattie (2008) and the EET Toolkit, to illustrate the point.

Enhanced feedback

Many reports or summaries of effective pedagogy identify feedback as a characteristic of effective teaching and learning (McBer, 2000; Harris and Ratcliffe, 2005; Coe et al, 2014). The EEF (2015) Teaching and Learning Toolkit recorded feedback strategy as having an impact equivalent to nine months of additional progress. Feedback was also singled out as one of the most effective teaching methods in Hattie (2008).

Hattie and Timperley (2007) reported a hyper-analysis of feedback based on synthesising the results of 74 meta-analyses that totalled 4,157 studies (reporting 5,755 different effect sizes). They did so without re-examining the original studies themselves or appraising their quality or appropriateness to be combined in this way. This calls such innovative approaches into question. The results of Hattie and Timperley (2007) were heavily influenced by the prior meta-analysis by Kluger and DeNisi (1996) because they said it was 'the most systematic' and 'included studies that had at least a control group, measured performance, and included at least 10 participants' (p 85).

This sounds good until the implications are realised. Other meta-analyses among the 74 presumably must have had studies with no control group, fewer than 10 cases, did not measure performance and/or were not particularly systematic. Even the studies in Kluger and DeNisi (1996) had an average of only 39 cases. Why were such poor studies in the meta-analyses, and why did Hattie and Timperley (2007) include these clearly even weaker meta-analyses in their hyper-analysis?

No account at all is taken of missing cases or data. When evaluating an intervention any attrition post-randomisation is a source of bias. Without consideration of the kinds of factors in the sieve described earlier in Chapter 2, these kinds of syntheses are heavily flawed from the outset. One could almost say that their overall trustworthiness is as good as the weakest study involved. For example, some of the studies in Hattie and Timperley (2007) are RCTs and some are based on convenience comparisons. Yet the former that should be much stronger are not given appropriately greater weighting.

It is well known that interventions evaluated using researcher- and developer- designed tests will tend to produce larger positive effect sizes, as will smaller studies, or those with non-randomised or otherwise inappropriate counterfactuals (Gorard et al, 2016a). Including such weaker studies without appropriate weighting in any overview will tend to make interventions such as enhanced feedback appear more powerful.

Most of the studies cited did not use random allocation or selection of cases and yet quoted p-values from significance tests (see Chapter 2), which must therefore be meaningless as probabilities. For example, one study had used MANOVA based on those students who agreed to participate compared to those who refused, presented as evidence of the impact of the intervention. If Hattie used meta-analyses based on such p-values (it was not traditional to present effect sizes until very recently) but did not eliminate the majority where they were computed incorrectly, then the meta-analytic results will be clearly incorrect (even if p-values were valid as a substitute effect size).

The hyper-analysis is based on studies of feedback used with young children up to students of traditional university age and beyond. The studies are based in psychology laboratory conditions and real-life settings. Some involve attainment tests, others cognitive assessments and some are based on behavioural or attitude outcomes. Some studies were targeted at sub-groups such as students with special needs or disruptive behaviour, which may lead to very different effect sizes to studies conducted with mainstream children. Some studies were nearly 60 years old and only a few were recent, using a wide range of approaches and understanding of what feedback is.

Several further problems arose for me when looking under the headline results to see what kind of studies were involved. Not all of the studies or effect sizes cited (see, for example, Table 1, p 83 in Hattie and Timperley, 2007) could be found. The hyper-analysis states the overall effect size of 54 studies in Lysakowski and Walberg (1982) was +1.13, whereas the original paper reports it at 0.97. Hattie (1992) reported that 'Skiba, Casey and Center (1986) used 315 effect-sizes (35 studies) to investigate the effects of some form of reinforcement or feedback and found an effect-size of 1.88' (p 8), but the later 2007 paper reports this review as having 35 effect sizes not studies, and an effect size of +1.24.

What these kinds of hyper-analyses have done is aggregate scores from a wide variety of research designs, practical approaches and educational settings, taking no account of the bias introduced by attrition, and treating a study with full response as equivalent to one with high dropout or missing data. This almost certainly inflates the apparent effect size for feedback and many other teaching approaches. Overall, the evidence for feedback is not as clear as commentators have suggested (Smith and Gorard, 2005). Over one-third of the studies in Kluger and DeNisi (1996) had negative outcomes. More recent large-scale studies of medium quality are divided about whether enhanced feedback makes any difference at all (Lang et al, 2014; Phelan et al, 2011; See et al, 2016).

There are proposed standards in place for reviewing prior evidence, but this is not really the issue here. Any such complex procedure is likely to face gremlins (Heywood et al, 2017), but bureaucratic rule-driven approaches to enhance quality are unlikely to be effective. Openness, transparency and acceptance of revealed limitations are crucial so that the next steps in progress can be made. Simply aggregating shoddy with good research is not the way forward here, appealing though its results may look.

Single-study trials and reviews

Closing the social class achievement gap or 'poverty gradient' in education is a prominent policy reform issue in the UK, as it is in many other developed countries. And billions of pounds of public money has been, and is being, spent on generic or tailored interventions to address it. However, these interventions are largely untested, or where they have been rigorously and independently evaluated, they have been shown not to work or even to be harmful. A much more promising approach to all of the above is based on working towards single robust evaluations of key approaches to teaching (Gorard et al, 2017a), leading to summaries of large numbers of these single studies, taking their relative quality into account (as well as their effect sizes). This is a successful approach, and is now being implemented in England by the EEF. This is not a panacea but it is a step further forward.

The results of my work on this for teaching approaches and a range of interventions is covered in Gorard et al (2016a, 2017c). Among other things, this work shows that a variety of individual and small group protocols work about as well as each other for helping low achievers in literacy and maths, and so perhaps it is the extra attention that matters more than the precise activity. It presents evidence that encouraging children to think and construct arguments is more effective than simply teaching them facts, even for literacy and maths outcomes. And the single-study review approach used suggests that the evidence for interventions like enhancing feedback (above) and peer mentoring is less secure than the big hyper-analyses portray.

This chapter reprises for readers some of my similar work on the impact of improving behaviour, attitudes and aspirations, proposed as a relatively cheap way of raising attainment, especially for disadvantaged students (Gorard et al, 2011).

Non-cognitive constructs as inputs to attainment

One of the main reasons for having universal, compulsory and free at point of delivery early education in the UK is to reduce the influence of social, familial and economic background, so promoting social mobility and a just and equitable society. There is perhaps no more important issue facing education and society today (Gorard and Smith, 2010). Understanding the reasons for the poverty 'gradient' (see Chapter 3) and devising approaches to help reduce it are therefore directly relevant to current policy and practice. But it would be unethical and inefficient to base real-life approaches on one study or on a clearly incomplete picture. An appropriately sceptical consideration of what the available evidence reveals about the causal links involved is a vital next step. It is needed to avoid wasted effort and opportunity costs, and to hasten the identification of feasible solutions.

There is already considerable policy and practice activity being undertaken on the assumption that aspirations and attitudes can be influenced to improve educational outcomes. For example, in 2009 the UK government introduced plans to lift the aspirations of 2.4 million children. There is an ongoing emphasis on raising aspirations so that no one is disadvantaged by their community and peers (St Clair and Benjamin, 2011). This is just one of many national, regional and local initiatives. To what extent are proposals like these, and the expenditure they entail, justified by the best available evidence? Do attitudes and aspirations *cause* educational outcomes?

My work reviewing the evidence from tens of thousands of studies on student attitudes and aspirations as determinants of attainment in education has led to quite clear results (Gorard, 2012c). Most such psychological constructs can be associated with differences in attainment, but there is no solid evidence of a causal path. For example, students with higher self-esteem tend to do better at school (and beyond). But in order to be sure that self-esteem was the cause of the better attainment, a different kind of study is needed to that commonly found in reviews. Such causal studies are rare, and where they have been conducted, the results are not promising. There is no good evidence showing that improving self-esteem leads to better academic outcomes, for example. It is possible to intervene and apparently raise the self-esteem of students, but this does not translate into better results at school or beyond (but see Chapter 12). Nor does raising self-esteem lead to subsequent participation in education or reduced dropout (Parr and Bonitz, 2015).

Many studies suggest that young people with higher educational aspirations have greater motivation and higher educational attainment than their peers (Lin et al, 2009; Jacob and Wilder, 2010). Similar claims are made for attitudes to school and educational expectations (Bui, 2007). A number of studies have suggested associations between self-reported learner motivation and attainment at school (Schwinger et al, 2009; Hayenga and Corpus, 2010). Some studies have claimed that there is a link between academic self-concept and/or self-esteem and achievement (Skaalvik and Skaalvik, 2009; Whitesell et al, 2009). However, other studies have included background factors such as family income, mother's occupation, family structure, housing tenure and parental education, and found no link from self-esteem to academic outcomes (Scott, 2004; Chowdry et al, 2010). There are also some studies that show a correlation between young people's reports of an internal locus of control or high self-efficacy and their school attainment (Gifford et al, 2006; Speight, 2010). However, as with many of these concepts, once other measures such as prior achievement were accounted for, locus of control was not linked to subsequent attainment (Tang, 2004). There is very little work linking these various concepts to post-compulsory participation, and none were found that specifically addressed the issue of overcoming disadvantage.

Therefore, there is limited but somewhat disputed evidence of an association between these attitudinal measures and attainment. This association arises largely when SES background and prior attainment are not accounted for.

There is even less secure evidence of the kind that really matters, where an intervention has been used to enhance one of these self-constructs and evaluate whether this led to improved attainment relative to a counterfactual group. The review found no rigorous evaluations of interventions explicitly concerned with raising aspirations or expectations and so influencing educational outcomes. There were five interventions involving changes to self-concept or self-esteem with attainment, of some sort, as a dependent variable (Cohen et al, 2009; Gordon et al, 2009 – note that citations in this section are examples from the larger number of studies found). None provide good evidence of a causal link. Four interventions were found that related to alterations in self-efficacy or locus of control and subsequent attainment. Together, these studies provide very weak evidence of an impact from self-efficacy, often with older students, on a small scale, and with far from convincing results (Blackwell et al, 2007; Miles, 2010). There were no studies relating to participation.

The review found four intervention studies in which extrinsic motivation was a major independent variable. Three of these concerned financial incentive payments with positive outcomes (Bettinger, 2010; Fryer, 2010; Riccio, 2010). However, the same studies also pointed out that incentives can only work if students know how to improve. This is an important point to note for all attitude and aspiration work. Confidence may be misplaced without competence. In each of these studies it is reasonable to infer that the students knew what to do (for example, they understood the school's definition of 'good behaviour'). There appeared to be a positive effect on maths scores, but not in reading. This may be because extrinsic motivation is more effective for some tasks. Students can memorise a series of facts or formulae to prepare them for the tests, but it is more difficult for students to prepare for reading a specific text or writing on a particular subject. However, paying students for inputs into the education production, such as for attendance, good behaviour, doing homework and wearing their uniforms, yielded moderate improvements in both reading and maths achievements. Paying students to read books yielded a noticeable increase in reading comprehension. There was no evidence that pupils' intrinsic motivation was affected either way.

Overall, the picture for using constructs such as attitudes to try and enhance attainment is that this does not work. One problem is that while the proposed definitions of such self-constructs have been debated by research in this field, the meaning and utility of these concepts remains unclear. Simply making people believe that they are more competent than they actually are may be ineffective or worse. But then making people more competent at gaining positive school outcomes, and so also making them more confident, is almost the same as simply improving their school outcomes. Self-efficacy, or whatever, by itself could be a red herring. At present, anyone with a sole concern to improve educational outcomes for those most at risk would be advised to seek interventions other than those based on altering attitudes or aspirations. Any money involved in research or policy in this area might be better spent on careful incentive schemes, or even just given directly to the families of disadvantaged young children.

Single summary reviews of evidence can provide useful insights for policy and practice, and will tend to be less misleading than the hyper-analyses.

Role of school leadership

Educational leadership is, understandably, a key conduit for school improvement evidence. Differences in the quality of leadership are the standard answer to why schools with supposedly equivalent SES and prior attainment get different examination outcomes and inspection results. From Rutter et al (1979) and probably before, management solutions such as a 'good school ethos' have been suggested as the way forward for improvement. It is seen as part of the leader's job to implement the findings produced by research about teaching and resource use, and so improve the attainment of students at their school. There are two related problems here. School and other educational leaders do not know very much about secure research evidence, and research into leadership itself must be among the weakest education research in the world (Gorard, 2005c).

Most published research in educational leadership/management has been non-empirical (not evidence-informed), and empirical pieces have been very small-scale. In 2005, when I studied this in detail, there was no published research on leadership in major UK journals using trials, research syntheses, longitudinal studies or statistical modelling. Papers in leadership and management journals were disproportionately submitted by universities gaining weak grades in the UK Research

Assessment Exercise (RAE) and subsequently. In the 2004 American Educational Research Association (AERA) conference (the largest in the world) there were 45 complete sessions on leadership alone and many more individual papers in other sessions. Most concerned the experiences or preparation of school leaders, with titles such as 'Using the Fullan leadership model to determine the meaning of leadership for four teacher leaders'. There were a few more promising titles, such as 'Instructional leadership: Principal *influence* on teaching and learning' and '*Effects* of educational leadership programs'. However, neither of these used a causal design, or even presented any evidence on student or organisation outcomes. No one seemed to want to test the actual impact of leadership.

In general, the impact of leadership on instruction or improvement (or indeed any measurable school outcomes) has not been the subject of research. Much of the work in the field is based on inappropriate theory, weak and producing large quantities of guff (Antonakis, 2017). In a few cases where suitable work has been attempted there is no good evidence that leaders can or do change school outcomes (Searle and Tymms, 2007).

There have been some attempted evaluations leading to a more positive picture, but even the best of these have the same problems as the usual school effectiveness-driven studies – not experimental, and often with no comparator at all. Louis et al (2010) make strong causal claims for an impact from leadership on outcomes based on teachers' surveys without consideration of prior attainment or pupil intake characteristics. As seen in the attitude work (see above) and throughout this book, where key variables are knowingly omitted from an analytical model, the results will tend to over-emphasise something else. Heck and Moriyama (2010) did use context and other factors, and found some small net differences linked to improvement-focused school leadership, but they used teacher reports for the leadership figures, meaning that the results could be a tautology, with teachers really reporting outcomes indirectly, 12 per cent of pupil scores are missing so creating a potential for bias, and there was no counterfactual at all.

The school inspection system in England (Ofsted) looks at leadership when inspecting and grading schools, and there is a correlation of 0.92 between school overall effectiveness (in their judgement) and effective leadership (also their judgement). Is this good evidence, then, that leaders matter in delivering school improvement? Or does it just mean that Ofsted is assessing the same thing in both cases?

Schools are assigned to one of four categories as a result of inspection – outstanding (20% in 2017), good (60%), requires improvement (18%) and inadequate (2%). These figures are based on the most recent 20,292 inspections, according to 'Inspections of maintained schools in England'. However, just as with school effectiveness modelling, the results are not independent of school intakes (see Table 7.1). The schools rated as requiring improvement and especially those deemed inadequate are larger on average, with much higher proportions of FSM-eligible and SEN pupils sited in considerably more disadvantaged areas (IDACI).

The schools rated 'outstanding' are more likely to be single-sex, especially girls-only schools. They are staggeringly more likely to be selective than comprehensive, and much less likely to be the majority secondary moderns left over after selection to grammar schools (see Table 7.2). This is very unlikely to be a real reflection of the situation, and, as shown in Chapter 6, does not reflect the true impact of these schools. It seems that Ofsted inspectors, overall, are unable to judge the quality of a school divorced from the kinds of challenges it faces. This is why schools deemed to be 'failing' are more likely to be in urban centres, and so-called good schools are more often in leafy suburban settings.

Using such school and pupil intake factors with others, it is possible to predict Ofsted overall school grades for over 71 per cent of schools

Table 7.1: Mean characteristics of each Ofsted outcome

	Outstanding	Good	Requires improvement	Inadequate
Total pupils	391	329	374	468
Percentage FSM	12	15	19	22
Percentage SEN	11	14	15	16
Average IDACI rank	18,201	16,819	15,387	13,999

Table 7.2: Percentage characteristics for each Ofsted outcome

	Outstanding	Good	Requires improvement	Inadequate
Boys only	34.1	44.7	18.8	2.4
Girls only	54.2	41.6	3.7	0.5
Mixed	19.3	60.7	17.9	2.2
Comprehensive	19.8	49.2	25.1	6.0
Secondary modern	12.5	57.5	24.2	5.8
Selective grammar	77.5	21.3	0.6	0.6

(without considering school quality at all). Some of these results could simply be read from the school location and intake characteristics (see Table 7.3). This model was created using only what was available from Ofsted reports. With more data, through linking to NPD, the predictions for Ofsted grades would be more accurate again.

The relevance of this for school improvement is that the correlation between leadership and school quality is most likely specious. Ofsted judgements of both leadership and school quality appear to be overly influenced by factors such as a school having high-attaining pupils (girls-only and selective). In fact, there is still no good evidence that leaders are yet the leaders of school improvement.

Table 7.3: Percentage of school Ofsted grades predicted correctly

Step	Grade predicted correctly
Baseline model	51.3
Pupil characteristics	66.2
Area and school type	71.0

Conclusion

Traditional approaches to researching school improvement and so helping students to learn better are not sufficient in terms of secure evidence, and may be misleading. Newer ideas such as the hyper-analyses of prior evidence are not working because they are insufficiently sensitive to the huge range in research quality of their material. Good research does exist, and it should not be wasted by simply aggregating it with inferior work. Too many ineffective ideas are still used in teaching and promoting improvement in attainment, whether this is learning styles and similar fashion items, or the kinds of attitudes and aspirations covered here. New teachers are not developed with a clear sense of the available evidence, perhaps because researchers are generally excluded from initial teacher education, even in universities (see Chapter 11). And as this chapter also shows, the situation for leaders wanting to use evidence to improve their schools is not promising. The field has let them down by not providing clear guidance on how to do it.

A much more interesting avenue was recently provided by some innovative schools and their research leads who applied for funding to conduct their own RCTs (Siddiqui et al, 2015; Gorard et al, 2016b). Schools are in a favourable position to run trials because of their ability to monitor pupil attendance and progress, access the personal and possibly sensitive data that schools record, keep their schools within the study, get permission to innovate, and hopefully having a lack of vested interest in what the findings say. If conducting such research were seen as a part of schools' functions, the overall cost of research could go down. It may even be possible to create some kind of nationwide ongoing trials with all willing schools contributing to an online database, which could adjust its synthesis of evidence with each new (small) study, much in the way suggested for medicine by Goldacre (2012). Who will take the lead on this?

EIGHT

Learning beyond institutions

Perhaps because school improvement research has traditionally been so weak (see Chapter 7), or because policy-makers have forgotten that a key component of the Education Act 1944 was for schools to minimise the impact of family background, there has been increased UK interest in education beyond formal institutions. In some respects, this could be a useful trend if followed to its logical conclusions (concerning informal learning, see below), but it can also be seen as a sign of defeat. According to some accounts, schools are not doing their job well enough. In response, the school day has been extended, more homework has been given, and there are breakfast clubs, after-school clubs and summer schools. The leaving age for schools was raised over decades from 14 to 15 and then 16. More recently the education and training leaving age has been raised to 17 and now 18 in England. There is more schooling than ever before. But this is, apparently, still not enough. So the problem is assumed to be lack of parental engagement in their child's education, and we have come full circle back to what the Education Act 1944 was trying to overcome by making schools compulsory, universal and free in the first place.

This chapter summarises my work in three strands with the common theme of learning or raising academic attainment outside of normal school (or other educational institution) hours. The strands concern out-of-school hours interventions (Gorard et al, 2015), trying to enhance parental involvement in their child's school work (Gorard and See, 2013), and learning or self-teaching entirely separate from institutions (Gorard et al, 1999c).

Evaluating out-of-hours interventions

As with the trials in Chapter 7, the out-of-hours evaluations summarised here are covered fully in Gorard et al (2017a). The first – Children's University (CU) – was an attempt to overcome a poverty gap in access to activities such as after-school clubs, arts and cultural events and volunteering and community-based projects (Southby and South, 2016). Whatever their other benefits, out-of-school activities (breakfast clubs, sports activities, music and art lessons, tuition, religious services) might also be able to improve attainment at school (Chanfreau et al, 2016).

The second – a summer school programme in three locations – was an attempt to reduce the summer learning loss for children moving to secondary school the following year, and so ease their transition from primary to secondary. Evaluations in the UK and elsewhere suggest that summer schools can be effective, especially for disadvantaged students (Matsudaira, 2008; Martin et al, 2013). And the approach used here was reported as one of the forms of summer schools with reasonable evidence of success (Terzian and Moore, 2009). However, several studies have also suggested that summer programmes yield no real academic benefit (Kim et al, 2016).

The summary results for the academic outcomes of both are shown in Table 8.1. The quality of the summer school evaluation suffered because of high dropout among students who volunteered in the summer term, were randomised to summer school, and then did not turn up. This is also why NNTD is listed as zero. It is not certain that the apparent effect in English is not created partly by the missing data (with the more motivated turning up in the summer). It was not possible to follow all missing cases to their new schools. The CU results after two years vary slightly from the interim results after one year as reported in Gorard et al (2017a). The CU trial had much lower attrition than summer school, but had an issue from the outset that not all children in schools randomised to treatment could take part. This was a capacity issue for the developer of the intervention and the funding they were provided with.

Nevertheless, the overall impression is that out-of-school activities such as these could have an impact on attainment. They show little or no promise of reducing the poverty gradient (because the effect sizes are generally smaller for FSM-eligible pupils), but they may have other potential benefits, as discussed later, in Chapter 9.

Table 8.1: Summary of results in two out-of-hours interventions

	Effect size	Effect size EverFSM6 only	Quality of evidence	NNTD-attrition
CU maths	+0.15	+0.03	3	0
CU English	+0.12	+0.05	3	0
Summer school maths	0	0	2	0
Summer school English	+0.17	+0.17	2	0

Parental involvement

The evidence on the relationship between parental aspirations, attitudes and behaviours is similar in many respects to that of children's attitudes (see Chapter 7). There is convincing evidence overall that parental expectations are associated with their child's attainment (Taningco and Pachon, 2008; Johnson et al, 2010), but not when SES and other factors are taken into account. The evidence for parental expectations falls well short of that needed to assume that it is a causal influence, because too few relevant successful interventions were found in review (See and Gorard, 2015a,b). Parental involvement may have many other benefits for both parties but, at present, the evidence suggests that anyone with a sole concern to improve attainment outcomes for those most at risk should seek an intervention elsewhere.

The review considered studies relevant to trying to raise attainment by increasing parental involvement in education that were of at least minimal standard in their reporting of scale and attrition, with a comparator and so on. Overall, these present a mixed and far from encouraging picture for the success of parental interventions. Of the best, some have suggested positive outcomes, some no effect, and some that parental involvement interventions may actually harm children's attainment. Many of the studies with positive outcomes involved complex interventions including more than parental involvement (such as additional classes at school as well). Where these different elements have been separated, it is those other aspects that are shown to be effective rather than the parental involvement itself.

Of the studies relevant to pre-school age, the results were almost perfectly balanced (see Table 8.2). The majority of studies were rated as low quality (0 or 1, according to the sieve in Chapter 2). Many of these were tiny, with group sizes for analysis as low as eight, as well as high dropout of cases after allocation to groups. One had a control group but ignored it. One researcher used changes in behaviour rather than tests to make claims about attainment, and one claimed positive results for teacher-reported outcomes but found no gains using a standardised test. The latter is instructive because it confirms that we should not

Table 8.2: Parental involvement interventions for children up to age 5

	Effective	Ineffective or harmful
Higher quality – 3 or better	0	0
Medium quality – 2	4	3
Lower quality – 0 or 1	20	22

rely on bespoke tests, indirect indications or simple self- or teacher reports. One study had 45 per cent dropout after allocation to groups, and another had 37 per cent attrition. One even quoted effect sizes for gains of children in a parental volunteer group compared to those parents who refused to participate, and claimed that these were the 'effects' of the programme.

Three medium-quality studies with positive outcomes were all of the same intervention, reporting after different times had elapsed (Reynolds et al, 2011). The successful intervention was the Chicago Child-Parent Center (CPC) Program, a federally funded pre-school for families in high poverty areas. It included parental training with a child-centred focus on developing reading and language skills. However, it also included teacher-directed whole-class instruction, small group activities, field trips and play, low child-to-staff ratios in kindergartens, outreach activities including home visits, staff development activities and an enriched classroom environment, plus health, nutrition and other services. Around 1,400 mostly African-American children were tracked through to age 28, with about 15 to 20 per cent dropout. The researchers claimed that the CPC had positive effects on the Iowa Test of Basic Skills, attendance and high school completion. However, because of the multiple components of the programme, it was not clear what the specific impact of parental involvement was, or even if it had any impact at all.

ParentCorps is a home–school partnership programme based on after-school group sessions where parents learn effective behaviour management (Brotman, 2013). This was a reasonable scale study involving 1,050 children randomised to treatment conditions. Participating children out-scored control children on standardised tests in reading and on teacher assessments of writing and maths. In some ways, ParentCorps is similar to the Chicago CPC in that it is a multiple component programme. It combines parenting skills, improving classroom quality and a family programme to teach parents and children strategies in managing children's behaviour. It involves enhancing teachers' skills in helping to identify and address the needs of children in early childhood settings.

Despite these few positives, it is difficult to conclude that there is much solid evidence of effective parental interventions for pre-school children, with almost as many evaluations suggesting no benefit.

The situation for studies of parental involvement with primary-age children is similar (see Table 8.3). Most studies are of poor quality. Again, a number of studies compared children of parents who volunteered for the programme with those who did not,

Table 8.3: Parental involvement interventions for children aged 5-11

	Effective	Ineffective or harmful
Higher quality – 3 or better	0	0
Medium quality – 2	1	2
Lower quality – 0 or 1	35	16

thus introducing a clear potential for bias in the results that went unremarked in the original reports (Calnon, 2005). Some had no good counterfactual, and again, many of these other studies were negligible in scale (Boggess, 2008), with as few as three cases per group. Other studies had high levels of attrition such as 31 per cent in one of the groups after allocation. Many completely misused the technique of significance testing. One dredged by trying to find a positive result through the removal of 'outliers' (possibly inconvenient results). In perhaps the best of these weak studies, the comparison group performed substantially better than the treatment group.

One medium-evidence study (Bradshaw et al, 2009) suggested a positive impact, but the study was again a complex one, and showed that the classroom aspect of the intervention was more important than the parent-focused component. The Family-School Partnership Program improved parent–teacher communication. It involved using teachers and health professionals to train parents in teaching literacy and numeracy, and child behaviour management skills. Teachers received a training manual, videotape and training aids, plus additional support after the training. Programme experts visited schools during the intervention to supervise and offer feedback. There were nine parent workshops run by first grade teachers, social workers and school psychologists, with weekly home-school learning and communication activities. The evaluation was a longitudinal study involving a total of 678 students from nine schools. Classes were randomly allocated to one of three groups who were tracked from first grade to age 19. One group received the parental intervention, one a classroom intervention and one acted as a control. Around 16 per cent dropped out after allocation.

Two studies that showed neutral or negative outcomes were deemed of medium quality. The LiFuS programme involved training parents to support their fourth grade children at home with their reading homework, and training teachers in cooperative learning activities at school to enhance children's reading motivation and comprehension (Villiger et al, 2012). The home reading programme was for 20 minutes three times per week. It emphasised supporting the child's autonomy in reading by avoiding controlling and interfering behaviour and using autonomy supportive strategies. Parents were asked to provide reading materials such as dictionaries and remain nearby to answer questions, but allow the child to read silently at their own pace. Instead of giving them the complete solutions to queries, parents were instructed to provide strategies for the child to use. Before implementation, parents attended two training sessions, each lasting three hours, held in the evening in the child's school. Parents were supported throughout the intervention with personal coaching, and received instructional booklets with the content of the training session (to refer to whenever they needed). Children were given a checklist to help them remember the steps of the strategy used. A total of 713 children took part in the evaluation, divided into three groups: school intervention, school/home intervention and a control group. The control group was merely matched with the intervention groups, and known differences between the groups controlled for. Although Villiger et al reported that the programme had 'significant' effects on students' enjoyment of reading and reading motivation, it did not have any positive effect on reading comprehension tests. Both interventions (school only and home/school) actually had small negative effects on text comprehension compared to the control group, suggesting that students might have been better off without the intervention.

The second study evaluated a school-collaborated programme involving parents helping their children to read at home using prescribed activities (Herts, 1990). Parents in the treatment group attended one training session, where they had to commit to a 14-week parental involvement programme. At the sessions they were given materials, and discussed the topics in handouts. The topics were about issues such as building self-esteem and how to support their child in their reading. Parents also received vocabulary and comprehension exercises and were shown, using role-play, how to reinforce reading skills at home. This is an important study because it is a straight comparison between parental involvement or not (and is the only such study of medium quality found in the review). In five schools, teachers and their 230 students were allocated in an unspecified manner to the 'treatment' or 'comparator' group, but around 15 per cent dropped out after allocation. The comparison group actually made greater improvements in reading attainment than the treatment children (ES = −0.20), as assessed by the standardised Gates-MacGinitie Reading Test (GMRT).

Overall, there is no evidence here that primary-age interventions to enhance parental involvement are generally effective in increasing children's attainment. In fact, the better studies suggest that the interventions may even be harmful. It may be important that the medium-quality negative studies are largely about training parents to act a little like teachers at home, whereas the medium-quality positive studies involve parents and other adults meeting and working together in an institution of some sort. It is also noteworthy that when parental involvement has been compared to a classroom intervention with the same purpose, if there is a difference, then it is the classroom programme that is more successful.

The review found few interventions aimed solely at young people of secondary school age. This is presumably because of the widespread belief that earlier interventions will be more effective. Most that do exist are of low quality. Problems with these studies included very small samples, and confusion about what the results really are. One study suggested that prior attainment was the key to outcomes. The latter is important because, if true, it means we cannot trust any studies that either do not take prior attainment into account, or that do not make it irrelevant by having large, randomly allocated groups.

One study with positive results was of near-medium quality. Bridges to High School/Puentes was a family-focused programme to reduce problems associated with transition to secondary school (Gonzales et al, 2012). It lasted for nine weeks in the eighth grade, and combined parent and child education with family support. It involved a parenting intervention, adolescent sessions and family sessions, plus two home visits (one pre- and one during intervention). Parenting sessions were aimed at helping parents understand school expectations, improving parent–teacher communication, enhancing parenting skills using positive reinforcement, monitoring and appropriate discipline and reducing harsh parenting. Students were taught coping strategies, managing interpersonal and school problems, exploring goals and motivations and balancing family relationships with other obligations/interests. Family sessions provided structured opportunities for mutual understanding, enjoyment and communication, and to practice skills learned in parent and adolescent sessions. Around 500 students were randomly allocated to treatment or not, and around 27 per cent dropped out later, especially in the non-treatment group. The authors reported positive effects on students' GPA. It is difficult to isolate the active ingredient as there are so many aspects to the intervention including parental training, home visits and adolescent behaviour training. The outcome measures are heavily dependent on self-reporting scales with less emphasis on independent observation/

records, and in the analysis no account was taken of the differential dropout.

Overall, on this evidence, it is currently not possible to conclude that parental involvement interventions will be effective in secondary phases.

Regrettably, the main conclusion of the review has to be that no one seems to have really tested whether parental involvement itself works in terms of enhanced attainment for children. There are *no* large, strongly designed studies on this topic despite considerable expenditure by policy-makers and practitioners and thousands of pieces of research by academics. In this respect at least, schools pushing their responsibility for education beyond their school boundaries does not work.

Informal learning

Informal, self-directed or leisure learning completely independent of educational institutions is an area of considerable interest, which I have examined in terms of individual computer-assisted learning, common-sense learning at work, and more widely in terms of hobbies and interests (Gorard et al, 1999c; Selwyn and Gorard, 2004). This is a tremendously difficult area to research accurately. It goes beyond schools trying to recruit parents to assist their children more, or schools and colleges offering extra-curricular activities. This section is about how some people report wanting to learn non-trivial things by themselves. They do not want to be taught, or to attend a course, and are not interested in qualifications. In this sense, talking to maintenance personnel at work about the operation of the photocopier or reading a weekly magazine at home about growing fruit in the garden would be examples of informal learning. On the other hand, attending a lecture on health and safety or learning to dance at an adult evening class would both be formal episodes.

When asked in their interviews, around one-quarter of the adults described in Chapter 3 reported at least one 'episode' of informal learning. As expected, these were more common among those who also undertook more formal episodes of education or training as well – the lifelong and delayed learners, as described in Chapter 12 (see Table 8.4).

Many interviewees reported no informal learning experiences and no leisure interests involving study or practice. In most cases, where a reason was given for this, it was attributed to a lack of interest by someone who had not attended school regularly and who had left at the earliest opportunity, for example, or to lack of time by someone

Table 8.4: Reports of informal leisure study, by trajectory

Learning trajectory	Percentage reporting informal study
Lifelong learners	29
Delayed participants	26
Transitional learners	15
Non-participants	18

like a consultant surgeon who had spent most of his life in formal study. In general, new episodes of informal learning here decreased over time.

The type of interests reported by informal learners have also changed over time. In the 1960s an interest in local politics or history, gardening, art or photography was common, but these have been largely replaced by learning sports, keeping pets and using a computer. Voluntary work and sewing (or related skills) have remained popular. In very general terms, where an interviewee described any genuine interest at length, they also described several others, both of a formal and informal nature. In a sense there were people who seek out things to learn and people who do not. Surprisingly, books and magazines were more frequently cited as sources of information than other people, or broadcasts, or IT. Magazines were used to learn sports like golf or how to build a radio transmitter, while the use of books included learning musical instruments, languages, calculus and practical skills such as building a garage or wiring a house. These activities were often undertaken by people with little or no formal education after compulsory schooling.

One man had taught himself pottery, electrolysis for metal work, simple electronics, wax casting and furniture modelling. He had a Perspex-cutting room in his house, a frog he had gold-plated in his living room, and had once made a scale model of the Challenger space shuttle that was then on the desk of a four-star general in NASA.

'I haven't got a GCE or a BSc or whatever they're called these days ... but as I say, you don't have to be academic to be able to do things.... Because of the books I read and I like reading science books et cetera, and with the television my favourite channel is the Discovery Channel.

It's the same with the French polishing, you see. I used to do it as a favour. I got a book from the library. I had a blind chappie who was a pianist, like, and he used to tune pianos and doing them up. He asked me if I knew anything about polishing and I said "not the foggiest". So I went to the library, got a book on it, we got the French polish and promptly went into business.'

Another man in his 60s had left school at 14 chiefly for economic reasons, like so many others:

'My father was mining underground. He had six months off, he went back for another month, and of course there was no dole or anything in those days, and myself and my sister still at home.... Then I took this job. Didn't earn a lot of money but of course anything in those days was better than what we had.'

He also had no lifetime qualifications, but a very successful career in what was then British Steel, being promoted several times and moving between areas of work, having received no formal training in his account:

'You learn as you get along.... You got to train yourself and you use your hands and ears. No one came along and said, you mustn't do this or you mustn't do that.... I mean, common sense will tell you not to do certain things.... I can pick up most things purely by someone else doing it.... I did my own wiring in my house.'

He and his wife support local opera and drama groups, and helped to reopen and refurbish an opera theatre in their village. He was a self-taught plasterer and electrician, and explained how he had read about the care of the 7,000 bedding plants he had in his garden:

'Well, you see, when I was doing those I used to send off for those books. Once a month you get books from them. They come in volumes. There are 12 volumes. So if ever I was stuck I look, I used to look through the books and say "oh". Read it up, oh that's the way to do it. It's the same with the bricklaying. I ordered a bricklaying book and I read it up ... with plastering, now a friend of mine is in the library and she got me a book, so ... if ... I'm not quite sure I get the book and read it up and say "oh well" this is the way.

Like, that wall was all different when I'd done it the first time. Then we went to Porthcawl one day and we see these walls and she [his wife] said "Yeah, it's nice – could you do that on the wall?" She said, "Well, there's a lot of cracks there." So we took the old wall off and I plastered it across, removed all the fittings, fitted them all in and plastered it all off and it's been there since.'

This extraordinary learner was labelled a non-participant in the trajectory analysis. Obviously many respondents who took an active role in developing their own skills and knowledge were not as accomplished as the individuals quoted here. There were also some differences in the sorts of learning reported by male and female respondents. Intriguingly, women may be even more likely than men to describe informal learning episodes as simply 'activities' and so to downplay their reporting of what must have transformative experiences in many ways.

One woman in her 60s taught herself to crochet and do quilting from books, building on skills in knitting and sewing she had gained as a child. She had organised a local 'ladies club' and a coffee club to raise funds for her children's school. There are similarities with her earlier work as a bookkeeper that she undertook with no reported training, and where she taught herself how National Insurance worked from pamphlets, for example.

A similar story emerges from a woman in her 50s who explained how she taught herself to play the organ:

'When we came here … there were two organists and neither could play at this funeral for some reason. He said you've got to play. Fortunately there was a week in between and every day I went down, this was a very old pipe organ. I went home in tears and said "I can't play it", it's a completely different ball game to playing the piano. You wouldn't believe it…. Middle C isn't middle C and when you take your finger off it stops. I just can't, but I did it.'

She runs a sewing class for the Mothers' Union, does all the brassing for the local church as well as their laundry. She is Brown Owl of the local brownie pack and governor of her local infant school. She reports no special training to take on any of these roles, which she describes as 'just inheriting'.

In some cases, people's ambitions are more prosaic but also more important to them. One woman who was illiterate when she left school and throughout her first marriage simply wanted to learn to read:

> 'Mine started to get better really when I was having my first son. I was in hospital for nigh on six months and I mean hospital is quite boring. I started to read. I read a lot now but I find I like to go over the books a couple of times because I'm always picking up things that I've missed before.'

A woman in a similar position taught herself to read in her 30s assisted by her husband, and can now read a tabloid newspaper, a skill of which she was understandably proud and keen to demonstrate during the interview.

According to respondents, even most of their new jobs involved no training of any sort. New tasks were picked up through 'common sense' by individuals in a wide variety of situations, from barristers in pupillage, to pharmacists on drug counters, to lathe operators, school teachers, sales representatives and care assistants. One woman became a clerk, then an assistant to a dog-breeder, and then a small-holding farmer without any formal training at any stage. Another was trusted with the accounts of a medium-sized firm, and later set up her own play group for children, both without any training. The point they were making is that, in their view, formal training was unnecessary and that experience was everything, despite being 'thrown in at the deep end'.

One man was a coal-cutter who had to give up when his local mine suffered a catastrophe:

> 'There was an explosion in Six Bells – can you remember it? And there was quite a few dead. Well, we was actually working, they were working towards us from Six Bells ... and we was only a matter of from here to that wall away from then when it happened. So I thought that was enough, so then, um, I came out and went to be a manager with Premier Cheques. Used to have a cheque and they could go into the shop and buy clothes. Premier Cheques it was called at that time and I was manager in Tredegar, and they moved me over to Brynmawr.'

The importance of this story is that this man received no training at all in order to switch from being a coalminer to catalogue shop manager (apparently successfully). He states that he could have had five or six jobs, and from an era of full employment there are many such examples of what would now seem extraordinary career changes involving no retraining. The interviews confirm that the very necessary skills and knowledge required to perform all sorts of jobs were not acquired in any formal way.

Similarly, a signalman on the railways in the 1950s became a station master with a staff of six, "doing everything, income tax, bills, pay, everything." He learned his tasks "just by spending a fortnight with the chap who was doing it before me ... and I'd issue all tickets."

A woman with several job changes had no training. She first worked as a typist in the car industry, and learned as she 'went along', and then moved to work as a clerk to an insurance firm:

> 'Well they gave me a manual to work the computer. I just learned myself. But I managed.... I had a manual to work it all out. And I wasn't computer-minded so I was right in at the deep end.'

She moved to become a branch administrator for a national sports company, a move that involved added responsibility, such as installing a new networked computer system with no training and with immediate effect.

In each of these accounts respondents were forced to rely on their own 'common sense' to do their jobs. These stories are also an indication of how the circumstances they faced in these jobs required them to learn in this informal way in order to do these jobs at all.

Earlier than the periods described in these interviews, the coal industry in South Wales depended on a system of informal learning by which the skills and knowledge of coalmining were transferred from one group of experienced coalminers to a new group of recruits attracted to the industry from poorly paid rural employment. In addition, this process of informal learning also applied to coalminers' families where the early socialisation of sons prepared them in a general sense for their future coalmining experience. According to the archive data, this system of mentoring was a matter of physical wellbeing and even survival – 'pit sense'. However, the educational opportunities that existed went further than coal-winning skills. It is clear from the historical evidence that the mining system of mentoring also included a desire on the part of the older generation to enthuse their younger counterparts about academic attainment. It should be noted that the archival evidence on informal learning is primarily concerned with the coalfield, and therefore with men rather than women.

If informal learning is a characteristic of later-life learners, surely it is a characteristic that policy-makers should seek to enhance rather than ignore merely because such learners do not certify their activities or start to pay external providers. If informal learning is less class-stratified than formal education, by only recognising formal episodes, policy may be excluding those it is purportedly setting out to include through widening participation. The results reinforce doubts about the efficacy of simply considering opportunities and barriers in attempting to encourage greater participation for other adults. The opportunities for informal learning are already so widespread, and the barriers so few, that there must be further reasons for those not continuing to learn (or at least not realising and reporting it). The finding that those who stay in formal education or training after compulsory schooling and those who do not are both unlikely to have undertaken leisure study suggests that simply extending the length of initial education, the policy of successive UK administrations, is not a sensible way forward for all (see Chapter 12).

Conclusion

Relatively formal activities seemingly unrelated to attainment, such as the CU discussed at the start of this chapter, can benefit attainment at school. However, they do not seem to be able to reduce the poverty gradient in attainment. Using parents more as a resource for their children's education may not have a beneficial impact at all, and will increase rather than reduce the poverty gradient, unless parents are brought into activities conducted in schools – which is then no longer 'education otherwise' but just more school. This is partly why countries move towards compulsory, universal schooling in order to reduce the impact of differences in home life and parental time and resources.

Although learning completely separately from formal participation – independent and informal learning – is still stratified in the same ways as formal educational outcomes, the patterning is far less. Many (not most) apparent formal non-participants teach themselves impressive and certainly non-trivial skills for work, life and leisure. Perhaps the stratification of educational outcomes is partly illusory and a consequence of an over-emphasis on taught, formal episodes and, above all, on certification. There is little evidence that indicators such as formal participation and qualifications are good predictors of a person's value for employers or to society. By ignoring informal learning commentators may misportray historical trends in skill formation, and in accessing wider elements of knowledge. This is a point taken up again later, in Chapter 12.

NINE

The wider outcomes of schools as societies

Following Chapter 4, this chapter looks at how education and experiences at school can influence outcomes and attributes other than cognitive attainment. Attainment is important but is only one possible educational outcome of schooling. Others such as wellbeing, enjoyment of learning, or preparation for adult life could be just as important. Although interventions and policies to enhance wellbeing, resilience or engagement may not convert into higher attainment (see Chapter 8), they can still lead to positive outcomes in their own right.

My work in this area falls into two main categories. I looked at formative interactions at school between adults and students, and between student peers, and their link to students' intentions for the future, their sense of justice and expectations of life (Smith and Gorard, 2006; Gorard, 2007c, 2010e; Gorard and Smith, 2010). I then conducted robust evaluations of interventions intended to improve students' non-cognitive outcomes such as communication, teamwork and confidence (See et al, 2017a; Siddiqui et al, 2017a,b). Both categories are summarised in this chapter.

The wider and non-cognitive outcomes of schooling are potentially very important but difficult to define, and so to research. The chapter beings with one of the easiest outcomes to assess.

School experience as a determinant of post-compulsory participation

Only just over half of 14- to 15-year-old pupils in England report that school encouraged them to want to learn more, and that they plan to continue in formal education of some sort (see Table 9.1). Since this work was done (Gorard and Smith, 2008), the leaving age for education and training in England has risen to 18, but the pattern remains, and is strongly linked to wanting a professional occupation as an adult.

Table 9.2 shows the result of logistic regression models using a number of possible explanatory variables to try and explain the

Table 9.1: Percentage of Year 11 pupils agreeing with each statement about participation

School has encouraged me to learn more	51
I plan to continue in education after age 16	55
I want a professional occupation	56

Note: N=2,700.

Table 9.2: Cumulative percentage of variation in responses to envisaged futures, explained by each stage of analysis

	School has encouraged me to learn more	I plan to continue in education after age 16	I want a professional education
Individual pupil background variables	12	30	21
School-level variables	6	4	6
Individual experiences of education	35	20	22

difference between pupils reporting the outcomes in Table 9.1 and the rest. Variable were entered in three groups, starting with individual student background. These personal and family background factors explain a substantial amount of the variation that can be explained in all three models. This is because the outcomes are stratified by SES to some extent. A smaller amount of variation is explicable by school-level factors. However, because adjusting the school mix would cost very little (see Chapter 4), it is worth taking into account. Much of the difference between those who have been encouraged by schooling and others is then related to their individual experiences of education.

The first stage in the regression analysis for all three models used only the potential explanatory variables related to pupil background. Those that were strongly linked to the three participation outcomes are similar (see Table 9.3). Pupils from professional family backgrounds are more likely to report being encouraged to learn more, plan to stay on in education after 16 and want a professional occupation. Pupils from families living in poverty, who are less likely to have professional parents, are correspondingly less likely to report plans or desires for participation of this kind. In addition, girls and pupils speaking a language other than English at home are more likely to want to continue to post-compulsory education and to have a professional occupation. Prior attainment is a factor in professional aspiration. Participation in education and training at age 16, or not, was not overtly selective in England at the time, and so prior attainment is less

Table 9.3: Individual background variables in model for envisaged futures

	Encouraged to learn more	Planning to continue in education	Professional aspiration
Sex (female)		2.79	2.21
EAL		2.70	1.47
Father has a professional occupation	1.35	1.56	1.47
Mother has a professional occupation	1.27	1.89	1.56
FSM-eligible	0.69	0.47	0.59
Attainment at KS3			1.46

Note: The figures are odds ratios. A pupil eligible for FSM is only 0.47 times as likely as other pupils to report planning more education.

of an issue for immediate participation itself. However, the educational system in England moves from being largely comprehensive at age 15 to mostly selective in HE, and it is the highest attainers who are more likely to have realistic professional aspirations.

Academic attainment was rarely valued in and of itself, but as a gateway to being able to do what pupils wanted in the future – FE or HE or employment. One pupil said:

> 'Grades are very important as they enable us to get further in our careers.'

Staff attitudes, approaches and reported priorities, overall school results at KS4, the ethnic mix of pupils, geographical location, curriculum offer, school type such as faith-based or single sex and the management organisation of each school are all unrelated to patterns of reported participation plans. There are only two notable school-level factors related to variation in outcomes. The first is a kind of gradient of schools relating to the level of government or local authority control. Once individual pupil background had been accounted for, pupils in community schools of all types were less likely to report wanting to stay on in education than pupils in maintained 'independent' schools like foundation and academy schools, and even less likely than pupils in fee-paying schools. This is described by a pupil who had previously not been keen on school but who had noticed a change over time as his school became an academy:

> ''cos they all treat you like you're adults, and that's actually good, 'cos … like, young adults, and they tell us, like, if you don't bother about your GCSEs you're not gonna end up

nowhere, so ... that's when I thought, just keep my head down, do my work.'

The same kind of transformation was noted by parents in several fee-paying schools:

'I can't say how pleased I am for having a daughter who wasn't confident at all, who left this school a changed person. It changed her character and gave her a feeling that she could achieve.'

A relationship of mutual respect between adults and young people is, therefore, a possible determinant of pupil desire to continue in education. For whatever reason, this kind of relationship is currently more likely in schools, and other institutions, outside direct community control. And the suggestion is that something can be learned from them by all schools.

The second school-level pattern relates to the aggregated intake to schools (or school mix). Once individual values are accounted for, there is still a small amount of variation (4-6%) explicable by the percentage of FSM and professional background pupils in each school. This could be evidence that one of the levers under our direct control in education is the mix of pupils between institutions. A link to the mix effect is pupils reporting contact with pupils on other courses or programmes, and so being more likely to want to continue in education. One reason could be that they become aware of the range of possibilities. This is a further reason for mixing pupils of different types within, as well as between, schools.

The final stage in each model, using individual pupil responses to their experiences of schooling so far, is at least as influential as pupil background. Participation-relevant outcomes are positively linked to the provision of good information and guidance for the future, a feeling of being in control, advice from immediate family and contact with pupils doing other courses (perhaps offering insights into alternatives, or even things to avoid). So the overall impression is that pupils want help from various sources, but to feel that the choice remains theirs. These outcomes are also enhanced by being in small classes with appropriately specialist teachers, indicating, perhaps, that the quality of the learning environment also plays a role (see Table 9.4). Aspiration (for professional occupations at least) is curtailed by lack of any necessary pre-qualification, and pupils also seem to react badly to pressure from their schools to participate in specific ways.

Table 9.4: Individual response variables in model for envisaged futures

	Encouraged to learn more	Planning to continue in education	Professional aspiration
Future guidance was good	2.01		
Encouraged to make up own mind	1.79		
Choice influenced by family	1.54	1.37	
Contact with pupils on other programmes		1.30	
Teachers for specialists subjects		1.30	
Choice influenced by school pressure		0.56	
Classes were small enough to learn			1.22
Not qualified for desired course			0.61

There were mixed views among young people about the quality of information, advice and guidance provided for them. Around 40 per cent reported that they had received clear guidance about employment, and around 55 per cent about their future learning. There was some concern that making curriculum choices sometimes seemed a perfunctory exercise, influenced by organisational demands or by teachers 'selling their subject':

'It seemed teachers were too fussed about timetabling and how many pupils were going to do each subject, rather than why we want to do subjects and how they will help with our future career plans.'

Treatment of pupils by teachers

The ways in which students are treated by teachers could have a big influence on how they view society. Young people generally gain skills and qualifications and learn to socialise during their compulsory schooling. They also learn how to assess whether something is fair or not (EGREES, 2008), and these attitudes to wider society can be fairly long-lasting or even lifelong (Gorard and Smith, 2007; Gorard, 2011c, 2012d; Smith and Gorard, 2012). PISA data shows that the type of school attended is linked to the nature of student relationships with teachers (Vieluf et al, 2015). Several small-scale and other studies around the world have suggested a link between experiences at school and civic activities such as voting in general elections (Engelmann, 2016).

Pupils' reported experiences at the hands of their teachers in school during the previous academic year are quite consistent across social, economic and family background groups, and in all countries I have looked at (England, Wales, Belgium, Spain, Italy, France, Czech Republic and Japan). In all the countries, males, females, high- and low-attainers, those from families with professional-educated parents and those with less educated or unemployed parents, recent immigrants and second language speakers all report pretty much the same experiences – there is almost no difference, for most items, between pupils from families with different occupational and educational histories. Pupils with potential disadvantages, such as those with parents in lower-status jobs, do not report experiencing greater potential injustice in these terms. Of course, the situation is not ideal, since the percentage agreeing that their teachers are trustworthy can often be low, but at least different kinds of pupils are not reporting different levels of agreement. The same lack of variation is also noticeable in some less desirable experiences – such as punishments being used unevenly, teachers getting angry with pupils and teachers having favourite students.

Table 9.5 shows five example logistic regression models, each based on one potential outcome, and the extent to which the models can improve on that percentage by adding variables representing pupil background and school experiences. So, for example, the model can predict which pupils considered teachers to be trustworthy with 50 per cent accuracy using both background and experience variables. This is a substantial improvement from the base figure.

Several things are noticeable about these models. Most obviously, the largest proportion of variation explained (over and above the base frequency) comes from the school experience variables. Despite being entered last in each model, and so giving the opportunity for patterns due to pupil and family background to emerge first, it is the

Table 9.5: Percentage of pupils correctly identified as agreeing with each outcome or not, by batch of variables

Outcome	Pupil background	Aggregated background	School experience
Teachers are trustworthy	9	0	41
Willing for others to be helped	19	2	15
Immigrants should adopt local customs	11	2	22
Trust other adults	10	0	12
I enjoy school	9	2	18

Note: Variables representing parental support add nothing of substance to any of these models, and this stage in the analysis is simply omitted in the reporting here. See also Chapter 8, which also suggests that parental involvement is not as key to success as sometimes envisaged.

pupil's experience of school that appears to matter most in all models. There is stratification in these outcomes, in that they are somewhat patterned by pupil background. The pupil mix variables, which are mostly the same pupil background variables aggregated to school level, then make little substantial difference to any outcomes. There is not much evidence of a school mix 'effect' here (as also found for other 'soft' school outcomes by van Houtte and Stevens, 2010). For these kinds of outcomes, the noticeably strong association is not what kind of schools a pupil attends, but what actually happens in interactions with teachers and others when at school.

Table 9.6 summarises the key interactions relating to the first four of these outcomes (enjoyment is discussed later). Interestingly, there is little overlap in the precise items that are linked to learning to trust teachers, and learning to trust adults outside school and more generally. Teachers have to be seen to be following the principles of equity properly by respecting all pupils, and their autonomy, and showing concern for all. They must also be prepared to reward and punish some pupils when this is warranted, and to remember not to carry this justifiable discrimination over into areas of school life where it is not. The trust (or not) of teachers is bound up with pupils' treatment by teachers, and interactional justice in marking, punishments, and the like. The reasons given for trusting teachers are similar to those for enjoying school generally (see below). Trusting other adults is linked to a few of these items, but more to social interactions with peers, and to a range of disagreeable experiences such as having something stolen.

Around 52 per cent of pupils reported that they were happy for a teacher to give extra help to a pupil with a specific difficulty (even at their own expense in terms of time). The remaining 48 per cent mostly reported that all pupils should have equal attention, regardless of their learning needs. In this case, therefore, pupils are almost evenly split about a crucial issue for equity. There is a relationship between pupils' reports of justice in school and their willingness for a pupil in difficulty to receive extra help. Being respected by teachers, with teachers not getting angry in front of others, not punishing pupils unfairly, being concerned for pupil wellbeing and prepared to explain until everyone understands are strongly linked to pupils reporting being prepared to support help for those with difficulties. Taken at face value this suggests a possible role for teachers in educating citizens who are tolerant and supportive of the difficulties of others. They do this not through citizenship pedagogy, but through their exemplification of good citizenship in action.

Table 9.6: Coefficients for pupil/school experience variables and social outcomes

	Trust teachers	Trust other adults	Willingness to help others	Immigrants should adopt local customs
Teachers punished bad behaviour fairly	1.72	1.23		
Teachers have been interested in my wellbeing	1.67		1.27	
Teachers treated pupils' opinions with respect	1.67			
Teachers treated my opinion with respect	1.67			0.81
My marks usually reflected the quality of my work	1.61	1.18		
Teachers encouraged me to make my own mind up	1.45			
My marks usually reflected the effort I made	1.43			
Teachers continued explaining until all understood	1.32			
I have good friends in school		1.16	1.70	1.67
I have a friend who gets low marks at school		1.14		1.32
All pupils were treated the same way in class		1.10		
Something of mine was stolen		0.89		
Teacher got angry with me in front of the class		0.86		
Teachers got angry with a pupil			0.81	
I have a friend who does not come from [country]				0.68
Hardworking pupils were usually treated best				1.15

Note: All coefficients are odds in relation to the 'strongly disagree' category.

The last 'outcome' variable relates to society beyond school, and the extent to which experiences at school might be relevant to pupils learning about the wider issues. Yet again, teachers apparently misusing or confusing two principles of justice and treating hardworking pupils better even where it is not relevant, and not respecting the opinions of pupils, are linked to what could be construed as a long-term negative outcome of schooling.

Pupils report that being treated differently is not necessarily problematic if this differential treatment is deemed appropriate and fair (Smith and Gorard, 2012). But teachers do not appear to be sensitive to the more subtle distinctions drawn by their pupils. One recurring example of apparent inequity stems from respondents' observations that teachers were inconsistent and unfair when punishing pupils, that teachers had favourites and that certain groups of pupils (for example, the hard working ones) were treated better than others. The issue of even-handedness generated the most complaints from a wide range of pupils:

> 'When a pupil can wear their own coat throughout the class and another pupil wears a ring and is asked to remove it. Certain pupils are allowed to sleep in lessons.'

> 'How the naughty children get more attention and get highly praised when they manage to produce the same amount of work as the rest of the class, which they should be doing anyway.'

> 'Some teachers in the school respect certain pupils and don't respect some others, and they wonder why kids get so rude to them and start swearing and that's when we get into trouble.'

> 'In history, the teacher's "favourites" don't get punished, can walk round the room, even walk out of the room, and not get punished. The rest of the class isn't acknowledged.'

> 'In the history class, I left my book and I got yelled at for five or ten minutes and the teacher hit my head about ten times, also, I was called back after the class. When another student, who was cleverer than I, left his book, he was told only to go home to bring it, but he was neither hit nor called back afterwards.'

'Some students dye their hair and behave aggressively, and teachers cannot deal with them and they are not disciplined. But teachers are very strict to some other people who did something wrong. Teachers are scared of some students and it affects our lessons.'

'It will go on forever once we start to count unfairness. What annoys me the most is some specific students always escape from being punished because of their excuses, while other students have to do some punishments such as cleaning for a week. It is teachers' fault, this unfairness. It seems impossible to change.'

It is episodes like these that help pupils decide that a school or a teacher is unfair. Appropriate discrimination in terms of need, effort and attainment are all accepted or even preferred, but to be punished more harshly than another for the same thing, for example, leads to lingering resentment.

Enjoyment of school

According to Ofsted (2007), around 42 per cent of students at school in England do not enjoy school, and their teaching is the source of greatest dissatisfaction. Apparently much of the teaching taking place in England is 'boring' (Marley, 2009). In my study, 58 per cent of students in Year 11 did not enjoy being at school (Gorard and See, 2011), and one of the reasons for this is clear. Only 38 per cent said that most of their lessons were interesting. A logistic regression model similar to those above was created to predict who reported enjoying school. The students' personal and family background explained some of the variation. Again, almost none of the variation in responses was explicable by school-level factors. The levels of enjoyment reported by students did not differ substantially by school type, and there is no real evidence of a school effect. This finding has important and beneficial consequences for attempts to increase and widen enjoyment of education. Most of the differences between those who enjoy and those who do not enjoy school are related to specific individual experiences of education.

Restrictions on choice at age 14 caused by school pressure and timetable blocking constraints reduce the likelihood that students enjoy their school and lessons. On the other hand, enjoyment of school is strongly enhanced by student sense of autonomy – including being allowed to work at their own pace, to discuss issues with staff and other students, and being encouraged to make up their own minds about issues raised. These outcomes are also linked to variation in delivery, including practical work, visits and field trips, and contact with students on other programmes. Many students referred to friends they have made, and the social aspects of learning, such as support from friends and discussion groups. Having friends at school and the social aspect of school were frequently suggested by students as key to their enjoyment valued in its own right, but also as promoting learning:

> 'I prefer to work in a group, because if you have one on one it's really, really nervous. But if you have a friend with you it's like you've someone else to talk to.'

> 'Yes, definitely! I've met a lot of new people and always had help and encouragement when I needed it. I know I can come back anytime and have felt very at home here.'

Some talked about fun activities in the classroom, while others referred to a relaxed atmosphere of teaching and learning or an adult relationship with teachers (being treated with respect and as young adults rather than as children). For some it was very simple things like addressing their teachers by their first names that made them feel they were being treated as grown-ups, and this could make the learning experience enjoyable. Students also referred to issues of respect and autonomy in learning, having the chance to discuss things in class, being given the opportunity to work in small groups, receiving individual attention and having a say in their learning.

The main setting for interactions between young people and teachers is in lessons, and pupils appreciate imagination and variation (see also Chapter 6):

> 'I had one teacher who would do, like, to show Women's Liberation he wore a bra and took it off, and ... I just ... that ... I will never ever forget that. And to do hippies we walked into the classroom and there were candles everywhere, he had his tie round his head, you know, and it was just so different and so funny that you won't ever forget it, so....'

> 'And sometimes they get us to do presentations, like us teaching the class so it sort of helps us to learn it as well ...

so it can be boring ... sitting there with a teacher and we just switch off so she gets us to actively teach the other person so that get us to know the textbook as well.'

There is little worse than struggling at school and finding no assistance. Happily, many young people reported additional support, whether one-to-one at the end of the lesson or more formal or permanent arrangements. They appreciated this help and it allowed them to enjoy school more. Some students spoke of the approachability of the teaching staff that helped to make school life pleasant:

'Yeah, all that I have to do is just go and speak to my teachers and say I'm struggling with this and the teacher will say come to me at a certain time and we'll see what we can do about it.'

'If you ask a teacher to explain something you don't understand.... I've had half an hour, just a one-to-one, before, them teaching me something I don't understand, or something I've missed. If you put in less, then you won't get the respect of the teacher, so you end up getting less. You get back what you put in.'

While other students are a welcome source of friendship and support for many, the behaviour of other students was also described as a major factor hindering enjoyment. The abusive behaviour of a minority of young people to their peers is perhaps the biggest single threat to genuinely inclusive and comprehensive schooling. In this study, however (Gorard and See, 2011), the concerns expressed were more about the frustration and wasted time of lessons disrupted by other students:

'Don't think it's anything to do with, like, lesson planning, ... it is just generally the class distraction. If they were willing to listen then I think we would learn. It's just ... teachers allow some students to get away with murder.'

Poor student–teacher relationships can be a cause of stress for students, while lack of teacher respect for students was widely cited as a cause, or justification, for bad behaviour. Sometimes the complaints were simply about poor basic technique. One common complaint was about audibility, one of the most basic elements of classroom craft:

'I am failing my [subject] because my teacher does not speak up and only talks to the front row.'

A linked complaint was lack of real engagement, such as eye contact, and continuing with a narrative almost like a recording, so missing the point that students could not engage and copy notes at the same time, and turning question and answer sessions into a farce:

'Sometimes if you're copying and the teacher is talking at the same time you can't listen to them, so you don't know what they are saying.'

'He doesn't say can you answer this question most of the time, because he just shouts.'

Unimaginative lesson delivery was easily the most common complaint. The experiences that were widely perceived to undermine enjoyment were passive pedagogy, such as listening to a teacher for lengthy periods, copying, note taking and having to sit still for a prolonged period. The connection between active learning and enjoyment and between passive learning and lack of enjoyment was widely but not universally made by students. Many did not like the classic style of lesson, as it would appear in a caricature of school:

'We're given a sheet and we're just spoken to and we write down notes and then the sheet is, at the end of the hour, two-hour lesson, is lost and never seen again. We don't really learn that way.'

It is noteworthy that none of the thousands of teachers taking part in the survey mentioned prioritising enjoyment for students. Very few alluded to it in the interviews. This is a shame because while enjoyment is presumably neither necessary nor sufficient for learning to take place, student reports of enjoyment are a kind of barometer of when things are going well in a lesson, and of when they are most definitely not.

Results of bespoke interventions

So far this chapter has presented results from descriptive and correlational studies using regression modelling. This final section looks at a few deliberate attempts to improve non-cognitive outcomes, especially for the most disadvantaged students in schools. One was based on encouraging philosophical dialogue in primary classrooms (Philosophy for Children, or P4C). The intervention is described in Gorard et al (2017d), and the full results of this quasi-experiment are outlined in Siddiqui et al (2017b). As shown in Table 9.7, as far as it is possible to tell, P4C leads to greater self-reported ability to work in a team and to communicate with others. More importantly this is at least as true for FSM-eligible pupils as the rest.

The other two interventions both involve trying to provide experiences for all pupils that are perhaps more frequent in high-SES and private schools – based on youth social action (Birdwell et al, 2015). The first of these is a range of uniformed activities such as Sea Scouts and St John's Ambulance Brigade, taking place as extra-curricular activities via schools, and run by Youth United (YU). The full account is given in See et al (2017a).

Such activities have a negative association for some students, and are seen as the preserve of the middle class (Bradbury and Kay, 2005). Other studies have claimed that social action and uniformed groups lead to greater employability, self-esteem and confidence (Ward et al, 2009; Kirkman et al, 2016). However, again, few actual interventions have been evaluated, and where they have, the evaluations have often not been rigorous enough to assess the impact convincingly (Booth et al, 2015).

Table 9.7 summarises the headline results of the work with YU, showing that there is a small benefit for the two key measures of teamwork and self-confidence. The YU participants also noticeably increased their empathy for others, and their professional aspirations, compared to the control group. The pupils who received the intervention wanted to know more about pathways towards professions than previously. However, unlike P4C, these benefits were smaller or non-existent for FSM-eligible pupils. This suggests that such uniformed activities are not the way forward here.

Table 9.7: 'Effect' sizes from three trials of non-cognitive outcomes

	Effect size	Effect size FSM only	Quality of evidence	NNTD attrition
P4C teamwork	+0.15	+0.11	2	0
P4C communication	+0.10	+0.23	2	0
Youth United teamwork	+0.07	−0.04	3	0
Youth United self-confidence	+0.10	+0.04	3	0
Children's University teamwork	+0.04	+0.17	3	0
Children's University social responsibility	+0.08	+0.10	3	0

The third intervention is Children's University (CU), which organises, supports and badges extra-curricular activities taking place via schools, leading to a graduation ceremony (see also Chapter 8). There was some prior evidence that volunteers with parents able to pay for the CU programme reported higher levels of satisfaction, attendance at school and subsequent attainment (literacy and numeracy) than those who did not volunteer or otherwise could not attend (MacBeath, 2012). However, the programme was not assessed in relation to a randomised control group. Children who are more likely to attend these activities are from families in a higher socio-economic group and so are already more likely to have better outcomes at school (Cheung, 2016). However, Table 9.7 shows a small benefit from CU in terms of their chosen headline measures of teamwork and responsibility, and a potentially larger benefit for FSM-eligible pupils in an RCT. In addition, the CU group became more empathetic than the control, and increased more in their professional aspirations as well.

The range of social action activities was wide including charity fundraising, making packs for donations to food banks, collecting unwanted household items for charity shops and participating in awareness walks. Pupils in one school grew vegetables that they sold to raise money for donations to a cancer research foundation. Others reported:

> 'We help younger children in our school learn new games in the playground. It is a real fun and we like helping them to learn exciting games.'

> 'I volunteered to help in a local library and it gave me a chance to meet new people. I also learned about books and how to place them in the bookshelves.'

> 'I volunteered to help organising a show for St John Hospice. It was a competition for the disabled. It was so great to help people who were helping others.'

> 'We want our streets to be clean and no litter around. We want no graffiti on the walls. We have made these posters so that people should see that we care about our area.'

> 'We know we can't see children living in countries where there is war but we can at least collect money for the charity so they can buy food and clothes for children in need.'

'My school is very nice. We play and do a lot of fun activities. We have raised funds for school buildings in Uganda so that children go to schools like mine.'

Conclusion

The similarities between the determinants of concepts such as aspiration, sense of justice, hope for later life, how others should be treated and enjoyment at school are remarkable. They are all generally less stratified by pupil origin than attainment outcomes, which should make them easier to improve. There is little evidence of a substantial school effect, even where pupils are educated away from mainstream settings. However, as with the poverty gap in attainment, mixing pupils from different backgrounds in schools costs little or nothing and could improve non-cognitive outcomes and benefits for society by up to 6 per cent, at a stroke. The biggest lever for change is improved interaction with teachers, and for policy-makers this lies in making schools act more like the kind of society that we want – not sectarian, overtly selective or clustered by SES, but with pupil autonomy in their learning choices, and mutual respect between young people and adults. These things are more easily demonstrated than taught. Those pupils treated best at school tend to have the most positive outlook on trust, civic values and sense of justice. With only half of all pupils enjoying their time at school, something can and should be done to improve the situation. And this is then likely to reduce the stratification of subsequent educational episodes.

Positive experiences of school tend to be associated with pupils having positive experiences of justice at school, with teachers who are tolerant, sharing and inclusive. Negative experiences of school tend to be associated with pupils who are then prepared to tolerate and countenance these kinds of injustices at school. Those who had experienced teachers giving extra help to other pupils who were struggling were more likely to be in favour of extra help being given to others. Those who had been bullied or hurt at school were less in favour.

The importance of this is that where students see schools as cooperative ventures, enjoyment is more widespread. Enhancing enjoyment of school through consideration of better and more consistent student–teacher relations may have an impact on learning, behaviour and attendance. But this is not to suggest that enjoyment of school is important primarily because it will help yield higher attainment. Enjoyment of life in school is clearly a good thing, even if it leads to no greater attainment. It would probably also have an impact on young people's lives outside and beyond school, and on their developing sense of what is appropriate and normal in wider society. It will almost certainly help produce generations of adults less wary of formal education and training in their future lives (see Chapter 12).

As shown earlier in Chapter 7, intervening to increase children's motivation, aspiration or attitudes related to education does not, in itself, improve attainment. But the three interventions described here show that giving pupils new experiences could enhance their empathy, confidence and aspirations as good things in their own right. And two of them also show that such school experiences can reduce the SES stratification of such non-cognitive outcomes.

TEN

Widening participation to higher education

Fair access to university has been an enduring theme of my work for over 20 years. I have looked at undergraduate student funding and hardship in Wales (Taylor and Gorard, 2001), the difficulties of deciding which social and economic groups might be under-represented in HE in the UK (Gorard, 2008b), what can be done to address under-representation (Gorard et al, 2017e), why some ethnic groups are over-represented (See et al, 2012), and what happens to students when they arrive at university (Selwyn and Gorard, 2016).

This chapter focuses on widening participation to undergraduate HE. The patterns of participation in HE in England were portrayed earlier in Chapter 3, although similar patterns appear in Wales, the rest of the UK and across the world (Gorard, 2005d). When in the 'pipeline' to HE do these socio-economic patterns first appear, when are they strongest, what causes them and what can be done about them? Can we overcome the stratification by using contextualised admissions (CA), as is ongoing policy in the UK at the time of writing (Gorard, 2016c; Boliver et al, 2016, 2017)?

Policy approaches to widening participation

Access to HE is patterned by inequalities worldwide, and it is difficult to change that pattern through compensatory education and similar approaches (Neve et al, 2017). In most countries and contexts the most important barrier to participation in HE is prior attainment (Raffe et al, 2006; Broecke and Hamed, 2008). Student intakes to universities in the UK are and have always been stratified in terms of SES and other characteristics (Gorard et al, 2007a) – perhaps more so than in other developed countries (Jerrim and Vignoles, 2015). Students from less advantaged social and economic backgrounds are under-represented, especially in the UK's most selective universities and in some subjects leading to professional occupations (Broecke, 2015).

Despite an increase in the number of students studying at HE level in the UK, and estimates place it at 43 per cent of the 18-30 age group

(Attwood, 2010), it is still the case that inequalities persist with regard to who participates and who does not. The home countries of the UK, EU member states and many countries worldwide have concerns about the stratified nature of the student body in first-time undergraduate HE (Triventi, 2011). This has led to a number of attempts to 'widen participation' for the kinds of students currently under-represented in HE, creating some widening of participation overall, but still less so in the 'top' universities (Harrison, 2011), and in demand areas like STEM subjects (DfE, 2016).

As with many countries, and because of these patterns, the UK is attempting to create wider participation in HE for all social groups. There are 164 HE providers (139 universities and 25 colleges) in the UK, catering for around 2.3 million students. For traditional undergraduates, entry to HE is based on prior attainment at KS5, currently taken by only just over half of the relevant age cohort. The applications of traditional age students are largely managed by the independent University and College Admissions Service (UCAS), but the actual places are offered by the universities themselves.

Policy attempts to widen participation have involved a number of approaches. In the context of up-front tuition fees and no maintenance grants for students, in England at least, universities are offering fees remission and bursaries (discussed further in Chapter 11). The simplest approach has been to expand the number of places available at universities. This has also been the most successful in the sense that the patterning of HE intakes became less marked as the numbers of entrants increased, and ironically the policy of widening participation really only began in earnest when that increase was halted (Gorard et al, 2007a). Until recently the most common approach to widening participation involved outreach work in relatively deprived schools and enrichment activities to encourage young people from disadvantaged backgrounds to apply to university. This approach has never been robustly evaluated, so there is no clear evidence of whether it works or not. Research has shown that many young people express a desire to go to university, including those from disadvantaged backgrounds, suggesting that limited aspirations play only a small role in the uneven social composition of university entrants (Gorard et al, 2011; Kintrea et al, 2011).

A much more significant role is played by the seeming intractability of social disparities in school achievement. A related approach therefore involves efforts within the secondary and further education sectors to improve the pre-university academic attainment of pupils from disadvantaged backgrounds in order to increase the pool eligible for university admission. But such activities are unlikely to have made much difference to the key issue of the number of disadvantaged students attending university. This is because universities are selective in their intakes, and generally demand the highest prior qualifications that they can get away with while still filling their planned places. Their position in the prestige pecking order is largely based on the grades they demand that young people have on entry. Because qualifications such as GCSEs and A levels are stratified by the same variables that widening participation is intended to address, such as social class and poverty, the selective nature of the system makes widening participation just about impossible.

None of these approaches have been evaluated very well, and some not at all. Where there is available evidence, many do not work. For example, alternative entry routes to HE in Sweden intended to help the most under-represented actually advantaged upper-middle class applicants the most, and so increased the class bias in HE.

Can contextualised admissions widen participation?

A further widening participation strategy is now being widely promoted – the use by universities of contextual data about prospective students' socio-economic and educational circumstances to inform admission decision-making (OFFA, 2015), usually by reducing the grade requirements for entry where it is clear that an applicant comes from a disadvantaged family, neighbourhood or school environment. CA policies are therefore a kind of positive discrimination within the current set-up (Clayton, 2012). Across the UK HE sector, many universities currently take into account the socio-economic context of applicants' attainment when deciding whom to shortlist, interview, make standard or reduced offers to, or accept at confirmation as 'near-misses' (Moore et al, 2013; Universities Scotland, 2016), and more plan to use contextual data in the future.

However, the indicators used are often chosen because they are readily available, without much consideration of the possible alternatives (SPA, 2016). Yet in order to be effective, the indicators must be accurate, appropriate and complete. The possible variables for use with CA must be easily and cheaply available to decision-makers at the time of application to HE. They must be true indicators of disadvantage, with an impact on attainment and progress, accurate, reliable, and have few or no missing values. They should be standardised (and so comparable) and officially verified. Their deployment must lead to increased fairness in admissions, and not to a different form of injustice, such as denying a limited place to a more deserving applicant, and ideally this should not substantially lower the overall retention, degree completion and degree classification rates of the universities concerned. Of course, no indicator will be perfect in all of these respects, but these are the interlocking criteria by which CA indicators can be judged.

Indicators not available at admissions stage

The range of possible indicators that could be considered for CA is almost limitless, but however attractive they may sound, most are of no practical use. Most commonly, they are not available to the admissions authorities in a secure form. These include whether an applicant is a young carer for others, has suffered a recent bereavement or similar disruption, and their sexuality. There are several problems with reliance on all such self-reported items, including the fact that the definitions and thresholds used by different applicants will be different and, most importantly, that once it is known that reporting one of these issues leads to preferential offers at university, there will be some gaming of the system. At present, many of the same problems arise with chronic ill health (other than disability/special needs) and gender status. Our review found no good evidence relating to transgender students and attainment at school, for example. None of these indicators appears in the NPD or similar official datasets at present, and they involve important ethical and legal problems concerning confidentiality and the protection of the data subjects. All of these ideas could be important, but the necessary evidence does not yet exist.

The latter also applies to family income/tax credits. Official data on family income is not readily available. Self-reported family income data can be available to university admission authorities via UCAS, but currently only after the institution has made a decision on the application, and with a high proportion of missing data.

At present none of these can or should be used as part of a valid national approach to contextual admissions.

Indicators with little or no promise

My review of indicators (Gorard et al, 2017e) showed that many of the additional tools used for admissions, such as entry tests, interviews and setting tasks for applicants, generally lead to more bias in offers and entry than simply using prior attainment (Yates and James, 2013; Gill and Benton, 2015).

Probably the most commonly used indicators for CA should not be used. These are the neighbourhood characteristics of where an applicant lives, whether based on low local participation in HE (POLAR) or indices of multiple deprivation (IMD, IDACI, Townsend). The problems of using the modal characteristics of where someone lives rather than their individual characteristics are many and serious. First, it is a kind of fallacy (Do et al, 2006; Harrison and McCraig, 2015). Most disadvantaged applicants do not live in the most disadvantaged areas (for example, around 60% of the most disadvantaged residents are not in the 20% lowest POLAR or IDACI wards), whereas a substantial minority of the wealthiest residents are. Some local area indicators are based on as many as 6,000 residents, who will vary considerably. The approach works especially badly in rural areas with low population densities, and in areas with high population density where rich and poor can live closely together.

Furthermore, an area measure can only be used if the address of the applicant is known. In practice, a large proportion of this address data is missing, which affects all such indices. For example, the school-age NPD has had around 11-13 per cent of student addresses missing in each year, and it is well-established that data is never missing by chance. Missing addresses are more common for recent immigrants, refugees, homeless people and Travellers, among others. For example, a total of 1,183 KS4 students were missing IDACI scores in 2015 (the year when most of them sat for 16+ examinations), and they are much more likely to be from poor families eligible for FSM, certain minority ethnic groups, with SEN or a disability, or to have been recent arrivals in their schools (see Table 10.1). They also have markedly lower attainment than average, at every stage including KS2 (age 11) and at KS4, when they decide whether to continue in formal education at age 16.

Therefore, ignoring cases with missing addresses when deciding which students are disadvantaged would be unjust because some of the most deprived and so most deserving of assistance would be put aside in favour of others. However, using the fact of missing data as an indicator

Table 10.1: Percentage of students with specified characteristics with and without IDACI scores, England, 2015

	Missing address	All students
FSM-eligible	21	14
SEN (any)	24	17
Joined school in last two years	8	3

in itself would also be unjust and would offer assistance to some of the least deprived students (who may simply have transferred from another home country of the UK). It would also provide an incentive for families not to provide clear data to schools and universities. And this missing data means that the neighbourhood scores themselves, even for those people whose postcodes are known, will tend to be biased since the characteristics of those residents missing addresses will also be missing from the averages of the local residents' characteristics.

Additionally, in order for the area measures to be accurate for all residents, there must be accurate records on all other relevant factors for all residents as well, but if such data actually exists, it is clearly more appropriate to use the data from individuals (as in Table 10.1) and not only about where they live. Even for the cases that do exist, and do have addresses, much of the data is self-reported and so unverified (such as ethnicity, via the Census of Population). It would also be possible to 'game' indicators based on postcode since wealthy families may be able to obtain an address in a disadvantaged neighbourhood for the purposes of increasing their child's university admissions chances (similar to what has happened in reverse for school choice and allocation processes). It is not clear which address should be used to reflect childhood and current disadvantage – for mature students, the most recent or longest inhabited for younger students, and so on.

ACORN and MOSAIC are area measures based on smaller geographical units than IMD and the others, such as 10-15 households, but the same issues still arise. In addition, both are commercial products and neither is available to universities without paying.

Another widespread indicator of possible disadvantage used by universities that should not be used is the nature of the school attended. Most of the same counter-arguments relevant to area indicators also apply to school-level indicators. Treating the modal characteristics of the students in a school as though they were true of every individual in that school is again an ecological fallacy. It is not clear whether it is the most recent school or the one attended for longest that is most relevant, and this is also open to games-playing (as when private pupils transfer to state-funded sixth forms). In any year there is a considerable number of students in the NPD with unknown schools (6,532 out of a cohort of 590,000 in 2015). Where data is available, these students with missing schools are clearly more disadvantaged, and have markedly lower than average attainment and progress. So, as with area of residence, the type of school attended is not justified as a contextual indicator, and similar problems arise for the average level of attainment, average poverty and prior HE participation rates in the school attended. Using a modal characteristic for an area or school can be a very misleading guide to individual disadvantage, and can lead to at least as much injustice as the stratification that widening participation is intended to reduce.

Indicators that are not clearly about disadvantage

There are a number of possible indicators listed by advocates of CA that *are* about the individuals themselves, but that are not clearly indicative of disadvantage in education.

For UK residents applying to HE, the clearest 'non-traditional' route is that taken by mature students using their prior experience as an alternative to KS5 or similar prior qualifications. First degree mature students are often, perhaps unintentionally, ignored in policy pronouncements and even research about widening participation to HE, which tends to focus on existing, traditional-age, full-time participants to the exclusion of all other relevant parties and comparators (Gorard, 2013d). In general, those entering HE with non-traditional entry qualifications tend to achieve higher degrees (Hoskins et al, 1997). Mature students also tend to do better after HE than their younger peers in terms of subsequent graduate employment and salaries (Woodfield, 2011). To be older is not necessarily to be disadvantaged in access to HE.

Immigrant groups vary considerably in their access to and success in HE, and some face clear barriers (Erisman and Looney, 2007) while others do not. It is not clear that being a recent immigrant is necessarily an indication of educational or social disadvantage. A student from an English-speaking professional family moving to the UK from the US, for example, would not be considered disadvantaged but would be a recent immigrant. Recent immigrant status would currently have to be based on self-report and is not an indicator available to higher education institutions (HEIs) before decision.

A recent refugee or asylum-seeker is more likely to be disadvantaged than a recent immigrant more generally, but this is still not necessarily so. Currently, HEIs only receive this data from UCAS after an institution has made a decision on the application, and the data is based only on how applicants chose to classify and identify themselves in their UCAS applications. A substantial number select 'I prefer not to say', and so there would be considerable missing data as well as uncertainty if this were used for CA. The review found no large-scale or authoritative evidence relevant to this indicator.

Having EAL can be an indicator of disadvantage given that instruction in the UK is generally in English. However, in most respects EAL students and the rest are very similar (see Chapter 3). They have lower than average KS2 results at primary age, but make considerably more progress, and have higher than average KS4 and KS5 results. They are then more likely to continue to KS5 (63% compared to 52% of first-language English speakers in 2008), and achieve good grades at A level or equivalent. Being an EAL student is usually only a temporary disadvantage, and for some individuals it is not even that. The NPD specifies the first language of the home or family, but a substantial minority of cases (9% or more) are missing a valid value in the NPD. None of this makes EAL a good indicator for CA.

Participation by minority ethnic groups overall, but not necessarily in the more prestigious universities, is higher than might be expected from the target population (Chowdry et al, 2008; Gallagher et al, 2009). However, the level of degree completion is then sometimes lower even after age, prior attainment and subject of study are accounted for (Broecke and Nicholls, 2007). Black and Chinese minority students are most likely to have withdrawn from their course after one year (HEFCE, 2013; Woodfield, 2017). It would probably be necessary to disaggregate minority ethnic groups in order to use this indicator to widen participation in an effective manner. Some ethnic groups, such as Chinese groups, are well represented across the HE sector of the UK. Others, such as Black Caribbean-origin students, are disproportionately in less selective or less prestigious HEIs, and others again, such as Travellers and White UK groups, are under-represented in HE as a whole.

In the NPD and UK Census of Population, missing ethnicity is the largest 'minority ethnic' classification. As with any indicator, the missing cases tend to be the most disadvantaged, with the lowest probability of continuing in education after the age of 16, and the lowest chance of any level of academic qualification at age 18 (see Table 10.2). In general, the known minority ethnic students are more

Table 10.2: Percentage of students continuing with post-16 education by ethnicity, England, 2008

	Other	Asian	Black	Chinese	Mixed	Missing	White
Continued post-16	61	67	58	84	55	49	51
Achieved EE+ at KS5	51	57	48	77	47	41	44
Achieved CCC+ at KS5	34	37	27	62	32	27	30
Achieved ABB+ at KS5	23	25	16	50	23	19	22

likely than the majority White students to continue to KS5, gain minimal A level equivalent grades (EE+) and gain the kind of high grades needed for entry to the most selective universities (ABB+). On average, Black students are currently finding it hardest to convert participation into the highest grades.

It is not clear how much any disadvantage is about ethnicity itself and how much is about the ethnic group acting as a proxy for other forms of disadvantage (see Chapter 3). Some studies suggest that ethnicity has only a minor link to educational outcomes once other factors such as SES are accounted for (Gorard and See, 2013), and others suggest that some apparently disadvantaged groups actually do better in some respects after controlling for social class and other factors (van Dorn et al, 2006).

Ethnicity does not have a clear legal definition, and even in official statistics such as the NPD or Census of Population it can only be based on self-report. It has a large and growing number of categories, that either fail to capture the real variation or produce unwieldy schemes and tiny cell sizes (Williams and Husk, 2012). The term is used in different and contradictory ways (Salway et al, 2010), based on common ancestry, memories of a shared past, a shared cultural identity that might include kinship or religion, language, shared territory, nationality or physical appearance (Lee, 2003). The classification is heavily dependent on the identification of sole ethnicities, with the mixed categories clearly intended to be for a minority. But it is hard to contend that there are many individuals who do not have a mixed ethnic origin of some kind. All of this does not make it a particularly reliable or valid indicator.

For all of the indicators above it is not clear that they are true indicators of disadvantage, although they will denote some very disadvantaged applicants who should be picked up in other ways using more valid indicators.

Indicators only available for applicants

At the time of admission, universities can have access to a number of variables about individuals that could denote relative disadvantage. Unfortunately, many of these are only available for applicants, which means that we cannot tell whether any of the groups indicated are under- or over-represented in HE compared to the more general population of young people (for whom equivalent figures do not exist). They are also all only self-reported, and have considerable missing data even for the applicants. These indicators include the otherwise promising items such as parental education, and parental occupation or social class. The proportion of HE applicants not stating a parental (or other) occupation on their application has grown over time to 26 per cent of all HE applicants in 2007 (Harrison and Hatt, 2009). This has made 'unknown' the largest social class group in the UK.

In general, indicators only available for the self-selected body of young people who enter and survive KS5 and then apply to a university in England are not to be preferred as a general solution to CA.

Individual indicators with more promise

In some respects, the indicator that an applicant has spent time living in care is not much better than some of those above. The indicator covers time spent by the applicant in local authority care, and is linked to the worst educational outcomes in the UK. It has a relatively simple, binary and official definition, and where known, this indicator is sent to universities with application data. However, at present the information is only self-declared by the candidate, and is otherwise unverified, and much relevant data is missing or unclear. Such information is likely to yield both positive and negative misclassifications. It would be better if this data could be made available from official records to a responsible central authority. This indicator covers only a relatively small number of cases, and any that are verified could simply be tagged for CA.

Young people with SEN or disabilities tend to have lower average attainment and make lower average progress in any phase of schooling (see Table 10.3). Only non-SEN pupils have positive VA scores (again, calling the disassociation of VA from absolute scores into question; see Chapter 6). In 2015, no students had a missing value recorded for SEN (although there are an increasing number of missing values when going back through each prior year at school for these students). Not surprisingly, students with the most serious SEN have the lowest average attainment and make the least progress. Students with any SEN

Table 10.3: Mean attainment scores of students by SEN category, England, 2015

	No SEN	SEN no statement	SEN with statement
KS2 average points	21	17	11
KS1-KS2 value-added progress	+0.22	−0.43	−0.65
KS4 capped points	330	225	114

are clearly more disadvantaged than those without, on most available indicators, and this is especially so for students with SEN statements.

This means that SEN students will, on average, be less likely to proceed to HE. SEN students are much less likely than average to continue in education post-16, and even less likely to obtain the sort of qualifications permitting uncomplicated entry to HE under the current system (see Table 10.4). Twenty-six per cent of non-SEN students achieved ABB+ at KS5 in 2008 compared to less than 3 per cent of those with SEN statements (5% of SEN students more generally). Whatever provision for help those statements put in place, it is clearly not enough to allow easy access to HE. All of this makes SEN a promising indicator for CA.

However, SEN is not a simple binary indicator and does not have a clear legal definition (Florian et al, 2004). It includes mental health difficulties, mobility issues, sensory impairment and unseen disabilities. A student with mild dyslexia should not be treated the same as one with both severe visual impairment and mobility problems. Multiple challenges are often ignored in recording the most serious one or two for any individual (DfES, 2003). It would be fairer to disaggregate this indicator into a number of categories of risk concerning participation in HE, and the kinds of support HEIs would need to provide after admittance.

There are serious concerns about the accuracy of SEN labelling, whether in classification or recording (Douglas et al, 2012). The accurate 'identification' of these challenges can itself be stratified by other indicators of relative disadvantage (as shown in Chapter 3). Historically, SEN, and especially the identification of learning or behavioural problems, has been more prevalent among lower-SES students. This stratification may be partly accurate, reflecting multiple disadvantages, but it may also be linked to differential diagnosis. Students in disadvantaged or more social segregated school settings are more likely to be diagnosed as having a behavioural disorder, for example, whereas those in more advantaged settings may be treated as being merely 'naughty'. However, this historical trend has

Table 10.4: Percentage of students continuing with post-16 education by SEN, England, 2008

	No SEN	SEN
Continued post-16	60	19
Achieved EE+ at KS5	52	15
Achieved CCC+ at KS5	36	8
Achieved ABB+ at KS5	26	5

changed with the rise of dyslexia and similar unseen disabilities. A disability statement based on dyslexia yields an increased chance in the competitive education system for the child (such as extra time in examinations), and it is the middle classes in the UK who have taken most advantage of this (Tomlinson, 2012). An overall disability flag indicator, most especially a self-declared one, is therefore vulnerable to abuse. Compared to the school and more general population, students flagged as disabled are actually slightly over-represented in UK HE (Gorard 2008b), are fairly evenly distributed across HEIs and increasingly completing their first degrees successfully (Pumfrey, 2008). All of these issues mean that SEN is a promising CA indicator, but cannot be adopted wholesale without considerable further work.

Eligibility for FSM relates to applicants from the poorest families in England (defined in Chapter 3). It is a reasonably secure and verified indicator of official relative poverty. Recording and reporting of it is a legal requirement for all state-funded schools, and the FSM status of each child is held as part of the NPD to which HEIs could have annual access. The measure is therefore available for nearly all relevant young people, irrespective of whether that person applies to HE or not. FSM is one of the most comprehensive and accurate measures of SES available.

It is clear that students eligible for FSM at any stage of schooling are more disadvantaged on average in all other respects as well. They are more likely to be recent arrivals, from minority ethnic groups, with EAL and SEN. FSM students have lower attainment at all stages of schooling, and make less progress between Key Stages, and the longer they have been eligible by age 16, the lower their attainment is (see Chapter 3).

Due to lower attainment at age 16, FSM students are far less likely to continue to KS5, and so apply to HE at age 18 (see Table 10.5). They are less likely to obtain the minimum entry qualifications for HE, and far less likely to get the higher grades required by the most selective universities. FSM may be the best single indicator of relative disadvantage for use as a CA variable.

Table 10.5: Percentage of students continuing with post-16 education by FSM, England, 2008

	Non-FSM	FSM
Continued post-16	56	31
Achieved EE+ at KS5	48	25
Achieved CCC+ at KS5	33	13
Achieved ABB+ at KS5	25	8

However, it is still not without some problems (Boliver et al, 2016). For example, the NPD has around 11 per cent of cases with unknown FSM status every year, of which around 7 per cent are in fee-paying schools that do not have to complete the school census (Gorard, 2012a). A small number of children will be home-schooled or otherwise simply missing from the register, rather than in fee-paying schools. Some of these can be assumed to be among the poorest in society. The remaining 4 per cent of students missing data on FSM eligibility in state-funded schools would also be ignored and so disadvantaged by a system that used FSM as a context variable for HE admissions. It has been shown from what we do know about these students that they could be among the most disadvantaged in society – with the lowest known rate of qualifications. Many are in special schools (while many of the rest are mobile students such as Travellers, or recent arrivals such as asylum-seekers perhaps without official papers). Given the level of inclusion of children with SEN in mainstream settings, those in special schools are more often those with very severe learning and other challenges. All of these groups could be among the most deserving of consideration in a contexualised admissions system, yet would be ignored if they were missing FSM data, and FSM was the criterion used.

Individual indictors currently ignored

As shown in Chapter 3, the age of a child within the year of their school cohort is linked to both labelling (of SEN and EAL) and to their relative attainment. It is therefore not surprising to find out that summer-born children in England are about 10 per cent less likely to go to university than their winter-born peers. The simplest way to deal with this clear injustice would be to routinely age-standardise all attainment scores, including for access to university. This would reduce unfairness for summer-born children. Age is a clear, valid and reliable indicator, collected officially, available from all applicants, and it can be easily verified. Age is probably the single best CA variable available for use. Age-in-year is currently ignored because for some reason it is not seen as an issue for widening participation.

Male and female students are, as would be expected, similar in levels of poverty, ethnic origin, first language, age-in-year and school mobility. However, males are much more likely to be labelled as having SEN, and have markedly lower attainment results at all phases of schooling. Substantially fewer male than female students continue in education post-16, and fewer again attain any KS5 qualifications (see Table 10.6). These differences cannot be explained by students' differential background, and if sex were almost any other characteristic, it would already have been proposed and widely used for CA. The variable is still a relatively clear one (perhaps the second clearest available after age), routinely collected and available to HEIs at the time of admission. As with age, there is an argument that all attainment results should be sex-standardised, using student sex for CA. This would help to balance the intakes to HEIs.

Table 10.6: Percentage of students continuing with post-16 education by sex, England, 2008

	Male	Female
Continued post-16	48	57
Achieved EE+ at KS5	41	50
Achieved CCC+ at KS5	26	35
Achieved ABB+ at KS5	19	26

The leaky 'pipeline' to higher education

Only just over half (52%) of all KS4 students in England have historically continued to immediate KS5 academic or equivalent vocational study. They do so in almost direct proportion to their KS4 attainment. Because KS4 attainment is stratified by student background characteristics, the KS5 cohort each year is also stratified by these same characteristics. The under-represented groups are students living in care (only 16%), with any SEN (11% with a statement), eligible for FSM (33%), males (48%) and those born later in the academic year (summer-born). Students with EAL are actually over-represented, as are all minority ethnic groups. Table 10.7 shows how the population of students at KS4 with each background characteristic becomes segmented by participation and attainment in post-16 education, up to degree classification such as a 2.1 or above.

The other 48 per cent not continuing to KS5 are the more disadvantaged and lowest attaining students in the country on average. Nothing done from thereon in terms of widening participation will make any difference to their chances of attending or being successful in HE. In fact, some will leave formal education with below functional literacy and numeracy. It is important to remember in any concern for educational justice that nearly half of each cohort is effectively ignored by widening participation activities, and that the focus of all that policy spending and effort is on the already more advantaged half

Table 10.7: Percentage of pupils continuing with post-16 education by background, KS4 cohort, England, 2006

	Continued post-16	Achieved EE+	Achieved CCC+	Achieved ABB+	Entered HE	Russell Group	2.1 or first
FSM-eligible	31	25	13	8	20	2	5
Non-FSM	56	49	33	25	36	7	17
White	51	44	30	22	31	7	15
Asian	67	57	37	25	55	9	19
Black	58	48	27	16	48	4	11
Chinese	84	77	62	50	72	22	35
Mixed	55	47	32	23	40	8	15
Other	61	51	34	23	51	9	15
Unclassified	49	41	27	19	30	6	13
Not English	62	54	34	22	52	7	16
English	52	45	30	22	31	7	15
SEN statement	11	8	5	3	6	1	2
School Action	24	19	9	6	13	1	4
School Action+	16	13	6	4	9	1	2
No SEN	60	52	36	26	39	8	18
Living in care	16	11	6	4	10	1	2
Not in care	53	46	31	22	38	8	15
Male	48	41	26	19	31	6	12
Female	57	50	35	26	38	7	18

Notes: Full data on all independent schools was not available. The Russell Group is used as a convenient proxy for selective universities.

of the cohort, and deals largely with the 'usual suspects' of those most like the students already attending, or on a trajectory towards, HE. Of course, it may be argued that the more successful students at KS4 deserve or merit their higher attainment, but this is not the approach used by traditional widening participation advocates when considering KS5 attainment. There is a huge inconsistency in policy here. If disadvantage affects attainment at KS5, then surely it equally affects attainment at KS4 and before. In which case, there is no justification for leaving the 48 per cent, not continuing to KS5, out of current widening participation arrangements.

Of those continuing to KS5, around 88 per cent attain results that would be equivalent to at least two E grades at A level and might be considered the minimum level for general entry to HE at traditional age (see Table 10.7). Within themselves, these results are much less stratified than at KS4, and much less stratified than continuation to KS5 itself. However, some groups identified by background characteristics continue to have lower average attainment. These, again, include students living in care (69% attaining EE or better), with any SEN (73% with a statement), eligible for FSM (80%), younger students and males (85%). Only Chinese-origin students are noticeably over-represented in this group (92%), but Black-origin students are under-represented (83%). This all confirms that KS5 is not the key problem, that the biggest opportunities to widen participation lie earlier in life, but that early disadvantage continues into KS5, and produces strong patterns at the highest levels of attainment (of the kind that are used by the most selective universities).

Around 65 per cent of those continuing to KS5, and 74 per cent of those attaining EE and equivalent or better, then enter HE. Dramatically, the stratification alters from the pattern above for most indicators. FSM-eligible students in KS5 are as likely as any other to continue to HE, and those attaining EE+ are *more* likely to continue to HE (80%) than students not eligible for FSM. Similarly, 91 per cent of those living in care who attain EE+ at KS5 continue to HE. This may be a result of prior widening participation actions. The difference between males and females also largely disappears. SEN students are still under-represented, but those with SEN statements who attain EE+ are slightly more likely (75%) to attend HE than those without SEN. White ethnic-origin students continue to be under-represented (61% of KS5 and 70% of those with EE+), and all other identified ethnic groups are over-represented − 97 per cent of Asian and nearly 100 per cent of Black-origin students with EE+ at KS5 continue to HE. This suggests that once students have been (self-)selected for KS5, continuation to HE is largely in proportion to numbers and attainment. If anything, the admissions process makes HE entry rather fairer for potentially disadvantaged groups − *but only for those that continue to KS5*.

Around 13 per cent of the KS5 cohort and 15 per cent of those attaining EE+ attend a Russell Group university − a simple but incomplete way of estimating those attending the most selective HEIs. These figures are balanced by sex. But they under-represent students eligible for FSM (6% of the KS5 cohort), of Black ethnic-origin (6%), living in care (6%), with SEN (9% for those with a statement) and for whom English is their first language (11%). These same indicators are still under-represented in Russell Group universities, even when considered only for those with at least ABB at A level. This suggests a problem with the most selective universities that seem to be directly or indirectly selecting even *among* high-attaining students on some other basis that leads to other forms of stratification. Having a selective HE system clearly does not prevent even those among the most disadvantaged KS5 students from entering HE somewhere. The main function of selection, whether intended to or not, is to hinder access to only some HEIs within the system, and in doing so, to emphasise differences in student background.

Around 29 per cent of the KS5 cohort and 35 per cent of those attaining EE+ then complete their studies with a 2.1 class degree or better (for those HEIs and subjects where degrees are graded), across all universities (see Table 10.7). And many of the earlier patterns re-emerge at this stage. These high grades are less likely to be obtained by students living in care (13% of the KS5 cohort), FSM-eligible (16%), with SEN (18% for those with a statement), Black origin (19%), males (25%) and speaking EAL (26%). Potential early disadvantage continues even on completion of HE.

Table 10.8 shows the situation slightly differently, using 'achievement' gaps (see Chapter 2) for each group relative to the overall KS4 cohort,

Table 10.8: 'Achievement' gaps between students with different characteristics, KS4 cohort, England 2006

	KS4 level EM[a]	Continued post-16	Entered HE	2.1 or first
SEN statement	−72	−65	−70	−76
SEN (School Action+)	−56	−62	−58	−76
Living in care	−54	−62	−55	−76
School Action	−44	−37	−45	−58
FSM-eligible	−27	-25	−26	−50
Male	−4	−4	−4	−11
Unclassified ethnicity	−4	−3	−6	−7
White	+1	−1	−5	0
EAL	+1	0	−5	0
Not in care	+1	+1	+6	0
Mixed ethnicity	−1	+3	+8	0
Non-FSM	+3	+4	+3	+6
Black	−9	+5	+17	−16
Female	+4	+5	+6	+9
No SEN	+7	+7	+7	+9
Other ethnicity	−1	+8	+20	0
Not EAL	0	+9	+21	+3
Asian	+3	+13	+24	+12
Chinese	+17	+24	+36	+40

Note:[a] EM = including English and Maths

and considering entry to KS5 and HE, and results in HE. Thus, SEN, FSM-eligible and living in care students are vastly under-represented in KS5, and this is maintained (or even worsened slightly) in HE. These three groups have a clear problem of access to KS5, and it is here that attention should be focused. By definition, students without these characteristics are more likely to enter KS5 and retain their advantage in HE. Asian, Chinese-origin and students with EAL are also more likely to enter KS5 and to retain their advantage in HE.

SEN, FSM and students in care are under-represented in post-16 education, but only to the same extent as their KS4 attainment results (at least until the degree result is considered). Other than these, the next biggest achievement gap in access to post-16 education is between male and female students. And as above, Black students are over-represented in KS5, especially in relation to their KS4 scores, and much more so in HE, but tend to achieve lower grades to almost the same extent.

Those students entering HE are predictably higher qualified than average, having started out with higher test scores and made more progress at school (see Table 10.9).

Playing around with the KS5 qualifications needed for entry to HE, such as dropping the equivalent of two A level grades for under-represented groups, will therefore make no difference at all to overall entry to HE. And most under-represented groups such as males, summer-born and those with severe or multiple SEN are not even considered as widening participation candidates (widening participation seems not be to about this at all). As a general widening participation strategy, such playing around will fail – because the most under-represented students do not even continue to KS5. The key way to include more of the most genuinely disadvantaged would be to drop KS5 attainment as an entry requirement. This would make little difference for the usual KS5 cohort, with most already obtaining at least minimal qualifications and attending HE. It might make a considerable difference for a few of the most disadvantaged students at KS4. But the biggest difference would be to the most selective

Table 10.9: Mean scores for pupils at each stage of post-16 education to HE, KS4 cohort, England, 2006

	All	Entered KS5	Achieved EE+	Entered HE	2.1 or first
KS4 capped points	292	358	364	372	393
KS3-KS4 CVA progress	+1.27	+13.85	+14.64	+14.12	+30.10
KS5 total points	348	660	752	762	889

universities. Put simply, selection does not operate as a gatekeeper to HE itself as much as a way of sorting students into the most selective universities – and in doing so, leads to an intake strongly stratified by other characteristics (Evans et al, 2017). This problem can be solved at a stroke simply by eliminating this kind of selection and making HE more open access. It could be non-selective just as the national school system is, but not compulsory, unlike the school system. It would be a proper national system – and every HEI could be funded and supported to be as good as every other (just as schools and colleges should be).

If qualifications at KS5 are deemed to be merited by the hard work and talent of the students taking them, the allocation to HEIs within the HE system is already largely fair. Its stratification *is* the stratification of prior qualifications. But if qualifications at KS5 are not deemed to be merited by the hard work and talent of the students taking them, it would make sense not to use such qualifications at all for selecting students to specific HEIs. Meddling with the usual suspects by foregoing a grade or two will not make any fundamental change, and although it may benefit some individuals, it will also lead to the thorny issue of who, with higher prior attainment, deserves not to be selected where there are limited places. Trying to judge to what extent a qualification is merited by any individual is a difficult task that will inevitably create new injustices, and it certainly cannot be judged more accurately by HEI admissions tutors than by the national, formal, moderated qualification system itself. To repeat, if we do not trust qualifications at KS5, then we must not trust them at KS4 and earlier. This would allow us to work with the much larger pool of true widening participation students with the lowest levels of qualification.

Predicting continuation to KS5, HE and degree result

Putting the variables together, it is possible to use prior attainment and all of the background variables to model whether a student continues to KS5 or not, to HE or not, and their eventual degree classification (for HEIs and subjects where this is possible). This is done here rather differently to usual because the concern is to see how unbalanced admission to KS5 and beyond is, once prior attainment has been accounted for. Therefore, prior attainment is entered into the model before SES and other factors. It is clear that the best predictors of KS5 participation are the various indicators of prior attainment (see Table 10.10). Once these are accounted for, the students in different categories of possible contextual variables participate to roughly the

Table 10.10: Percentage predicted correctly for KS5/HE outcomes, by each step

Step	Enter KS5	Enter HE	2.1 or better
Base	53.1	66.7	53.2
Step 1: KS3 attainment	77.1	69.4	60.5
Step 2: KS4 attainment	83.0	72.7	64.4
Step 3: KS5 attainment	–	76.3	65.5
Step 4: Student background (school)	83.3	78.1	65.9
Step 5: Student background (HE)	–	–	65.9

same extent. Around 53 per cent of these KS4 students continue to KS5, and so an attempt to predict whether a large group of students would continue to KS5 or not would be correct around 53 per cent of the time just by chance. Adding their KS3 prior attainment would increase the accuracy to 77 per cent, and so on. Student background, in this way of reckoning, only contributes a further 0.3 per cent.

A similar pattern appears for continuation to HE. Only around 33 per cent of students continue to HE at this age. Most of the variation can again be explained by prior attainment. However, the overall model is less accurate, and prior attainment only adds 9.6 per cent. There is a slightly larger 'role' (1.8%) for student background here. Unlike the first two models, analysis of degree outcomes is only possible with the minority of students who do eventually attend HE. Predicting whether a student gains a first or 2.1 is harder than the previous steps, partly because not all degrees are classified, and partly because so much other data is missing or unclear. But again, once prior attainment is accounted for, there is little or no difference between students of different backgrounds. Around 47 per cent of students in HE for whom there is a result obtain a 2.1 classification or better (meaning 53% do not). Their attainment before HE adds 12.5 per cent to the accuracy of prediction, and their contextual background only adds a further 0.4 per cent. Students are gaining HE results in almost direct proportion to their prior attainment and largely unrelated to their SES background.

To the extent allowed by the model, poorer students, and those living in care or with SEN, are marginally less likely to continue to KS5. But this is not true for EAL and minority ethnic students who are actually over-represented in KS5 given their qualifications (see Table 10.11). Clearly, those with higher prior attainment are more likely to attend HE. Again, minority ethnic groups (of all categories) and EAL students are considerably over-represented in HE, while males and those living in care are under-represented. Poor students

Table 10.11: Coefficients for variables in final step of each model

Variable	Step 3 odds	Step 4 odds	Step 5 odds
KS3 average points	1.01	1.03	0.97
KS4 entries	0.86	0.93	0.88
KS4 capped points	1.02	1.01	1.01
Number of AA* passes	1.15	1.05	1.003
Number of passes A*-C	1.17	1.06	1.12
KS5 total points	–	1.004	1.001
Female (vs male)	1.02	0.87	1.26
In care (vs not)	0.65	0.80	0.59
FSM-eligible (vs not)	0.88	0.98	0.91
EAL (vs not)	1.67	1.99	0.96
SEN (vs not)	0.86	0.72	0.93
Other ethnicity (vs White)	2.04	3.42	0.70
Asian (vs White)	2.41	3.83	0.78
Black (vs White)	3.24	5.02	0.68
Chinese (vs White)	2.94	3.53	0.95
Mixed (vs White)	1.56	2.04	0.83
Higher managerial professional	–	–	1.15
Lower managerial professional	–	–	1.16
Intermediate occupations	–	–	1.14
Small employers and own account workers	–	–	1.09
Lower supervisory and technical occupations	–	–	1.06
Semi-routine occupations	–	–	1.03
Routine occupations (vs unclassified)	–	–	0.99
Never worked and long-term unemployed	–	–	0.63
Parental HE	–	–	1.10
POLAR 1 (vs 5)	–	–	0.91

and those living in poorer areas appear to participate in almost direct proportion to their earlier qualifications. Insofar as background is a factor in degree classification, the outcomes for minority ethnic groups reverse, with all groups doing slightly worse than the White majority, as do EAL students. To some extent, of course, this balances the situation for entry to HE.

Conclusion

Similar analyses to those above have been conducted with the national KS4 datasets from 2006 to 2012, and in all important respects the results are the same.

Most students completing KS5 are capable of obtaining a place in HE somewhere in England, with few (or even no) qualifications. The overwhelming majority of students with minimum-level KS5 qualifications continue to HE, and they do so largely without systematic differences in their background or family characteristics. The stratification of HE is almost entirely the stratification of pre-university, indeed, pre-KS5, attainment. Therefore, where CA are used, it is not because many similarly qualified students with different backgrounds are being treated differently on entry to HE. It is clear that making it easier for disadvantaged students to gain entry to HE squeezes out others, and that those losing out are not the most advantaged but those just above whatever level of disadvantage is operationalised (Adventures in Evidence, 2017). If it is fair to deny a place to one student with noticeably higher grades in favour of another, this suggests a lack of trust in the prior assessment system. In this case, it is pertinent to consider whether we should use qualifications in this way at all (Gorard et al, 2007a).

Given that success in education is predicated on success at the previous educational stages, and because young people from less affluent social groups have lower achievement throughout schooling, on average, it is unsurprising that entry to HE is also stratified by social characteristics such as occupational class background and economic activity. This leads to a kind of education-based discrimination, which is too often overlooked (Tannock, 2008). In England, it is illegal to select people for occupations or educational places on the basis of age, sex, social class, ethnicity and so on. Yet countries and universities continue to select on the basis of academic attainment, despite knowing that attainment is clearly stratified by these same 'illegal' variables (Gorard et al, 2007a). In many ways this makes no sense (Walford, 2004).

Recently, the growing use of contextual admissions has seemed to offer a possible half-way house, keeping the system selective, without fully agreeing on the validity of qualifications. Applicants are still assessed as they always have been, with their prior qualifications the key factor, but with greater consideration of the context in which those qualifications were obtained. Young people who have clearly faced considerable challenges, and who have succeeded against the odds, are given some leeway – perhaps offered a place with a slightly lower grade than other applicants to the same university. In this way, the theory goes, we can widen participation without upsetting the whole system. The trouble is, we do not know if CA work either. The foregoing all suggests that they do not.

Getting more under-represented groups into university via CA is not easy. Currently the wrong kinds of indicators are being used. For example, the Scottish Government has committed itself to the Scottish Index of Multiple Deprivation (SIMD) that is among the least useful of all indicators of disadvantage. The safest and clearest indicators could be the sex (male), age-in-year (summer-born) and years FSM of a student, but none of these is currently considered in widening participation. Perhaps prior attainment results should be standardised by all three variables for consideration as part of the admissions process.

At present, not all universities and colleges use the CA approach to the same extent or with the same indicators. In the absence of a centralised procedure or a commonly agreed set of indicators, universities use a range of different indicators to identify hardships faced by learners for admissions decision-making. To some extent, HEIs are simply using widening participation as part of a larger competition to promote enrolment to their own programmes rather than to promote system-wide or national objectives. Older universities tend to ask for high A level grades and demonstrate a willingness to be more flexible where there is a low demand for courses. Less prestigious institutions tend to recruit more students from working-class backgrounds because of the markets they are able to recruit in rather than because of their widening participation policies as such (Greenbank, 2006). Often the rhetoric and justification for selection on the basis of merit or otherwise does not fit the observed practice in the same institution. And universities rarely use or used the same system for selecting candidates anyway, whether they use context as part of it or not (ECU, 2012).

One possible approach would be a modelled one, in which all available explanatory and background factors were used as context to create a national model for each qualification level. This would have to be done centrally, with access to a full dataset of all relevant students. The achieved qualification level for each candidate could then be adjusted up or down (for those who have substantially better or worse than their circumstances would predict), to create a more truly contextualised grade. Where the contextualised grade was higher than the achieved grade, the admissions tutor could treat the contextualised grade as the entry requirement. Exactly how this would be done requires a lot more work, but it would be similar in several ways to CVA analyses for school outcomes, and these throw up almost as many problems as they solve (see Chapter 6). This would not deal with the fact that CA are focused entirely on traditional age (and full-time) students, as though increasing the number of older, less traditional, students would not be widening participation.

Further than that, the CA process misses out the overwhelming majority of students who will not ever go to university in order to focus on the 'usual suspects' of those most like those who traditionally attend. CA must not be a replacement for work to reduce the impact of disadvantage on educational outcomes earlier in life. This is where the key difference must be made. Such work could not only have benefits for widening participation, but would also help those never likely to go to HE under any system.

ELEVEN

The supply of professionals

One of the reasons given for widening participation to HE, as discussed in Chapter 10, is that societies need more trained professionals in certain areas such as doctors, nurses, engineers and social workers. The two areas I have researched in greatest detail involve reported shortages of scientists (Gorard and See, 2008, 2009; Smith and Gorard, 2011) and of school teachers in the UK (Gorard et al, 2006; Gorard 2013e) and US (Smith and Gorard, 2007b). This work includes detailed accounts of the 'pipelines' from early years to employment and retention in STEM or as a teacher.

Shortage of scientists

STEM subjects, students and teachers occupy a privileged position in UK government education policy because of their economic importance and apparent shortages (HEFCE, 2008). Scientists are deemed crucial to any economy and the health of any nation, but to be in short supply and/or reducing in proportion to the number of available opportunities (CBI, 2010). The funding for STEM subjects, students and teachers has been retained, even in economic downturns. The UK and other developed countries are trying to maintain or even grow the number of scientists that they train and employ. The US also has its version of the 'science problem'. In 2004, 32 per cent of first degrees from US HEIs were awarded in STEM subjects compared with 56 per cent in China, with the proportion of 'foreign-born' scientists and engineers in the US growing rapidly. However, their numbers have decreased, leading to alternative concerns that the US will lose out in the global marketplace for the best STEM scholars to emerging economies such as India and China (NSF, 2008). The purportedly reduced uptake in science has been variously attributed to poor initial education in science, high levels of dropout once science becomes optional at school, and poor pay and promotion for scientists in comparison with other professions (Butz et al, 2006).

As with the US, different countries are worrying about recruiting and retaining fewer scientists than their competitors, and this has led to considerable government spending on related interventions in the

UK and elsewhere. As early as 2004, the UK STEM Mapping Review reported 470 STEM initiatives run by government departments and external agencies designed to engage young people, and in particular, under-represented groups, in STEM subjects. The number has grown considerably since then. The UK Space Agency alone identified or was involved with over 1,000 educational interventions about one space mission (See et al, 2017b). There are now tens of thousands, possibly hundreds of thousands, of STEM initiatives in the UK alone (Banerjee, 2017). All are intended to promote interest in science, largely reflecting industry's concerns about the lack of a suitably skilled workforce. Many of these strategies focus on teaching and learning and in particular, the nature of the school science curriculum.

However, perhaps because of recent initiatives, there seem to be too many people studying science for the labour market to cope with, or perhaps it is that graduates are considered no longer of sufficient quality. It is more likely, however, that many scientists are without related employment every year because the shortage thesis is wrong and there are not enough STEM jobs waiting for all of them, or because they are 'dropping out' having learned that they do not enjoy their subject areas, or they can get better pay elsewhere (which is itself an indication of how much or little STEM jobs are valued in comparison to the service sector).

My review of evidence in this area shows that, in spite of the proliferation of research, numerous theories (speculations really) still abound, and no conclusive evidence has been put forward as to how exactly SES impacts on students' academic achievement or their uptake of post-compulsory STEM subjects. While a lot of work re-discovers the link between SES and attainment, very little goes further than speculation in explaining why this link exists. But this situation is not unique to science. There is a role for schools and teachers in inspiring students to continue with the study of science, but the studies in the review only allowed this role to be a small one. In general, students are not encouraged to continue with science unless they have been successful in previous stages.

Students can be put off continuing with science by repetition from earlier stages and rote learning at low levels (Osborne and Collins, 2000). Some students may move away from science because it is not intellectually challenging enough. Perhaps non-compulsion at an earlier stage of schooling could lead to greater interest later – especially as students are reported as being more interested in areas of debate (more prevalent in post-16 study) than certainty (more prevalent pre-16). Ironically, it is possible that making science and maths core subjects is at least partly responsible for their later stratification.

At KS4, the differences in attainment between social groups are no larger in science than in all subjects. But many other subjects do not require, or appear to require, such a high level of KS4 attainment in order to continue study. If prior attainment is taken into account in any analysis, there is a very limited role indeed for SES in subject choice at school (Mwetundila, 2001).

The science pipeline to employment

One reason that was given for maths and science being core subjects at school along with English is their apparent economic relevance. In England, science and maths are key subjects from primary stage up to the age of 14. Participation is therefore not an issue at this stage. However, tests for children as young as seven have shown that attainment in science is already stratified by pupil background, with boys and poorer pupils doing worse. This is not a new phenomenon and there is no evidence that it has worsened over decades. The differences in attainment by sex and poverty are no larger, and often smaller, than the differences for all subjects or for English (see Table 11.1). There is not a specifically STEM problem.

Once students are faced with a choice of whether and how to study science (usually at age 16 but increasingly at 14), there is a drop-off in participation, especially in the separate subjects of physics and chemistry. Students are not encouraged to continue with science unless they have been relatively successful in previous stages, and so given the chance, most pupils do not study the 'hard' sciences. Those taking maths or science in any combination after age 16 have, on average, higher prior attainment scores than students taking other subjects for A levels or equivalent (see Table 11.2). They also obtain higher KS5

Table 11.1: Mean capped points scores (all subjects and sciences) and percentage attaining grade C or above (maths and English), all students, KS4, England, 2005/06

	All subjects points	Science subjects points	Grade C+ maths (%)	Grade C+ English (%)
Male	338	33	50	49
Female	378	34	52	64
Not-FSM eligible	373	35	55	61
FSM eligible	266	25	27	31

Table 11.2: Prior and post-attainment points scores, KS5, all entrants, England, 2005/06

	Mean total KS4 points	Mean total KS5 points
Science	484	844
Not science	427	663
Maths	487	925
Not maths	434	674

qualifications, of the kind that permit entry to selective universities (see Chapter 10).

The number and proportion of traditional-age students continuing to HE has risen over the past 50 years, while the share of candidates applying to study all science and science-related subjects at UK universities has remained relatively stable – almost half of the students applying through UCAS apply for the sciences. There is no evidence of a major 'swing' away from science subjects, because there are slightly more science students each decade than ever before. Science subjects as widely envisaged, to include computer science, psychology, forensic science and medicine, for example, have almost kept up with the increase in the number of students studying at university.

The apparent 'problem' is that the absolute number of students taking the separately named subjects of physics, chemistry and biology has remained about the same. This is only a problem if subjects like computer science, and the increasing number of science-related degrees without science in the title, are not treated as real science somehow, or if there is a huge unmet demand for the employment of STEM graduates for these three subjects especially.

STEM graduates have relatively high levels of subsequent employment or further training. A high proportion of graduates in maths and the physical sciences continue to further study, including initial training as teachers (see below). Most engineering graduates, however, enter some form of employment as their first destination (75%), and this makes them suitable for consideration of the type of employment involved. Of the rest, 15 per cent continue to further immediate study, and around 10 per cent are unemployed.

Interestingly, only around 45 per cent of engineering graduates with an occupation are employed in jobs directly related to their degree (see Table 11.3). Even though this is only their first destination occupation, it is astonishing in light of claims of science graduate shortages that so few new graduates go into clearly related employment (in addition to the 10% unemployed). A further 20 per cent are in jobs

Table 11.3: Percentage of recent engineering science graduates in each occupation, 2003 and 2009

Occupation	2003	2009
Employment directly related to degree subject		
ICT, research and science professionals	6	5
Science/engineering technicians	3	2
Engineering professionals	34	38
IT service delivery occupations	2	1
Employment indirectly related to degree subject		
Design and media associate professionals	3	4
Public service and other associate professionals	1	1
Teaching professionals	2	2
Business, statistics and finance professionals	3	4
Architects, town planners, surveyors)	1	1
All managers and senior officials	10	8
Non-graduate employment		
Sales and related associate professionals)	2	3
Elementary administration and occupation	4	5
Sales occupations	6	9
Customer service occupations	2	2
General administrative occupation	3	2
Skilled metal and electrical trades	1	1
Elementary trades	2	1
Administrative occupation records	3	1
Unknown or other	11	9

like management and business, 25 per cent in jobs that are officially considered to be non-graduate jobs such as sales and the service sector, and 10 per cent are not known. Of course, for graduates, many of these jobs could be temporary, and it is perfectly proper for engineering graduates to get jobs in banking and service industries that often pay better. But this is not what most people would envisage as happening with a crisis shortage of scientists.

Supply of teachers

As with scientists, there appears to be a constant demand for more teachers in the UK and other developed countries. Much of my work on this was done in the 2000s (Gorard et al, 2006, 2007b), but it is an area I have revisited recently, and the same situation applies (Gorard, 2017e).

Teacher shortages

In the UK there have been regular reports of insufficient teachers, and concerns about the quality and subject specialisms of some of the trainees that are recruited (Smithers and Robinson, 2000). Recruitment is often lower than the targets set, and has been for some time, especially in reputedly shortage subject areas like STEM (Schoolsnet, 2001). There have also been reports of a considerable loss of potential teachers during and after training, with only 71 per cent of those who completed teacher training courses going into teaching in state-maintained schools, and too many of these then leaving teaching within five years (Howson, 2001). According to press and government reports, more teachers are leaving the profession than ever (Scott, 2016). This means that even if enough teachers were in training, there could still be a shortfall in practice.

Comments to the media from the Chief Inspector of Schools in England suggested that the teacher 'shortage' in 2001 was the worst for nearly 40 years. In 1999, more teachers were leaving than entering the profession, resulting in a net loss of 14,300 practitioners in England and Wales, and those leaving were increasingly unlikely to return (School Teachers' Review Body, 2001). Reported teaching vacancies in secondary schools doubled between 2000 and 2001, and the pupil-to-teacher ratio (PTR) was the highest it had been since 1976 (Smithers, 2001). Headlines appeared proclaiming that the 'Country has run out of teachers' (Dean, 2000). Schools were reported as being forced to go on four-day weeks due to lack of staff, and pupils were being sent home because there were no teachers to teach them.

Academics have also generally written as though teacher shortages are a well-established empirical phenomenon (Reid and Caudwell, 1997; Kyriacou et al, 2002). Studies of teacher shortages point to the difficulties of recruiting and retaining teachers as the reasons for the prevailing problem. The same issues appear in other developed countries (Ingersoll, 2001), and have been the subject of discussion by policy-makers and academics for some time (Shankler, 1992).

Almost exactly the same situation applies in the UK today (Santry, 2017). There were 920 teacher vacancies in November 2016 compared to 730 the year before, and more schools were reporting vacancies – and over 3,000 teaching posts were being held temporarily by staff on a short-term contract. The primary school pupil population has been growing for years, and the secondary school population is now projected to rise until 2025. Even worse, the *Independent* (Pells, 2017) reported that 'staggeringly high numbers of teacher [are] threatening to quit the classroom.' This could be around 40 per cent of young teachers in the next five years. As I write this, there are unconfirmed stories on Twitter about schools in England being so short of teachers that there are class sizes of over 40, and in one case, of over 100. The reported 'crisis' never really seems to go away.

As well as having too few teachers, there have also been complaints about the quality of the teachers that do exist. A survey by the National Association of Head Teachers suggested that 70 per cent of secondary school vacancies in one area had led to the appointment of teachers without the necessary qualifications. Many secondary teachers had not studied their specialist subject beyond A level (Henry and Thornton, 2001). Ofsted has suggested that teacher trainees following employment-based routes have only a narrow experience of teaching strategies, limited subject knowledge and find it harder to teach high-attaining students. Lessons taught by unqualified and temporary teachers are often rated 'unsatisfactory' (House of Commons, 2000).

What causes teacher shortages?

A popular explanation for changes in teacher supply relates to the economic cycle, which is part of the justification for attempted solutions based on financial incentives, such as those aimed at attracting more high-quality trainees, including tax-free bursaries for trainees on postgraduate ITT courses, as well as sizeable 'golden handshake' payments for those who successfully complete their induction teaching period in priority subjects.

It was widely believed that the failure to meet recruitment targets in the late 1990s was the result of a buoyant economy, resulting in high general employment (Slater, 2000). A number of policy studies have claimed that the state of the graduate labour market can affect the proportion of graduates going into training in general (House of Commons, 1997). A similar pattern appears in England today. High teacher vacancies have been generally attributed to an employment market with high rates of employment, particularly graduate employment, in which teaching is thought to be a less attractive career, meaning that fewer graduates enter teaching because of lower wages relative to other occupations (Dolton, 2005). In times of economic recession, on the other hand, teaching becomes a more attractive proposition, and vacancy rates fall. If such explanations were true, we would expect to see an increase in the number of teachers during a period of economic recession.

In fact, real GDP is mostly unrelated to the overall figures for teacher supply in both the UK and US, and there is growing recognition that the problem is neither cyclical nor related to economic performance (Horne, 2001). Teacher numbers actually declined a little after 1992 in the UK, while the economy was faltering. A more direct factor influencing the increase in teacher vacancies is changes in school funding. Around 85 per cent of any school budget is allocated to staffing costs (Johnson, 2001). The number of teacher posts in any school is, in part, dependent on how many teachers a school can afford to pay for. Funding-per-pupil fell between 1995 and 1997, the period of lowest teacher vacancies. From 1997 to 2001 pupil funding increased, coinciding with the period when teacher vacancies also started to rise. In 2001 there was a sudden annual increase of 107 per cent in teacher vacancies (more than doubling), even though the number of teachers had started increasing faster than pupil numbers.

Advertised vacancies are, therefore, the natural accompaniment of any increase in funding. With more money, schools can create more posts. Consequently there is an increase in the apparent demand for teachers, which is translated into advertised vacancies. These temporary vacancy figures are more likely to cause public alarm than the underlying PTRs. Therefore, we are in the paradoxical situation that the purported crisis may be more a product of increased funding per pupil than of increased pupil numbers and, therefore, demand. Those bemoaning the shortage of teachers may have fallen into the trap of bemoaning an increase in money to schools. Similarly, high levels of resignations and teacher turnover may be inconvenient for school leaders but are not, in themselves, evidence of a crisis. Most resignations are caused by teachers moving schools for career or personal reasons, and are more nearly a sign of a healthy national profession than of a problem.

Another part of the explanation lies in school numbers. By closing very small schools with surplus places after 1990 there was greater efficiency in the deployment of staff, since teachers were then more likely to be in larger schools with a higher PTR. Fewer but larger schools led to fewer teacher vacancies from 1990 to 1996, partly explaining the high PTRs and low vacancy rates during this period. However, after 1996, as the number of schools continued to decline, teacher vacancies increased. The year 2001 showed the first increase in the number of schools for decades, and vacancies then rose again abruptly the following year. Two factors may have been at play here. One is that the decline in the number of schools in England slowed down; the other was the increase in pupil funding (indirectly linked to the economy).

In its calculation of recruitment targets, using the formula that is publicly available, the DfE did not take into consideration regional differences, claiming that 'the number of teachers needed minus the number in post and those known to be returning to teaching will give the number to be trained nationally' (Dean, 2000, p 4). It has been assumed that trained teachers will automatically fill available teaching vacancies wherever they appear. As this is not true, there will still be shortages in some regions, even if overall teaching recruitment targets are met. If targets must be used, regional factors need to be incorporated into their calculation, and UK funding needs to be truly national. We should try to move away from the situation where the National Assembly for Wales sees teachers trained in Wales and teaching in England as money wasted, and vice versa.

Another limitation on teacher supply, given the insistence of training institutions on named subject specialisms for most secondary and even many primary places, is the number of home UK students pursuing 'shortage subjects'. For example, Table 11.4 compares total UK-domiciled maths graduates with the teacher supply targets and recruitment from 1995 to 2001. It shows that the number of home maths graduates was between 3,000 and 3,500, with the low point in 1997. In 1996, the target for recruiting teachers from this relatively small number of individuals was an unachievable 85 per cent. The equivalent of over half of the entire graduate cohort in maths actually entered teacher training, but this was still not enough to get anywhere near the target. The targets are unrealistic.

Given that the number of people being trained in shortage subjects is apparently not enough for a good supply of teachers, and the fact that teaching as the major employer of graduates has to compete with

Table 11.4: Maths degrees awarded and initial teacher training (ITT) intake targets, England and Wales, 1995–2001

	1995	1996	1997	1998	1999	2000	2001
Maths degrees, home students	3,280	3,181	2,962	3,154	3,378	3,315	3,490
ITT target	2,380	2,700	2,370	2,270	1,810	1,980	2,065
Targets as % of degrees awarded	73	85	80	72	54	60	59
ITT recruitment	1,888	1,741	1,538	1,191	1,390	1,390	1,660
Recruitment as % of degrees awarded	58	55	52	38	41	42	47

other industries, the number recruited is remarkable. According to the (then) Teacher Training Agency, more than two-thirds of employers had difficulty recruiting graduates of the right calibre between 2000 and 2001 (School Teachers' Review Body, 2002). Even meeting the PGCE targets in modern foreign languages and religious education required that over 40 per cent of the UK graduate output in these subjects entered teaching each year. But this pressure is largely circular. We need the specialist graduates to provide the teachers, and we need the teachers to grow the number of specialist graduates. But if most maths graduates enter teaching, as they do, even discounting those teaching outside the maintained sector or in HE, this considerably weakens the extended argument that we need more maths teachers, because maths is a key school subject and because maths is important for the economy and society in general (see above). Similar arguments can be made about school-level science and almost any curriculum subject.

Perhaps the apparent crisis in teacher supply, starting in the 1990s, was partly the result of continued government policy to reduce class sizes and improve PTRs, which inevitably increased the demand for teachers. Such policies that need advanced planning for increased teacher recruitment cannot be implemented within the lifetime of one administration. Changes in many areas of the educational system or policy can have implications for teacher demand and supply (revised curricula, introduction of new methods of teaching or changes in subject emphasis, for example). The difficulty lies in ensuring that any changes in teacher supply take effect in time to achieve the intended objective. Williams (1979) suggests a timescale of five to six years between changes in recruitment to teacher training courses and the time when the teachers will be needed, but this is generally beyond the life, and therefore the concern, of most political administrations. Education policy-making is rarely, if ever, joined up.

The quality of teachers

The concern is not just for more teachers, but also for more high-quality and motivated applicants. A problem here is that most studies of teaching as a career focus on those already teaching or training to be a teacher. Most of what we know in this field is, therefore, distorted by being based only on the views and qualities of those already involved. Looking at career decisions earlier and beyond teaching, the decision to become a teacher or not is a long-term one for most individuals. Early background characteristics, such as parental occupation and a student's prior qualifications, are able to predict which undergraduates will enter the teaching profession with around 80 per cent accuracy (Gorard et al, 2006). Once these differences are taken into account, the students who decide to become teachers tend to be more motivated by intrinsic factors such as job satisfaction and the opportunity to share their knowledge. Equivalent students who do not want to become teachers are more likely to be motivated in their career choice by extrinsic factors such as salary and job status, or more likely to report having had negative personal experiences of their own schooling. This means that very different policies would be needed to attract the marginal applicants, who nearly become teachers, or those individuals who report being 'uninterested' in or never considered teaching careers. The former may only need more information or adverts, and perhaps a short-term financial incentive. The latter would need more radical change in teaching careers, including perhaps noticeably higher salaries in later careers.

Nevertheless, the situation is not as bad as being portrayed by others. Interest in teacher training in England and Wales is high. The prior qualifications of applicants and trainee teachers are improving over time, and the vast majority of postgraduate trainees from 1999 to 2002 had a first or second-class degree (Smith and Gorard, 2007a). The number of people considering teaching as a career is, therefore, not a major problem for teacher supply. But half of all applications to postgraduate ITT in the UK are rejected, dependent chiefly on the local availability of funded places at individual institutions. One outcome is that some of those applicants rejected by some institutions are much better qualified than those accepted by others. A more centralised national system of allocating training places to applicants, rather than leaving so much of the decision in the hands of institutions, might overcome this variation in quality, and prevent loss of high-quality applicants at this stage.

Most teacher trainees are then successful, in terms of qualifying and obtaining a post, irrespective of their prior qualifications, subject specialism, sex, ethnicity or disability. Few trainees fail, and the majority of those who do not complete the course do not cite financial factors or academic failure as the reason for their non-completion. In one sense, then, the training system is efficient and fair, mostly weeding out those who have unrealistic ideas of the challenge presented by teaching in practice. In another sense, though, the system is inequitable. Students with poor entry qualifications, rated as poor at teaching by external inspections and trained in institutions judged by Ofsted (external inspections) as unable to make fair assessments of student quality have as much chance of a qualification and a teaching post as everyone else (Smith and Gorard, 2007b). If the quality of teachers is to be improved, such inequities need to be addressed first. Otherwise the job market may lead to differences in employment opportunities for differently trained teachers, and so exacerbate the segregation of high-quality teachers in the most desirable schools (see Chapter 4).

Different routes into teaching

Gilroy (1998) argued that the trend away from university-based teacher education towards employment-based routes in schools would be an important cause of the recruitment 'crisis' experienced in subsequent years. In England there is an ongoing change in the balance of routes to becoming a newly qualified teacher (NQT). Given this, and widely reported problems with teacher supply, it is important to consider whether there are discernible differences between the routes in terms of their uptake and outcomes (Gorard, 2017e). The average levels of satisfaction for NQTs are largely un-stratified by sex, disability, age and ethnicity. Within the two main routes of school- and university-led training there is almost as much variability as there is between them. Once other factors are taken into account, the differences in reported satisfaction between routes and providers are small. There is, therefore, no particular reason to promote or support one route at the expense of the other – at least in terms of NQT satisfaction. In both primary and secondary routes, those on school-based initial teacher training (SCITT) are more satisfied with their preparation overall. For secondary routes, NQTs are more satisfied if their route/provider had a higher Ofsted grade, and if previous NQTs had expressed higher satisfaction. Therefore, all other things being equal, successful SCITT courses and the most traditional university routes should be favoured.

Bullock and Scott (1992) reported that the articled and licensed schemes (now the standard approach) that involved experienced secondary school teachers more extensively in the training of new teachers would have implications in terms of demands on teacher time and require a higher overall TPR. This started a chain of events whereby students might apply to courses but were rejected because no schools could be found to place them in for SCITT. The net results are fewer universities running ITT education courses and fewer students that can be accepted on to courses. The withdrawal of a relatively large programme previously run by the Open University may have been an example of this. On the other hand, these are not very plausible explanations for teacher shortages. The expansion of school-based experience for traditional HE courses long pre-dated the purported crisis in supply, and the scale of fully school-based courses has, until now, been insufficient to explain such an apparently major national problem as reported in crisis accounts.

Conclusion

Whereas UK public spending has declined in real terms since the economic downturn of 2008 onwards, one area where policy-makers have claimed that spending has been sustained and even increased is encouraging the supply of new STEM graduates. The UK government proposals to develop the nation's scientific skills base largely lie in increasing the supply of young people into the STEM professions through attracting well-qualified people into teaching, increasing the science content of the National Curriculum in schools and reforming the curriculum to encourage talented young people to remain in the 'science stream' and subsequently study the subject at university. However, it seems that decades of well-funded and well-targeted initiatives have had little (if any) impact, and even requiring that more young people study the sciences up to the age of 16 has had a limited long-term effect on recruitment at the next educational levels. For example, students with the lowest attainment scores at age 16 (or none at all) continue to be less likely to continue with post-16 full-time study – whether of science or not. Changing the nature of opportunities available post-16 will have no impact on these non-participants.

Furthermore, the proportion remaining in education and training continues to be stratified in terms of social class, ethnicity and region. STEM graduates are stratified by social origin and prior attainment, and this sorting takes place during compulsory schooling, in the same way as it does for other high-status subjects. Traditional science, unlike psychology, for example, is not taken as an additional new subject but as one in which the student has not failed before. To some extent this is a matter of choice, but it is also often a criterion imposed by schools and colleges. Either way, it leads to physical sciences being dominated by those with high GCSE-level attainment or equivalent, which is, in turn, linked to high attainment at each previous Key Stage and to social class background. These are patterns that appear impervious to policy interventions, however wide-ranging or well-intentioned.

Students who would be likely to study physics or chemistry, which require relatively high entry grades and a commitment to the subject at age 16, would always have entered HE and would have been largely unaffected by the recent widening participation agenda or other initiatives to increase recruitment. Perhaps what is required is a more objective examination of the demands of the STEM sector for suitably qualified workers along the lines of that advocated by Lowell and Salzman (2007). It would also enable schools to focus on what many argue are the primary goals of science education – 'to educate students both about the major explanations of the material world that science offers and about the way that science works' (Osborne and Dillon, 2008, p 8) – rather than the current emphasis on preparing a minority of students to be the next generation of STEM professionals. It may be that education policy has been as much a creator of the science 'problem' as its solution.

Similarly, a whole range of policy initiatives have been proposed and tried to increase the supply of teachers in the UK. These include Teach First and similar schemes (where graduates move directly to school posts without teacher training), converting workers from other areas with a surplus such as the armed forces, allowing non-graduate teachers, training teaching assistants to be teachers, taking the cap off admissions to ITT in universities, offering flexible working hours, and the usual array of financial inducements for some. As with STEM supply, these ideas have not been properly evaluated for either direct impact or unintended consequences. It is not clear that they will work or that supply is really the problem. Even when 'hard-to-fill' teacher vacancies are considered, any problems tend to reflect the regional and subject dispersion of teaching staff rather than any national shortages. There are many unemployed qualified teachers in the UK and many more working outside of the education sector, or in education otherwise, who would rather be teaching in schools.

According to pupils, there is clearly huge variation in the quality of their teachers (see Chapter 8). How could this arise? One possibility is that some of the better candidates for teacher training in England are being turned away while some others are accepted, because of the institutional nature of the application process. Another, related, possibility is that teacher trainees are being passed in some institutions who would fail in others. This is because a quota of places was awarded to each teacher training institution, and they have the responsibility for accepting trainees. More trainees apply every year than are accepted, but most of those rejected by some high-prestige institutions are actually better qualified than the best-qualified trainees accepted at some lower-prestige institutions. Only a more coordinated national system of application and selection could prevent this. The problem of such variability in teacher quality may also arise because each training institution is permitted to decide on trainee outcomes. There is no relationship at all between the intake qualifications of trainees and their outcomes. Ofsted inspections suggest that several of these institutions just do not have the capacity to judge teacher quality for themselves, even though they are responsible for qualifying teachers.

While research conducted with teachers suggests that intrinsic motivation of the kind appealed to by TV teaching adverts in the UK is important for them, my work (with colleagues) suggests that those who reject teaching as an option have more prosaic concerns, about money, career prospects and pupil discipline. These could all be addressed by evidence-informed policy. There are more applicants for teacher training than places available, and no evidence that those turned away by some institutions are inferior in potential to those accepted by others. If funded places were increased, more students would be available for training, whenever needed. Additionally, there are teachers fully capable of teaching in shortage subjects for compulsory age groups, but who have a degree whose title (such as economics or engineering) does not match the title used in the National Curriculum (such as maths). Much of employed teachers' time is used in bureaucratic and managerial tasks, and there are some indications that teachers in shortage subjects are more likely to be promoted 'out' of the classroom to undertake more management. Areas with high PTRs still manage to generate the smallest average class sizes, and keeping the number and type of schools to a minimum, in urban areas, would lead to a more efficient use of teachers. At each stage, from career choice to the deployment of teachers in classrooms, there is considerable slack in the system. The key issue in teacher supply involves running this system as efficiently as possible. There is no great crisis, either passing or looming, and so no need for further minor but headline-grabbing policy initiatives at a national level. As with STEM supply, shortages of high-quality teachers may be created by the very education policies intended to solve them.

TWELVE

Widening participation to other opportunities

A major strand of my work over 20 years so far has been the investigation of lifelong trajectories of education and employment past initial schooling. This has involved changes due to IT, and the ways in which this has or has not made learning, especially informal learning, more accessible (Gorard and Selwyn, 1999, 2005a,b; Gorard et al, 2000, 2003b; Selwyn and Gorard, 2002, 2003). While there is insufficient space here to cover this aspect in any detail, a rough summary of the results over 20 years would be that the online learning world is roughly the same as the offline world in terms of who has access to the latest technology. The stratification of learning is not, apparently, open to a technical fix.

This chapter brings place and time more strongly to the fore in explanatory models of learning, added to the more usual mix of sex, ethnicity and so on, and distinguishes between biographical and historical changes (Gorard and Rees, 2002; Selwyn et al, 2003). I have been doing this work since long before intersectionality theory became fashionable among those who had previously focused on only one stratifying variable at a time. I also try to distinguish between the determinants of, and barriers to, participation. Chapter 3 showed the patterns of educational outcomes lifelong. In a sense, this final empirical chapter pulls it all together.

Trajectories and determinants

The idea of typical learning 'trajectories' that encapsulate individual education and training biographies was introduced in Chapter 3. Some people leave formal education at the earliest opportunity. Some of these leavers return to formal learning at some time as adults, but a high proportion do not. Other people continue into extended initial education, but never return to formal learning once this is over. Others remain in contact with formal learning for a large proportion of their lives. Which of these patterns, from lifelong non-participation to lifelong learning, an individual follows can be accurately predicted on the basis of characteristics that are known by the time an individual reaches school-leaving age. This does not imply that people do not have choices, or do not face barriers, but rather, that these choices occur within a framework of opportunities and expectations determined by the resources that people derive from their background and upbringing.

Logistic regression analysis is used to identify those characteristics of respondents that enable good predictions of which 'trajectory' they follow. I have conducted the same analyses with several different datasets totalling 10,000 adults across the UK, and each shows the same determinants of post-compulsory participation (Gorard, 2003b).

Whether any individual reported extended initial education or training can be predicted with at least 84 per cent accuracy (that is, the prediction would place the individual on the correct trajectory 84 per cent of the time). Predictions of their later episodes of participation have overall accuracy of 77 per cent (see Table 12.1). In both cases, therefore, the accuracy of predictions improves by around 50 per cent compared to the baseline. The explanatory variables are entered in batches representing periods in the individual's life, from birth to the present. In this way, each batch of variables can only improve the prediction based on the previous batch(es). This provides a clue as to which variables are the determinants of learning episodes and which, like qualifications, are largely proxy summaries of others. The vast majority of variation in patterns of participation that can be explained is explained by variables that could have been known when each person was born. Other than that, a key issue in explaining continuous post-compulsory learning is the experience of initial schooling, whereas a key issue in explaining later life learning is early experience of work and family life as an adult.

Even when the interaction with other variables is accounted for, younger respondents are more likely to have continued with initial education and training of some sort, as are those from a minority ethnic background (see Table 12.2). Those aged 21-60 are nearly three times as likely to have taken part in later education or training as those aged 61 or over, and so on.

Table 12.1: Predictability of learning trajectories at each life stage

	Baseline	Birth	Schooling	Adult	IT access
Continuous	62	79	84	84	84
Later life	54	71	71	77	77

Table 12.2: Personal characteristics as determinants of trajectory

	Continuous	Later life
Year born	*1.03*	
Ethnic group		
White British	0.57	2.24
White other	1.24	0.82
Male/born in ward	0.56	
Male/born in site	0.62	
Male/born in area	0.81	
Male/born in UK	1.66	
Male		1.95
Age 21-40		2.90
Age 41-60		2.81
Nationality		
Welsh		0.21
English		0.23
Scottish		0.20
Irish		0.20
British		0.51
Male age 21-40		0.45
Male age 41-60		0.49

Note: For clarity, real-number variables have been written in italics, meaning that the reported coefficients are multipliers for that variable. For example, someone born in 1975 is 1.03 times as likely continue in education or training after school as someone born in 1974. All other coefficients are for categorical variables, and represent a change in odds compared to a base category. For example, a male is 1.95 times as likely as a woman to undertake an episode of education or training as an adult in later life.

The influence of parental background and age of parents finishing initial education is strongly linked to trajectory (see Table 12.3). A respondent from a family with a service class father is nearly four times as likely to continue with education, and nearly three times as likely to undertake formal learning in later life, as one from a family with a non-working father. The picture for mothers is very different. Once other factors are taken into account, the occupation of mothers is unrelated to continuous learning. But a respondent with a non-working mother is nearly seven times as likely to report later life learning as one with a mother from a skilled manual occupation. This represents the historical and class patterns of employment by sex. All of these patterns decline somewhat over time (as represented by the age of the respondents).

Table 12.4 shows the model coefficients for variables relating to schooling, and then the initial occupational class of the learners

Table 12.3: Parental characteristics as determinants of trajectory

	Continuous	Later life
Age father left education	*1.14*	
Age mother left education	*1.28*	
Father service class	3.82	2.87
Father non-manual	3.06	3.40
Father skilled manual	2.01	3.22
Father part-skilled	1.18	2.12
Mother service class		0.82
Mother non-manual		1.51
Mother skilled manual		0.14
Mother part-skilled		1.21
Father lives in ward		0.62
Father lives in site		1.07
Father lives in area		2.06
Father lives in UK		1.43
Mother born in ward	0.50	
Mother born in site	0.52	
Mother born in area	1.61	
Mother born in UK	1.25	

Table 12.4: End of compulsory schooling as determinants of trajectory

	Continuous	Later life
Regular school attender	4.03	1.79
School attended at 16		
Comprehensive	4.71	
Grammar	11.94	
Secondary modern	2.99	
Private school	27.45	
First occupation		
Service class	13.00	1.89
Non-manual	2.65	3.37
Skilled	1.03	2.14
Part-skilled	0.80	1.47

themselves. Those respondents who did not attend school regularly were only one-quarter as likely to continue to education or training at school-leaving age as the others. Those attending private or grammar schools were considerably more likely to continue learning at school-leaving age than those attending elementary, and other, schools. While occupational class is strongly linked to both continuous and later learning, the patterns are different. Whereas service class respondents are more likely to continue with full-time education, later learning is even more common for the non-manual and skilled manual occupational groups (in comparison to those without paid employment).

The model coefficients representing the later adult and work-life of learners do not improve the quality of prediction of participation (see above). Those with children are less likely to report continuous learning, and those reporting later learning tend to have had any children while younger (aged 21–40). In these models I also added a final batch of variables relating to access to and use of computers and the internet. As was apparent in Table 12.1, these also make *no* difference to the accuracy of predictions. Once all of the preceding variables are taken into account, the model explains both continuous and later learning as accurately as possible. The use of IT, therefore, cannot be said to widen participation in learning, and is patterned in just the same way.

In summary the key determinants of extended initial education are age, sex, place of birth, parental occupation and education and school attended. The key determinants of later formal participation are, in addition, ethnicity/nationality, area of residence, occupation and age of having children. The full model includes key variables that explain patterns of adult participation that can be grouped into five main themes – time, place, sex, family and school. It is important to note that all of these factors reflect characteristics of respondents that are determined relatively early during the life course.

Time

The first theme is the historical time period. When respondents were born determines their relationship to changing opportunities for learning and social expectations, so that respondents with similar social backgrounds from different birth cohorts exhibit different tendencies to participate in education and training (Rees et al, 1997). There is considerable evidence that the pattern of typical 'trajectories' has changed substantially over time. The archival research, for example, shows that, during the early decades of the 20th century in South Wales, the dominant forms of post-school learning were employment-based and largely restricted to men. Within coalmining, the pervasive method of acquiring knowledge and skills was working under the tutelage of an experienced worker, usually an older family member. This came to be supplemented by organised evening classes, which enabled individuals to acquire the technical qualifications that became necessary for career advancement in the industry. However, with the intensification of conflict between miners and owners during the inter-war years and later, the nature of participation was also transformed through the rise of 'workers' education', aimed at raising political awareness and feeding the labour movement with activists.

Since then, there has been a clear trend away from non-participation over the period since the oldest respondents left school. The training and socialisation available in the three local nationalised industries – coal, steel and rail – disappeared along with local job opportunities for many. The age of respondents, and therefore the periods at which they left school or moved jobs, is a major determinant of participation. Generally, the frequency of participation in formal education or training increased over the 50-year period of the study. More respondents in each generation report staying on in school or college after school-leaving age (partly because this legal age has also increased twice during the same period). More respondents in each generation also report brief work-based training.

The proportion of each cohort reporting no formal learning has decreased. However, this is due to increases in extended initial education and transitional learning, and has not proportionately increased later or lifelong learning. These patterns of change suggest the possibility that some elements of past practice in education and training were superior to the present, especially for men who left school during the 1950s and 1960s.

Place

The second main theme is to do with place. Where respondents are born and brought up shapes their expectations and access to specifically local opportunities to participate. In the same way that it does not make sense to consider why someone did not take an option that was non-existent at the time, it makes little sense to ask about opportunities that were non-existent in the place that someone lived or was able to travel to. Those who have lived in the most economically disadvantaged areas are least likely to participate in lifelong learning. However, those who have moved between regions are even more likely to participate than those living in the more advantaged localities. Partly this is a function of occupational class and educational attainment for those in national labour markets, or who had been to university elsewhere. However, since most respondents had not left their area of birth, the biggest influence of place was a direct one based on the availability of local opportunities for education and job-related training. One man in his 40s and unemployed after temporary work in a factory, left school at 15:

> 'I went into the coalmines [like all my school friends], but that was closed then in 1969. I had an accident just before it shut ... and it was while I was out that Llanhilleth shut, and everybody was transferred to other pits.'

He was clear that most of the jobs he was likely to encounter required no special skills or training, and equally clear that there was little point in learning except for a job. To some extent, such local views of the value of training are clarified by a training-for-work manager in one of the research sites:

> 'People can't move out of the area, to Newport, for example, because of the house prices, and there is no public transport at night or early morning for shift workers, so unless they have a good car people can't commute.... XXXX are always advertising for jobs, as their workers leave through boredom with the conveyor belt production. But they go on to another similar job hoping it will be less boring, or to benefit, and not to training.'

Table 12.5 contains one of a number of indicators that show how participation is strongly related to geographic mobility. In general, participation increases with the distance between current area of residence and area of birth. The most mobile individuals are the least likely to be non-participants.

Table 12.5: Area of birth, by trajectory

Trajectory	Neighbourhood	District	Area	UK	Abroad
Non-participant	50	47	24	24	14
Transitional learner	17	12	19	21	24
Delayed learner	23	29	30	20	24
Lifelong learner	10	13	26	35	38

Sex

A third factor is the sex of the individual. For men, the big increase in post-school participation took place chiefly for those completing initial education during the 1950s and 1960s, while for women, it occurred for those finishing school during the 1970s and 1980s. Men consistently reported more formal learning than women, and although the situation is changing rapidly, these changes are different for each sex. Women are less likely to report participation in lifelong learning, but are increasingly likely to be 'transitional learners', and this may be partly due to remaining differences in the nature and structure of work, with women more likely to work part time. It is also, presumably, linked to the higher attainment of girls at school (see Chapter 5). Sex is one of the strongest predictors of participation in lifelong learning, and it could be influential in several ways, perhaps in terms of opportunities or barriers, but a regular story that most dramatically displays the difference between men and women is a kind of enforced altruism:

> 'The thing was my husband was in the Air Force you see, so as soon as we got married we went to live in Germany and were just travelling around.... [I had no further jobs while married because] well, we had the children, you see, and in those days people didn't. It was almost a, in some spheres, a slight on the husband implying that ... he couldn't support you.'

This woman in her 60s has separated from her husband, taken a new career as a teacher with regular training, become an inspector of schools, and since retirement, has taken classes in Welsh, Spanish, antiques appreciation and contract bridge. She is therefore an 'ideal-type' lifelong learner, thwarted earlier in her trajectory by custom. As evidence that this altruistic phenomenon remains prevalent (although perhaps less widespread), a similar story was told by a woman in her 20s, who obtained a diploma in Business Studies (the first formal qualification in her family):

> 'Well, I found work then. We moved away to Birmingham ... [as a management trainee], but Steve [my partner] didn't like it up there. And he was promised a job back here, so we came back but it fell through and then the kids came along.'

This couple are now living in a depressed mining valley, and her husband is still unemployed. The respondent works part time as a packer in a local factory, and helps voluntarily with a local playgroup where she is learning Welsh, and taking qualifications in childcare.

Family

The fourth element is family background. Parents' social class and own educational experiences are perhaps the most important determinants of participation in lifelong learning (Gorard et al, 1999a). Family background can be about income and the material advantage this brings, but is it also about what are considered to be the 'natural' forms of participation. In some eras and regions it may be the characteristics of the father that are dominant, and in others, those of the mother (Bynner and Parsons, 1997). In this study, the father's occupation, and the mother's education and place of birth, seem to be key. Parents can be a big influence on their children's approach to education. Parents in the 1940s and 1950s were reported to have been concerned more with the outward appearance of school, to want their children to be as neat and tidy as possible, and to try and avoid 'the Board Man' coming to see them (about school truancy). Schooling itself and learning were not seen as important, and one reason may have been the ease with which jobs were available locally. One man left school at 14 with no qualifications, went over to the local tin works, asked for a job and started the next Monday:

> 'I don't think they [parents] cared one way or the other. They used to encourage you in as much as they would buy you ... the best clothes they could afford ... but once you left the house ... they wasn't worried until you came home then whether you'd been to school or not.... Myself, I couldn't have cared either way at that time whether I was learning or not.'

School

The fifth element is therefore initial schooling. As the book has demonstrated so far, experience of initial schooling can be crucial in shaping long-term orientations towards learning, and providing the kinds of qualifications deemed necessary to access many forms of further and higher education, as well as continuing education and training later in life. A sense of failure at school has been found to reduce the chance of FE (Gambetta, 1987).

The type of school attended (or not attended), the initial trajectory towards taking qualifications or getting a job and any particularly good or bad experiences of school are also associated with later attitudes to learning. For example, this man is now in his 50s, still living in the coalfield valleys, never been away and is now unemployed, having not been allowed to take the 11+ (see Chapter 6):

> 'When it came to my 11+ I was in a family that had nothing kind of thing, you know. I was in a very poor family. My father and mother was afraid in their hearts that I would pass for county school because it meant then that they would have to get me a uniform. Where I could go with the holes in the back of my trousers to an ordinary school. But then you had to have your books and your satchels and you know, so they kept me back from my 11+. I didn't go to school that day.'

Those who reported not attending school regularly were less likely to report adult participation in learning of any sort (see Table 12.6). Indeed, 60 per cent of them reported no adult education or training at all. It is notable that 22 per cent did report a return to some formal learning at a later date, and it is important therefore that this 'delayed' route back into learning remains feasible in future funding and qualification regimes.

Table 12.6: Attendance at school by trajectory

Trajectory	Regular school attender	Not regular attender
Non-participant	35	60
Transitional learner	18	10
Delayed learner	25	22
Lifelong learner	22	8

Possible solutions

The analyses in this book and others like them suggest that the idea of a trajectory is a useful one when analysing participation in lifelong learning and trying to model events in biographical order. To a great extent, the trajectories and their determinants summarise the patterns and problem for equity and effectiveness appearing in the previous chapters. Many of the possible policy solutions, assuming that the situation is agreed to be unfair, have been presaged in those chapters – including creating more mixed SES intakes to schools, reducing the importance of prior qualifications in educational decisions and giving more respect to non-taught learning. These and other themes are picked up again in the final chapter. Hereon the focus is more on attempted policy solutions specific to adult learning. There include overcoming barriers to adult participation, setting national targets for qualification and the use of anytime, anyhow access to opportunities via computers.

Barriers to participation

To the extent that participation in learning opportunities depends on the actions of individuals, people are deemed, by the economists so loved by policy-makers, to participate according to their calculation of the net economic benefits to be derived from education and training. Therefore, in order to attain fair access to learning opportunities for all, government policy focuses on the removal of the impediments or 'barriers' that prevent those people from participating in education who would benefit from doing so (Dearing, 1997; NAO, 2002). The barriers that are suggested to be holding people back from wider post-compulsory participation are largely those of the patterns of adult learning – such as buildings unsuitable to handle disability and lack of transport for learners in rural areas (Hudson, 2005). Transport is a barrier that might apply to all forms of participation (Hramiak, 2001). Proximity to home and convenience for travel were strong factors apparently influencing adult learners using learndirect centres (Dhillon, 2004).

The costs of formal, full-time study may disproportionately affect potential students from low-income families and non-traditional students in general (Metcalf, 2005). There may be more debt aversion for families with low incomes, lone parents and some minority ethnic groups (Callender, 2003). The cost of continuing in education can be indirect, such as expenditure on transport and childcare, or foregone income (Hand et al, 1994). Benefit entitlement in the UK has been generally incompatible with formal learning episodes, even when all of the costs of training are met by the individual. Many people have reportedly left learning episodes before completion because of uneven interpretation of the rules by benefits offices. Payment of fees to institutions by instalments is not generally allowable, or increases the overall cost, and many new learners are surprised by the level of other expenses, such as examination fees. For some full-time students, part-time work is considered essential to enable them to complete and finance their course. So the pressure of having to work could also lead to individuals missing sessions, which may then play a role in some of them subsequently deciding to leave their learning episode.

If anything, the situation is even worse for many part-time students with full-time jobs, and who may also have childcare responsibilities.

During the last two decades the costs of adult, further and higher education in England have gradually been shifting from the general taxpayer to the students and their families. Restrictions on access to unemployment and housing benefits were later accompanied by reduction of grants for HE, the introduction of means-tested contributions towards fees and upfront tuition fees that are now generally over £9,000 per annum. The increase in students continuing to HE has been accompanied by an increase in the number reported to be in debt. This debt situation is often worse for mature students (Gorard and Taylor, 2001b). As it is observed that potential students from lower-income families have lower rates of participation, it can be hypothesised that cost is a barrier, and removal of cost a solution to widening participation. This is the logic underlying policies such as the Education Maintenance Allowance (EMA), grants, fees remission and means-tested bursaries.

Not having enough time is another potential barrier to participation. Taking a course often involves an adjustment in lifestyle that may be more of a problem for those with dependants or in long-term relationships. Partners as well as children can reduce the time available for learning, in women's lives more than for men, perhaps (Abroms and Goldscheider, 2002).

However plausible these ideas about barriers sound, it is important to recall that the research evidence is almost entirely based on the reports of existing participants in education. Whatever those participating say about finance (and it obviously has not totally prevented them from accessing education), non-participants usually cite other reasons for not continuing with formal education. Importantly, the case presented here for barriers does not provide evidence that overcoming barriers makes much difference in practical terms. In fact, much of the available evidence points the other way. The widespread provision of free tuition for adults without Level 2 qualifications did not increase numbers. Rather, it changed who did what where (Lee, 2006). This attraction or re-direction of the 'usual suspects' is common. In the UK, the school-leaving age was raised in 1972 from 15 to 16, producing an inevitable but not total increase in staying on in education past the age of 15. A similar growth in post-16 participation took place in the 1990s, despite the lack of further legal compulsion. The Youth Cohort Study shows a steep growth in full-time education post-16 after 1989 (Payne, 1998). However, this is largely a question of robbing Peter to pay Paul, because government-funded training showed an almost equivalent drop over the same period. Other commentators have observed the same, and increases in staying-on rates in FE often replace work-based training, full-time participation replaces part-time participation and so on (Denholm and Macleod, 2003).

Finance is unlikely to be an important factor in generating stratified access to HE (Dearden et al, 2005; and see also Chapter 10). Financial incentives and income-contingent charging systems seem to increase the overall participation rate but leave the proportion of students from poor backgrounds largely unchanged (Chapman and Ryan, 2002). The introduction of tuition fees and the replacement of grants with loans did not significantly affect entrant behaviour. The proportion of students leaving their course who reported finance as the problem was very low – around 1 per cent (Gorard and Taylor, 2001b). Furthermore, when HE was free to students and living costs were more fully covered by a grant, participation in HE by social class was not more proportional, nor more equitable, than it is now. One explanation is that so many of the potential students qualified for entry to HE are relatively advantaged (Forsyth and Furlong, 2003; Taylor and Gorard, 2005). Similar doubts can be cast on the purported barriers of time, travel and institutional behaviour (Gorard et al, 2007a).

Targets

The setting of targets for attainment and participation from school to retirement age was a policy initiative in the UK in the 1990s onward. Targets generally took the form of specifying a group of the population and stating a level of qualification that a certain percentage should attain by a certain date. For example, a national target might be that 80 per cent of the working-age population should be qualified at Level 2 (KS4 equivalent) by 2005 (or whatever). Such targets for school leavers and for adults were intended to be both aspirational and a way of measuring the uptake of qualifications.

However, the actual impact of targets on the growth of related indicators appears to have been minimal (Gann, 1999). The first National Targets in Wales were set in 1991. If the policy of setting targets had been a useful one, this would have been reflected in improved progress in terms of levels of qualifications since they were introduced. For example, NACETT (1994) claimed that 'We have made real progress since the National Targets were launched in 1991', but without making clear against what criterion this progress was measured. NACETT were formed in 1993, and it was only then that targets began to become known to employers and educators, and policy changes are anyway generally slow to register any impact and are incremental in effect. In this context it may be noteworthy that the lowest annual growth in the indicator for the original Lifelong Target 3 was in 1996 (actually negative), and the growth in 1998 was otherwise the lowest since 1991. The average growth since 1992 has been 7.5 per cent per year, and the average growth until 1992 was 8.7 per cent. Overall, then, it is likely that not much has improved as a result of target-setting.

Although the National Targets for Education and Training in England and Wales included indicators for lifelong learning, and progress towards the targets set for these indicators was lauded by politicians and other observers, much of this apparent progress was actually accounted for by changes in these same indicators at foundation (school) level. Changes in the qualification indicators for schools will, in time, produce changes in the equivalent qualification indicators for the adult population. Once this 'conveyor belt effect', of passing increasingly qualified 16- to 18-year-olds into the working-age population instead of less qualified 60- and 65-year-olds (retirement ages at the time) is taken into account, progress in qualifying those of working age is much less (Gorard et al, 2002a). In Wales, for example, the number of working-age adults without Level 2 qualifications drops by about 0.5 per cent every year simply because older people with fewer qualifications retire. In fact, there is limited evidence that lifelong learning targets have had any impact at all. Certainly work-based training has not increased, and may even have declined over the last decade, while some socio-economic inequalities in adult participation in education and training have worsened (Gorard et al, 2002b).

Information technology

Through initiatives such as the Digital College, learndirect and UK Online, UK governments have suggested that IT can help establish an inclusive learning society. Each generation believes that it has cracked the solution to anytime, anywhere, anyhow learning – via microcomputers, dial-up modems, broadband, smartphones and tablets, to name a few. Access to IT is growing both at work and in homes. However, there is no evidence of IT having a widespread and sustained effect in terms of widening participation in adult education. Access to IT or to the latest IT of value for learning remains stratified by the same variables as more traditional participation, and often costs a lot more. At best, IT is increasing levels of participation within the social groups that were learning anyway (the 'usual suspects'), and this is true in the UK and elsewhere as well (Selwyn et al, 2001).

Learner identities

An overarching tentative explanation for the failure of these policies and others like them lies in the idea of a learner identity. Naturally, when interviewees describe their own patterns of learning (or not), they tend to emphasise not the patterns seen at large scale, but specific incidents and influences. However, many of the latter can still be summarised as family and local labour market circumstances that constrained or assisted them. For example, some older women describe the ways in which the learning opportunities available to them were limited by local employment, social expectations as to what was appropriate or by a 'forced altruism' with respect to family commitments (see above). Many people who had stayed on in some form of education after school saw this as a product of what was normal within their family or even their local community rather than a clear choice made by them. For example, they had discussed with their peers what to study at university but not whether to go at all. Others assumed that they needed to leave education in order to earn a wage. In order to make sense of each trajectory it is important to view the situation not just in terms of the objective opportunities available in that era and place, but also in relation to the subjective opportunity structure as seen by each individual in their own context.

Each interviewee had developed a kind of learner identity, shaped, perhaps, by the trajectory determinants mentioned so far, and others that filtered out some choices for them and enhanced the allure of others. For example, those who said they had 'failed' at school often saw any further episodes of post-formal learning as irrelevant – and this included work-based learning as well as further and continuing education.

The relevance of this idea is that it means, as with the supply of teachers (see Chapter 11), policies to improve participation need to take learner identities into account. Simply providing more opportunities will lead to them being taken up by those already likely to be involved in learning. Changing a negative learner identity, if that is what is intended, would require more.

Conclusion

Trying to decide between an explanation based on choice and one based on structural and other determinants may be something of a red herring. Either explanation, or both, is possible. People's patterns of participation may be determined by prior (and future) events in their lives, or these events may create a personal culture that colours the objective opportunity structure in such a way that people's choices are frequently predictable. In fact, rather than seeing these two mechanisms of agency as alternatives, they could be different descriptions of the same events, with both contributing to our understanding. The first appears more naturally when analysing in-depth data as narratives, while the second appears more naturally when the same data is used to create predictive models. To characterise patterns in the data covering many individuals does not negate the varied experiences of the individuals involved, and describing individual stories and key events still allows these to be patterned in a wider perspective. Philosophically the two accounts, although different in surface appearance, may be regarded as eliminatively identical. This, perhaps most obviously of the all of the points in this book, is why I say in Chapter 2 that it is absurd to try and do research that uses only one approach or method for collecting data. It leads to impoverished understanding and so harms the evidence that policy needs, or should need.

For example, the predictability of trajectories and the relative permanence of learner identities mean that qualifications and everything that follows from them make much less difference than is commonly supposed. When modelled in biographical order, qualifications such as at KS4 and beyond make very little difference to subsequent educational participation and outcomes. Often a 'learner identity' has already been formed, with a subjective opportunity structure that either includes or excludes a particular form of participation in learning. Family poverty, lack of role models and a sense of 'not for us', coupled with poor experiences of initial schooling, can conspire to create a negative lifelong attitude to learning. This would make the obvious barriers such as cost, time and travel largely irrelevant, and the same is true for any solutions to those barriers such as the internet. In the same way that most of the population is not deterred from HE by lack of finance (largely because most young people with the requisite entry qualifications already attend HE), so most non-participants in adult learning are not put off by 'barriers' but by their lack of interest in something that seems alien and imposed by others. How policy-makers could address this is picked up in the final chapter.

Part 3:
Conclusion

THIRTEEN

Where now for equity and effectiveness policy?

Examples of specific policy proposals

It is clear from this book, and long before, that educational participation and outcomes are strongly linked to era, place, social class, sex and family background. It is important to recall that these same inequalities appear just as strongly in other areas of public policy like housing, health and crime. In the same way, most of the datasets used in this book portray long-term, sometimes erratic, improvements in equity over time. Such historical improvements are common to the UK and other developed countries. They are more likely to result from long-term social and economic changes in the population than from improvements brought about by education policy itself. There are, generally, no abrupt changes in the data trends following policy implementation of the kind we would expect if investment, legislative changes, new curricula and so on actually made much of a difference. Education mostly appears to reflect society, which suggests that the root cause of inequality is at least partly not educational. Education policy cannot be expected to solve issues such as child poverty alone, in the short term, or even at all. This means that education policy has to be humbler, but it still has important roles to play – in ensuring that inequalities are not worsened by the education system, and by promoting structures and interventions that can 'compensate for society', to some extent (Pring, 2009; Gorard, 2010f). Pushing for quality and equality are in union here, and it is much more efficient to invest in disadvantaged rather than already advantaged learners (Chiu and Khoo, 2005).

There are several more specific recommendations that emerge when viewing, and re-reading, the whole body of lifelong evidence in this book. Each of the preceding chapters leads naturally to several specific recommendations for policy changes, only some of which are repeated here. For example, the proportion of time spent in education while living below the poverty threshold (years FSM% in England) would be a better indicator for allocating the pupil premium or contextualising results than whether a student is currently or has ever been FSM-eligible. This would be fairer, and would help address the poverty gradient between schools, types of schools and regions. All attainment should be age-standardised even for entry to HE. Young children in multi-form entry schools can be taught in age-adjusted classes, as is current practice in some early years settings, to minimise the summer-born problem. And the labelling of SEN needs re-visiting in relation to age-in-year. Where young people have serious and chronic SEN, it needs to be realised more clearly that whatever support is being provided is currently not sufficient to reduce the attainment gap with their mainstream peers.

The school mix effect on attainment and participation outcomes may be small (of the magnitude of 5% improvement in results). But it is clear that schools and other education institutions could easily become more mixed over time via direct policy interventions, and that they could gain that 5 per cent bonus for overall outcomes both cheaply and easily. There is a role for schools in reducing or at least not enlarging the poverty gradient (Crawford et al, 2017). There is also a school mix 'effect' on wider outcomes such as enjoyment, aspirations and role models and sense of justice, and this would be an added bonus from enhancing the social and academic mix of school intakes. Finally, there would be lifelong advantages in terms of appropriate trust as adults, citizenship and civic participation, and perhaps even learner identities (see Chapter 12). There is no benefit from clustering students in different schools and colleges in any way, whether by ability, faith or social class. There are only disadvantages for the system as a whole. This does not mean that bespoke activities cannot be used or created for sub-groups of students in schools, as happens with SEN students in mainstream settings at present. But the practice of every new Education Secretary trying to create a new type of school to cater for only some of the national population should cease. Then we can truly say that it does not matter where people live or which school any child goes to.

The procedures and structures of schooling are as important in shaping an individual's future as the pedagogy. For example, we cannot as easily teach civic responsibility using harsh discipline, healthy eating if the canteen serves junk, religious tolerance in a rigid sectarian system or respect for others if no respect is shown to students. In one sense, this whole book is about learner identities, and how these are shaped by families, schools, school peers, success and relative failure, treatment by adults, expectations of what is appropriate for 'people like us', and even how self-regulated learners are increasingly ignored by a system that ought to laud them. Education research and policy need to value learning a bit more and emphasise teachers a bit less.

In a welfare state such as the UK, benefits payments are at a universal level, and healthcare is provided nationally and is not intended to be better in some areas or for some people than others. Perhaps what is needed in education is more of an emphasis on a minimum entitlement for all. There will always be variation in outcomes, and presumably in learners' talent, motivations and effort as well, but everyone should be entitled to educational outcomes up to a certain level of education. This kind of equal outcomes policy is not the same as simply offering the same to all within a mixed mainstream school system. The state must be prepared to spend much more on those for whom the minimum level will be the most difficult (as happens with pupil premium funding, one of the most well thought-out of recent policy innovations). For example, the current minimum could be that everyone is entitled to a level of educational outcome equivalent to the expected levels at KS2, even where this is not achieved for some until long after primary school. Once this target is reached nationally, the minimum could be raised for all, meaning that what we understand by fairness in education would evolve and improve over time.

I feel that too much policy attention is devoted to HE, which is only ever intended to be appropriate for a minority of the population and attracts the most advantaged, most successful and most highly qualified students. The overwhelming majority of KS5 students obtain at least minimal qualifications for entry to HE, and then do indeed enter HE. The selection problem in HE is largely about which specific HEI accepts each of these KS5 students, but as with the health service (see above) and the school system, this is absurd. CA are not really needed for entry to HE, and probably would not work for selection to specific HEIs. We should not create or defend a national system of universities where the experience of going to one is deliberately made to be better or worse than any other. This idea, that a higher grade is needed to study English Law at Bristol than Sunderland University, for example, just needs to stop. The key problem for continuation to FE and HE lies at the KS5 gap, and the UK government has already taken one step to address this in England by raising the education and training leaving age to 18. Perhaps Wales, Scotland and Northern Ireland should follow suit.

However, viewed in biographical order it is not clear that school and later qualifications themselves are determining agents – except to the extent that we make them so by artificially insisting on them at every juncture. Some of the most impressive learners encountered in the research in this book had no qualifications at all, and, of course, some with qualifications had little or no real education. Qualifications are used as a substitute variable summing up the prior individual, social and economic determinants of 'success' at school and beyond. Educators do not select their potential students, or employers their employees, on the basis of their SES, ethnicity or age, as this is both unfair and illegal. However, they do select them on the basis of a substitute variable – prior education – that sums up and, as this book shows, is very heavily correlated with, such background factors. The international education Olympics are alluring, but policy-makers need to steel themselves against being seduced into the idea that qualification and education are the same thing. Education is much more, while the use of qualifications to select people may be increasingly seen as unethical and eventually illegal.

The build-up of a learner identity may help explain why policies like school improvement via the engagement of parents, widening participation through incentives or removing barriers do not work.

When policy-makers get it wrong

In summary, education policy is often the problem for equity and effectiveness rather than the provider of solutions. How can this be prevented? I once wrote a paper called 'Does policy matter in education?' (Gorard, 2006e). It looked at a range of education policies lifelong and worldwide where, like the target setting in Chapter 12, there was no difference in the long-term historical trend for the outcome that each policy was supposed to improve. These included the National Literacy Strategy used by the National Audit Office as an example of an effective policy lever, but which did not alter longer-term levels of literacy (Tymms et al, 2005). Early interventions such as Head Start and Sure Start have not really cut the link between the family background of a young child and their subsequent attainment (Merrell and Tymms, 2005). In 1993, the post-16 staying rate in England was 73 per cent. By 2000, after changes in policy encouraging extended education, labour market pressure, improvements in the nature and structure of provision and a steady rise in 16+ qualifications, the staying-on rate was 72 per cent. The strongest trend towards widened participation in HE came before the most prominent and vocal policies for widening participation (Gorard et al, 2007a). The provision of school choice within the Education Reform Act 1988 may have recognised an element of the local allocation of school places that already existed rather than introduced a new one (Gorard et al,

2003a). There are many more examples like these where nothing improves in terms of the stated outcomes. Policy is, at least sometimes, merely an epiphenomenon providing a legislated basis for what already increasingly exists.

It was explained in Chapter 6 that when the academy schools were created in 2002, their KS4 results were seized on by the then Labour Schools Minister as evidence of their clear superiority over the prior results of the schools that the academies replaced. In 2004, the BBC reported that, 'The government has released GCSE figures from three of its new flagship Academies in England. All the schools, which were set up in deprived areas, showed remarkable improvements in results'. At this stage there were only three academies with before-and-after results, one of which was Bexley Business Academy. The Prime Minister at the time stated that he had 'seen the future of education'. 'In its first year, the Business Academy, Bexley achieved an increase in pupils attaining 5 or more A*-C grades at GCSE from 7% in 2002 to 21% in 2003' (DfES, 2004). Similar claims to success were made by the academies themselves and their sponsors (Gorard, 2009b). As illustrated in Chapter 6, Bexley Business Academy's predecessor school had KS4 results of 24 per cent at Level 2 (five or more GCSEs grade A–C or equivalent) in 1998, and 21 per cent in 2003 after the intervention. This is despite the national rise in KS4 results over those five years, and the fact that the school intake had gone from 53 per cent FSM-eligible to 42 per cent. Faced with this evidence, the same policy commentators who had lauded the rise began to say that the signs were promising but that it was too early to tell!

The Conservative manifesto for the 2017 UK General Election tried to argue that increasing the number of grammar schools and selective places would increase the number of 'good schools for everyone' (an inherent contradiction). This was justified by saying:

> Contrary to what some people allege, official research shows that slightly more children from ordinary, working class families attend selective schools as a percentage of the school intake compared to nonselective schools. (Conservative Manifesto, 2017, p 50; see https://s3-eu-west-1.amazonaws. com/2017-manifestos/Conservative+Manifesto+2017.pdf)

The work of many researchers was written off as merely 'allegations'. I asked what the 'official research' was, and was pointed to the DfE (2017, p 39):

89. For grammar schools, the key differences are again amongst disadvantaged children and those from families with above median incomes. Here the variation is at its largest, with less than one in ten pupils in selective schools from disadvantaged backgrounds and over half from the most affluent group. The percentage of children at selective schools from below median income families, who are not considered disadvantaged, (36%) is almost the same as the percentage for non-selective schools (35%). This is shown in figure 29.

Their figure 29 is reproduced here as Figure 13.1. The work by the DfE (2017) was a useful attempt to look at the full range of family income (not just FSM) in relation to school intakes. Their figure 29 confirms that grammar schools are dominated by 'the most affluent group' in a way that non-selective schools are not. It also shows that grammar schools take very few pupils from families on benefits compared to other schools, but that they take the same proportion of non-affluent and non-poor pupils. To make this sound as though grammar schools have been especially inclusive of working-class pupils, as the manifesto did (without either citing the source let alone reproducing figure 29), is a completely unwarranted use of decent evidence.

Figure 13.1: Proportion of pupils attending grammar and non-grammar schools, by income group

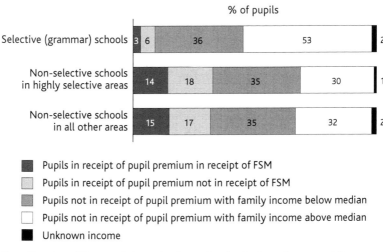

Note: Contains public sector information licensed under the Open Government Licence v3.0. This data can be found in DfE (2017).

These two examples from two very different UK political administrations are presented not to single them out especially, but to illustrate a wider point that some policy is, and presumably always has been, evidence-resistant rather than evidence-informed or even just evidence-neutral.

It is hard to decide whether the policy commentators who point to the higher raw-score results for only one type of school, such as academies, grammars or faith-based schools, are simply unconcerned with the truth, or not astute enough to see the really basic problem with their 'analysis' – that the school intakes differ wildly. Either interpretation is quite alarming because of the power or influence these people often hold. Chapter 6 explained that the design of VA analyses intended to account for differences in school intakes is zero-sum. This means that all schools could be improving or performing well, but half would still have negative VA scores. Schools can only succeed in VA because an equivalent number are deemed to fail. And this has practical consequences for inspection grades, jobs and lives. Yet the then School Minister who introduced the scheme told me later that he had no idea that VA was zero-sum and had these dangerous implications. This is to be evidence-ignorant rather than evidence-informed, or evidence-resistant, as above.

At one stage I was an adviser to the Digital College of Wales Access Board, looking to see how internet access to learning opportunities was possible for the most disadvantaged and remote families in Wales. This was in 2001, when broadband was scarce, much access was via dial-up modems and over 10 per cent of people in Wales did not even have access to a shared payphone at home. A well-meaning member of the board claimed, in all seriousness, that:

> 'Surely most people have broadband or two phones at home now.'

The point I made was that those remaining without such technology would be the very people the college was meant to assist. The college was intended to attract those most excluded from education, but these are the ones also most excluded from research about access, and carelessly (again through ignorance, perhaps) neglected by those policy-makers trying to make things better.

At about the same time the Welsh Government introduced targets for adult learning, clearly intended to increase adult participation and to lead to higher qualifications. One target was that by 2000 at least 50 per cent of those aged 16 to 64 should be qualified to Level 2. And there was progress towards the target. As I pointed out in Chapter 12, every year some people left the pool being aged over 64, and some joined on becoming aged 16. The older people had lower average qualifications than the younger ones, and this alone was enough to explain the apparent 'progress'. Not one more adult had to be educated as an adult for this progress to occur. When I presented this evidence to the government, the civil servants were genuinely surprised and said they would deal with it. About 18 months later I was in the Welsh Assembly for another study and asked about it. Not only had nothing been done, the same people had forgotten and the whole thing was repeated, including the surprise and the determination to act.

Again, these examples are not intended to mark out the individuals concerned especially. The CBI recommendation against the Northern Powerhouse infrastructure project is another example (see Chapter 5). They are illustrations that even when policy-makers are well intended towards evidence (not evidence-resistant), they tend to make assumptions and mistakes, which mean that their policies are still not actually evidence-informed. Nor are these examples meant to convey the idea that policies are never successful. Many are. Examples I have encountered recently in my reading include the move towards comprehensive schooling in England after Circular 10/65, the curriculum entitlement element of the Education Reform Act 1988, the school de-zoning laws in New Zealand in 1990, the incorporation of polytechnics as universities in 1992, and so on. On the other hand, there are areas covered in this book where the policies have almost created or sustained the very things they were intended to overcome – such as the weak supply of scientists and teachers. How could we improve the success rate for new policies?

How policy could work with research

In educational day-to-day practice, there have been clear moves since 2000 towards more, and more appropriately critical, use of evidence (Gorard et al, 2017a). And in other areas of policy, such as crime prevention, health and housing, it seems to an outsider that more progress has been made than in education policy. It is easy to attribute the stubbornness of education policy to the fact that so many people believe they are experts simply because they attended or taught in education themselves. But there is more to it than this. As with practice and research, it is not easy for policy to use research, especially without an intermediary or conduit (Honig et al, 2017).

The relationship between research evidence, education and policy is a strange one. It is constrained by the historical 'accidents' that have shaped the education systems in a certain way around the world, with a modified Victorian version of schools, and a mediaeval/Victorian model of universities, for example. And the interrelationship is curtailed because so many policy-makers appear uninterested in, or even hostile to, evidence. One of the reasons why money is being directed towards unproven, ineffective or harmful interventions is that the quality of the evidence available to policy-makers is generally so poor, and the fact that educators and policy-makers are not usually equipped to discriminate between the poor and the acceptable studies. And this is despite billions of pounds of public money spent on generating such evidence. It is crucial that there is, in future, greater discrimination between studies providing good research, and the rest.

An important example is the huge national impact in the UK of a study reported by Blanden et al (2005). This study claimed that social mobility in Britain was worse for a cohort of infants born in 1970 than for one born in 1958, and that social mobility in Britain was worse than in a range of other countries such as Norway. All three main political parties made these 'facts' the basis for their 2010 elections manifestos, a mobility tsar was created, followed by a cross-party Social Mobility Commission, and billions of pounds of taxpayers' funding was and still is being allocated to solve the problem. I am not arguing against the work done by these well-intentioned bodies, especially in addressing child poverty, when I say that all of this activity was trying to solve a problem that did not actually exist.

Most other research in this field shows little change over time in social class mobility, but this does not get the same media and so political attention. The data presented by Blanden et al (2005) actually shows a high level of income mobility in Britain (about 17% of those born to the poorest 25% of parents grow up to be among the richest 25%, and vice versa). Their paper presents and compares the data for the 1958 and 1970 British birth cohorts in order to claim there is a difference over time (with the 1970 data worse). The data for Norway are from 1958 with father's income for parents and son's income for children. This is the exactly same format as for the 1958 data for Britain. And this 1958 British data shows income mobility about the same as Norway and other Scandinavian countries. Yet Blanden et al (2005) used the worse British figures for mobility in 1970 to compare with the 1958 data from Norway, despite the 1970 figures being based on average parental income (and having further differences as well). And despite publishing the more comparable 1958 figure in the same paper, they use the less comparable 1970 figures in order to make the claim that the situation is worse in Britain. This mistake should be obvious to anyone reading their paper, but it is, apparently, much more appealing to imagine that things are getting worse. The paper did show that when considering the earned income of sons, and so ignoring all females and anyone on benefits, around nine people, or 0.004 per cent of the total cohort of 17,000 neonates born in 1958, were more mobile than their peers born in 1970. None of this provides a serious or valid evidence base for such expensive and wide-ranging policies (Gorard, 2008c).

A more positive current example would be selection for admissions to individual universities. All of the research evidence is clear that using prior attainment at KS5 or anything similar to decide whether to admit applicants to over-subscribed undergraduate courses leads to selection by SES at well. In a sense, researchers have done their job now. The facts are clear. It is up to policy-makers to debate and seek national votes on whether we want such an *internally* selective system (remember that mere admission to any HEI is not a major problem). If the ideology is that, for some reason, we want a system where it is harder to study English Law at Bristol than Sunderland (to continue an earlier example), we must accept the SES stratification of intakes that will result. If, as seems to be the public mood at present, such internal barriers are not deemed acceptable, the issue of widening participation to the most selective universities can be solved at a stroke, by not using such selection within the national system.

It is clear to me that a different approach to policy-making is needed, with a better relationship between researchers and policy-makers. Put crudely, policy-makers have budget constraints, priorities, manifesto commitments, ideas, values and promises that help determine what they want to achieve. They know what to do, but not usually how best to achieve their aims. Researchers have or can provide evidence on what works best, barriers to implementation and so on, and the unintended consequences of any policy aim, whether they agree with that aim or not. As individual citizens they will have opinions about policy and ideology, but these are no more important than those of any other voter. They are not the ones to judge what to do, but are or should be the best placed to advise on how to do it. Of course, it remains crucial that policy research is better conducted (or better discriminated), and that all policy-makers want to be evidence-informed (which should be an essential requirement for office). Once this is clearer to all concerned, both groups can work together more easily and more fruitfully, with trustworthy evidence informing and supporting, but not determining, policy.

References

Abel, E., Sokol, R., Kruger, M. and Yargeau, D. (2008) 'Birthdates of medical school applicants', *Educational Studies*, 34, 4, 271-5.

Abroms, L. and Goldscheider, F. (2002) 'More work for mother: How spouses, cohabiting partners and relatives affect the hours mothers work', *Journal of Family and Economic Issues*, 23, 2, 147-66.

Adams, R. and Weale, S. (2016) 'Ofsted chief calls for radical shakeup to close widening skills gap', *The Guardian*, 1 December (www.theguardian.com/education/2016/dec/01/england-faces-widening-skills-gap-says-outgoing-ofsted-chief).

Adventures in Evidence (2017) 'Student debt and grants in Scotland: A summary', 30 May (https://adventuresinevidence.com/2017/05/30/student-debt-and-grants-in-scotland-a-summary/).

Alegre, M. and Ferrer, G. (2010) 'School regimes and education equity: Some insights based on PISA 2006', *British Educational Research Journal*, 36, 3, 433-61.

Allen, R. and West, A. (2011) 'Why do faith-based schools have advantaged intakes? The relative importance of neighbourhood characteristics, social background and religious identification amongst parents', *British Educational Research Journal*, 37, 4, 631-55.

Amrein-Beardsley, A. (2008) 'Methodological concerns about the education value-added assessment system', *Educational Researcher*, 37, 2, 65-75.

Antonakis, J. (2017) 'On doing better science', *The Leadership Quarterly*, 28, 1, 5-21.

Attwood, R. (2010) 'Mind the gap', *Times Higher Education Supplement*, 26 February.

Ballatore, R., Paccagnella, M. and Tonello, M. (2016) 'Bullied because younger than my mates? The effect of age rank on victimization at school' (www.bancaditalia.it/pubblicazioni/altri-atti-convegni/2016-human-capital/Ballatore_Paccagnella_Tonello.pdf).

Banerjee, P. (2017) *Impact assessment of STEM initiatives in improving educational outcomes*, Bloomington, IN: AuthorHouse.

Barber, M. and Mourshed, M. (2007) 'How the world's best-performing school systems come out on top', McKinsey & Company, September (http://mckinseyonsociety.com/how-the-worlds-best-performing-schools-come-out-on-top/).

Belfi, B., Goos, M., Pinxten, M., Verhaeghe, J., Gielen, S., de Fraine, B. and van Damme, J. (2014) 'Inequality in language achievement growth? An investigation into the impact of pupil socio-ethnic background and school socio-ethnic composition', *British Educational Research Journal*, 40, 5, 820-46.

Bettinger, E. (2010) *Paying to learn: The effect of financial incentives on elementary school test scores*, NBER Working Paper No 16333, Cambridge, MA: National Bureau of Economic Research.

Birdwell, J., Scott, R. and Reynolds, R. (2015) *The double benefit of youth social action could help to tackle some of our social problems: Service nation 2010*, London: Demos.

Blackwell, L., Trzesniewski, K. and Dweck, C. (2007) 'Implicit theories of intelligence predict achievement across an adolescent transition: A longitudinal study and an intervention', *Child Development*, 78, 1, 246-63.

Blanden, J., Gregg, P. and Machin, S. (2005) *Intergenerational mobility in Europe and North America: Report for the Sutton Trust*, London: Centre for Economic Performance (http://cep.lse.ac.uk/about/news/IntergenerationalMobility.pdf).

Boggess, R. (2008) 'Educating parents to increase student achievement in a high-poverty school', *Dissertation Abstracts International Section A: The Humanities and Social Sciences*, 69, 11, 4235.

Boliver, V. and Swift, A. (2011) 'Do comprehensive schools reduce social mobility?', *British Journal of Sociology of Education*, 62, 1, 89-110.

Boliver, V., Gorard, S. and Siddiqui, N. (2016) 'Will the use of contextual indicators make UK Higher Education admissions fairer?', *Education Sciences*, 5, 4 (www.mdpi.com/2227-7102/5/4/306).

Boliver, V., Gorard, S. and Siddiqui, N. (2017) 'How can we widen participation in higher education? The promise of contextualised admissions', in R. Deem and H. Eggins (eds) *The university as a critical institution? An introduction*, Higher Education Research in the 21st Century Series (CHUR), Springer, pp 95-109.

Bolton, P. (2016) *Grammar school statistics*, House of Commons Library Briefing Paper 1398.

Bond, R. and Saunders, P. (1999) 'Routes of success: Influences on the occupational attainment of young British males', *British Journal of Sociology*, 50, 2, 217-39.

Booth, C., Shrimpton, H., Candy, D., Di Antonio, E., Hale, C. and Leckey, C. (2015) *National Citizen Service 2014 evaluation*, Ipsos/MORI (https://www.ipsos.com/sites/default/files/migrations/en-uk/files/Assets/Docs/Publications/sri-cent-gov-ncs-2014-technical-report.pdf)

Bradbury, A. (2011) 'Equity, ethnicity and the hidden dangers of "contextual" measures of school performance', *Race, Ethnicity and Education*, 14, 3, 277-91.

Bradbury, S. and Kay, T. (2005) *Evaluation of the pupil-centred stages of phase one of the Step into Sport project*, Loughborough: Institute of Youth Sport.

Bradshaw, C., Zmuda, J, Kellam, S. and Ialongo, N. (2009) 'Longitudinal impact of two universal preventive interventions in first grade on educational outcomes in high school', *Journal of Educational Psychology*, 101, 4, 926-37.

Broecke, S. (2015) 'University rankings: Do they matter in the UK?', *Education Economics*, 23, 2, 137-61.

Broecke, S. and Hamed, J. (2008) *Gender gaps in higher education participation: An analysis of the relationship between prior attainment and young participation by gender, socio-economic class and ethnicity*, DIUS Research Report 08 14, London: Department for Innovation, Universities & Skills (http://webarchive.nationalarchives.gov.uk/+/http://www.dius.gov.uk/research/documents/DIUS-RR-08-14.pdf).

Broecke, S. and Nicholls, T. (2007) *Ethnicity and degree attainment*, Research Report No 92, London: Department for Education and Skills (http://webarchive.nationalarchives.gov.uk/20130401151715/http://www.education.gov.uk/publications/eOrderingDownload/RW92.pdf).

Brotman, L., Dawson-McClure, S., Calzada, E., Huang, K., Kamboukos, D., Palamar, J. and Petkova, E. (2013) 'Cluster (school) RCT of ParentCorps: Impact on kindergarten academic achievement', *Pediatrics*, 131, 5, 1521-9.

Bui, K. (2007) 'Educational expectations and academic achievement among middle and high school students', *Education*, 127, 3, 328-31.

Bullock, K. and Scott, W. (1992) 'Teacher shortages in mathematic, physics and technology', *Educational Review*, 44, 2, 167-79.

Burgess, S., Wilson, D. and Lupton, R. (2005) 'Parallel lives? Ethnic segregation in schools and neighbourhoods', *Urban Studies*, 42, 7, 1027-56.

Burstein, L., Fischer, K.B. and Miller, M.D. (1980) 'The multilevel effects of background on science achievement: A cross-national comparison', *Sociology of Education*, 53, 4, 215-25.

Butz, W.P., Bloom, G.A., Gross, M.E., Kelly, T.K., Kofner, A. and Rippen, H.E. (2003) *Is there a shortage of scientists and engineers? How would we know?*, Santa Monica, CA: Rand Corporation.

Bynner, J. and Parsons, S. (1997) *It doesn't get any better: The impact of poor basic skills on the lives of 37 year olds*, London: Basic Skills Agency.

Callender, C. (2003) *Attitudes to debt: School leavers and further education students' attitudes to debt and their impact on participation in higher education*, London: Universities UK.

Calnon, R. (2005) 'Family involvement at home: Increasing literacy achievement of diverse at-risk kindergarten students', Unpublished EdD dissertation, Boise, ID: Boise State University.

Camina, M. and Iannone, P. (2013) 'Housing mix, school mix: Barriers to success', *Journal of Education Policy*, 29, 1, 19-43.

Campbell, T. (2014) 'Stratified at seven: In-class ability grouping and the relative age effect', *British Educational Research Journal*, 40, 5, 749-71.

Capron, C. and Duyme, M. (1989) 'Assessment of effects of socioeconomic status on IQ in a full cross-fostering study', *Nature*, 17 August, 552-3.

Casey, L., Davies, P., Kalambouka, A., Nelson, N. and Boyle, B. (2006) 'The influence of schooling on the aspirations of young people with special educational needs', *British Educational Research Journal*, 32, 2, 273-90.

CBI (Confederation of British Industry) (2010) *Ready to grow: Business priorities for education and skills. Education and skills survey 2010* (www.educationandemployers.org/wp-content/uploads/2014/06/ready-to-grow-cbi.pdf).

Chanfreau, J., Tanner, E., Callanan, M., Laing, K., Skipp, A. and Todd, L. (2016) *Out-of-school activities during primary school and KS2 attainment*, Centre for Longitudinal Studies, Working paper 2016/1, London: UCL Institute of Education, London (www.nuffieldfoundation.org/sites/default/files/files/CLS%20WP%202016%20(1)%20-%20Out%20of%20school%20activities%20during%20primary%20school%20and%20KS2%20attainment.pdf).

Chapman, B. and Ryan, C. (2002) 'Income contingent financing of student higher education charges: Assessing the Australian innovation', *Welsh Journal of Education*, 11, 64-81.

Cheng, S.C. and Gorard, S. (2010) 'Segregation by poverty in secondary schools in England 2006-2009: A research note', *Journal of Education Policy*, 25, 3, 415-18.

Chetty, R., Hendren, N., Kline, P. and Saez, E. (2014) 'Where is the land of opportunity? The geography of intergenerational mobility in the United States' (www.equality-of-opportunity.org/assets/documents/mobility_geo.pdf).

Cheung, P. (2016) 'Children's after-school physical activity participation in Hong Kong: Does family socioeconomic status matter?', *Health Education Journal*, doi:0017896916660863.

Chiu, M. and Khoo, L. (2005) 'Effects of resources, inequality, and privilege bias on achievement: Country, school and student level analyses', *American Educational Research Journal*, 42, 4, 575-603.

Chowdry, H., Crawford, C. and Goodman, A. (2010) *The role of attitudes and behaviours in explaining socio-economic differences in attainment at age 16*, IFS Working Paper 10/15, London: Institute for Fiscal Studies.

Chowdry, H., Crawford, C., Dearden, L., Goodman, A. and Vignoles, A. (2008) *Understanding the determinants of participation in higher education and the quality of institute attended: Analysis using administrative data*, IFS report, London: Institute for Fiscal Studies (www.ifs.org.uk/publications/4279).

Clark, M., Gleeson, P., Tuttle, C. and Silverberg, M. (2015) 'Do charter schools improve student attainment?', *Educational Evaluation and Policy Analysis*, 37, 4, 419-36.

Clayton, M. (2012) 'On widening participation in higher education through positive discrimination', *Journal of Philosophy of Education*, 46, 3, 414-31.

Clotfelter, C. (2001) 'Are whites still fleeing? Racial patterns and enrolment sifts in urban public schools', *Journal of Policy Analysis and Management*, 20, 2, 199-221.

Coe, R., Aloisi, C., Higgins, S. and Major, L. (2014) *What makes great teaching? Review of the underpinning research*, London: Sutton Trust.

Coe, R., Jones, K., Searle, J., Kokotsaki, D., Mohd Kosnin, A. and Skinner, P. (2008) *Evidence on the effects of selective educational systems*, London: Sutton Trust.

Coffield, F. (2012) 'Why the McKinsey reports will not improve school systems', *Journal of Education Policy*, 27, 1, 131-49.

Cohen, G., Garcia, J., Purdie-Vaughns, V., Apfel, N. and Brzustoski, P. (2009) 'Recursive processes in self-affirmation: Intervening to close the minority achievement gap', *Science*, 324, 5925, 400-40.

Coleman, J., Campbell, E., Hobson, C., McPartland, J., Mood, A., Weinfeld, F. and York, R. (1966) *Equality of educational opportunity*, 2 volumes, Washington, DC: Office of Education, US Department of Health, Education, and Welfare, US Government Printing Office, OE-38001; Superintendent of Documents Catalog No FS 5.238-38001.

Collado, D., Lomos, C. and Nicaise, I. (2015) 'The effects of classroom socioeconomic composition in students' civic knowledge in Chile', *School Effectiveness and School Improvement*, doi:10.1080/09243453.2014.966725.

Crawford, C., Dearden, L. and Greaves, E. (2011) *Does when you are born matter? The impact of month of birth on children's cognitive and non-cognitive skills in England*, Report for the Nuffield Foundation, London: Institute for Fiscal Studies.

Crawford, C., MacMillan, L. and Vignoles, A. (2017) 'When and why do initially high-achieving poor children fall behind?', *Oxford Review of Education*, 43, 1, 88-108.

Cribb, J., Sibieta, L. and Vignoles, A. (2013) *Entry into grammar schools in England*, London: Institute for Fiscal Studies (www.ifs.org.uk/docs/Grammar_Schools2013.pdf).

Danhier, J. (2017) 'How big is the handicap for disadvantaged pupils in segregated school settings?', *British Journal of Educational Studies*, doi:10.1080/00071005.2017.1322682.

Danhier, J. and Martin, E. (2014) 'Comparing compositional effects in two education systems: The case of the Belgian communities', *British Journal of Educational Studies*, 62, 2, 171-89.

Darling-Hammond, L. (2015) 'Can value added add value to teacher evaluation?', *Educational Researcher*, 44, 2, 132-37.

David, M., Weiner, G. and Arnot, M. (1997) 'Strategic feminist research on gender equality and schooling in Britain in the 1990s', in C. Marshall (ed) *Feminist critical policy analysis: Volume 1*, London: Falmer Press, pp 91-105.

Dean, C. (2000) 'Country has "run out" of teachers', *Times Educational Supplement*, 8 September, p 4.

Dearden, L., Emmerson, C., Frayne, C. and Meghir, C. (2005) *Education subsidies and school drop-out rates*, IFS Working Paper W05/11, London: Institute for Fiscal Studies.

Dearing R. (1997) *Higher education in the learning society. Report of the Committee under the Chairmanship of Sir Ron Dearing*, London: The Stationery Office.

Dench, S., Iphofen, R. and Huws, U. (2004) *An EU code of ethics for socio-economic research*, Brighton: Institute for Employment Studies (www.respectproject.org/ethics/412ethics.pdf).

Denholm, J. and Macleod, D. (2003) *Prospects for growth in further education*, Wellington, New Zealand: Learning and Skills Research Centre.

DfE (Department for Education) (2016) *Provisional destinations of Key Stage 4 and Key Stage 5 students in state-funded institutions, England, 2014/15*, London: DfE (www.gov.uk/government/uploads/system/uploads/attachment_data/file/559888/SFR47_2016_text_2.pdf).

DfE (2017) *Analysing family circumstances and education: Increasing our understanding of ordinary working families*, April, London: DfE (http://dera.ioe.ac.uk/28896/1/Technical%20consultation%20document.pdf).

DfES (Department for Education and Skills) (2003) *Consultation: Classification of special education needs*, London: DfES.

DfES (2004) *Schools, pupils and their characteristics*, London: DfES (archived, available via http://webarchive.nationalarchives.gov.uk/20120506052914/http://www.education.gov.uk/rsgateway/sc-schoolpupil.shtml).

Dhillon, J. (2004) 'An exploration of adult learners' perspectives of using learndirect centres as sites of learning', *Research in Post-Compulsory Education*, 9, 1, 147-58.

Do, P.C., Parry, J., Mathers, J. and Richardson, M. (2006) 'Monitoring the widening participation initiative for access to medical school: Are present measures sufficient?', *Medical Education*, 40, 8, 750-8.

Dolton, P. (2005) *The labour market for teachers: A policy perspective*, University of Newcastle Working Paper, Newcastle: University of Newcastle.

Domovic, V. and Godler, Z. (2005) 'Educational systems' efficiency evaluation on the basis of student performance: Comparison of Finland-Germany', *Drustvena Istrazivanja*, 14, 3, 439-58.

Douglas, G., Travers, J., McLinden, M., Robertson, C., Smith, E., Macnab, N., et al (2012) *Measuring educational engagement, progress and outcomes for children with special educational needs: A review*, Trim, Ireland: National Council for Special Education (NCSE) (http://ncse.ie/research-reports).

Driessen, G., Agirdag, O. and Merry, M. (2016) 'The gross and net effects of primary school denomination on pupil performance', *Educational Review*, 68, 4, 466-80.

Duncan, O., Cuzzort, R. and Duncan, B. (1961) *Statistical geography: Problems in analyzing area data*, Glencoe IL: Free Press.

ECU (Equality Challenge Unit) (2012) *Equitable admissions for underrepresented groups*, London: ECU (www.ecu.ac.uk/wp-content/uploads/external/equitable-admissions-for-underrepresented-groups.pdf).

EGREES (European Group for Researching Equity in Educational Systems) (2005) 'A set of indicators', *European Educational Research Journal*, 4, 2, 1-151.

EGREES (2008) *Developing a sense of justice among disadvantaged students: The role of schools*, Birmingham: EGREES.

Engelmann, K. (2016) 'Who is the engaged citizen?', *Educational Research and Evaluation*, 22, 5-6, 339-49.

Erisman, W. and Looney, S. (2007) *Opening the door to the American dream: Increasing higher education access and success for immigrants*, Washington, DC: Institute for Higher Education Policy (http://files. eric.ed.gov/fulltext/ED497030.pdf).

Evans, H. (2008) *Value-added in English schools*, London: Department for Children, Schools and Families (https://pdfs.semanticscholar.org/ d53d/8e149eafba6d7b5d2813ac439781b5a60dd9.pdf).

Evans, C., Rees, G., Taylor, C. and Wright, C. (2017) '"Widening Access" to higher education: the reproduction of university hierarchies through policy enactment', *Journal of Education Policy*, DOI: 10.1080/02680939.2017.1390165

Everson, K. (2017) 'Value-added modelling and educational accountability: Are we answering the real questions?', *Review of Educational Research*, 87, 1, 35-70.

Fernandez-Mellizo, M. and Martinez-Garcia, J. (2017) 'Inequality of educational opportunities: School failure trends in Spain (1977-2012)', *International Studies in Sociology of Education*, 26, 3, 267-87.

Financial Times (2016) 'Education better than roads to cut north–south divide, says CBI', by A. Bounds and C. Tighe, *Financial Times*, 1 December (www.ft.com/content/0c06cec2-b6f4-11e6-961e-a1acd97f622d).

Fitz, J., Gorard, S. and Taylor, C. (2002) 'School admissions after the School Standards and Framework Act: Bringing the LEAs back in?', *Oxford Review of Education*, 28, 2, 373-93.

Florian, L., Rouse, M., Black-Hawkins, K. and Jull, S. (2004) 'What can national data sets tell us about inclusion and pupil achievement?', *British Journal of Special Education*, 31, 3, 115-21.

Forsyth, A. and Furlong, A. (2003) *Socio-economic disadvantage and access to higher education*, Bristol: Policy Press.

Frankenberg, E. (2013) 'The role of residential segregation in contemporary school segregation', *Education and Urban Society*, 45, 5, 548-70.

Fryer, R. (2010) *Financial incentives and student achievement: Evidence from randomized trials*, NBER Working Paper No 15898, Cambridge, MA: National Bureau of Economic Research.

Gallagher, J., Niven, V., Donaldson, N. and Wilson, N. (2009) 'Widening access? Characteristics of applicants to medical and dental schools, compared with UCAS', *British Dental Journal*, 207, 433-45.

Gallagher, T. and Smith, A. (2000) *The effects of the selective system of secondary education in Northern Ireland*, Bangor: Department of Education (www.education.gg/CHttpHandler.ashx?id=97491&p=0).

Gambetta, D. (1987) *Were they pushed or did they jump? Individual decision mechanisms in education*, London: Cambridge University Press.

Gann, N. (1999) *Targets for tomorrows' schools: A guide to whole school target-setting for governors and headteachers*, London: Falmer.

Gifford, D., Briceno-Perriott, J. and Mianzo, F. (2006) 'Locus of control: Academic achievement and retention in a sample of university first-year students', *Journal of College Admission*, 191, 18-25.

Gill, T. and Benton, T. (2015) *The accuracy of forecast grades for OCR A levels in June 2014*, Statistics Report Series No 90, Cambridge: Cambridge Assessment (www.cambridgeassessment.org.uk/Images/243087-the-accuracy-of-forecast-grades-for-ocr-a-levels-in-june-2014.pdf).

Gilroy, P. (1998) 'The future of teacher education: England and Wales as a case study, A keynote paper for the UK/Japan Education Forum held in Tokyo in 1998', *Bulletin of the UK-Japan Education Forum*, 3, 1998/99, 7-33.

Ginsburg, H. and Pappas, S. (2004) 'SES, ethnic, and gender differences in young children's informal addition and subtraction: A clinical interview investigation', *Journal of Applied Developmental Psychology*, 25, 2, 171-92.

Glass, G. (2004) *Teacher evaluation: Policy brief*, Tempe, AZ: Education Policy Research Unit.

Gleason, P., Clark, M., Tuttle, C. and Dwoyer, E. (2010) *The evaluation of charter school impacts: Final report*, Washington, DC: National Center for Education Evaluation and Regional Assistance, ED510574.

Glenn, W. (2011) 'A quantitative analysis of the increase in public school segregation in Delaware: 1989-2006', *Urban Education*, 46, 4, 719-40.

Goldacre, B. (2012) *Bad pharma*, London: HarperCollins.

Gonzales, N., Dumka, L., Gottschall, A., McClain, D., Wong, J., German, M., et al (2012) 'Randomised trial of a broad preventive intervention for Mexican American adolescents', *Journal of Consult Clinical Psychology*, 80, 1, 1-16.

Gorard, S. (1996) 'Fee-paying schools in Britain: A peculiarly English phenomenon', *Educational Review*, 48, 1, 89-93.

Gorard, S. (1997a) 'A choice of methods: The methodology of choice', *Research in Education*, 57, 45-56.

Gorard, S. (1997b) 'Who pays the piper? Intergenerational aspects of school choice', *School Leadership and Management*, 17, 2, 245-55.

Gorard, S. (1997c) *School choice in an established market*, Aldershot: Ashgate.

Gorard, S. (1998a) 'Reflections of the past: The generation of school choice', *Education Today*, 48, 3, 25-32.

Gorard, S. (1998b) 'Social movement in undeveloped markets: An apparent contradiction in education policy studies', *Educational Review*, 50, 3, 249-58.

Gorard, S. (1998c) 'Four errors ... and a conspiracy? The effectiveness of schools in Wales', *Oxford Review of Education*, 24, 4, 459-72.

Gorard, S. (1998d) 'Schooled to fail? Revisiting the Welsh school-effect', *Journal of Education Policy*, 13, 1, 115-24.

Gorard, S. (1999) '"Well. That about wraps it up for school choice research": A state of the art review', *School Leadership and Management*, 19, 18, 25-47.

Gorard, S. (2000a) 'Questioning the crisis account: A review of evidence for increasing polarisation in schools', *Educational Research*, 42, 3, 309-21.

Gorard, S. (2000b) *Education and social justice*, Cardiff: University of Wales Press.

Gorard, S. (2000c) '"Underachievement" is still an ugly word: Reconsidering the relative effectiveness of schools in England and Wales', *Journal of Education Policy*, 15, 5, 559-73.

Gorard, S. (2001a) *Quantitative methods in educational research: The role of numbers made easy*, London: Continuum.

Gorard, S. (2001b) 'International comparisons of school effectiveness: A second component of the "crisis account"?', *Comparative Education*, 37, 3, 279-96.

Gorard, S. (2002a) 'Political control: A way forward for educational research?', *British Journal of Educational Studies*, 50, 3, 378-89.

Gorard, S. (2002b) 'Can we overcome the methodological schism? Four models for combining qualitative and quantitative evidence', *Research Papers in Education*, 17, 4, 345-61.

Gorard, S. (2002b) 'The role of secondary data in combining methodological approaches', *Educational Review*, 54, 3, 231-37.

Gorard, S. (2002c) 'Ethics and equity: Pursuing the perspective of non-participants', *Social Research Update*, 39, 1-4.

Gorard, S. (2002d) 'The missing impact of marketisation re-visited', *Research Papers in Education*, 17, 4, 412-14.

Gorard, S. (2003a) 'Understanding probabilities and re-considering traditional research methods training', *Sociological Research Online*, 8, 1.

Gorard, S. (2003b) 'Lifelong learning trajectories in Wales: Results of the NIACE Adults Learners Survey', in F. Aldridge and N. Sargent (eds) *Adult learning and social division: Volume 2*, Leicester: NIACE, pp 37-54.

Gorard, S. (2004a) 'The British Educational Research Association and the future of educational research', *Educational Studies*, 30, 1, 65-76.

Gorard, S. (2004b) 'Scepticism or clericalism? Theory as a barrier to combining methods', *Journal of Educational Enquiry*, 5, 1, 1-21.

Gorard, S. (2004c) 'Comments on modelling segregation', *Oxford Review of Education*, 30, 3, 435-40.

Gorard, S. (2004d) 'The international dimension: What can we learn from the PISA study?', in H. Claire (ed) *Gender in education 3-19: A fresh approach*, London: Association of Teachers and Lecturers, pp 26-32.

Gorard, S. (2005a) 'Revisiting a 90-year-old debate: The advantages of the mean deviation', *The British Journal of Educational Studies*, 53, 4, 417-30.

Gorard, S. (2005b) 'Academies as the "future of schooling": Is this an evidence-based policy?', *Journal of Education Policy*, 20, 3, 369-77.

Gorard, S. (2005c) 'Current contexts for research in educational leadership and management', *Educational Management Administration and Leadership*, 33, 2, 155-64.

Gorard, S. (2005d) 'Where shall we widen it? Higher education and the age participation rate in Wales', *Higher Education Quarterly*, 59, 1, 3-18.

Gorard, S. (2006a) *Using everyday numbers effectively in research: Not a book about statistics*, London: Continuum.

Gorard, S. (2006b) 'Towards a judgement-based statistical analysis', *British Journal of Sociology of Education*, 27, 1, 67-80.

Gorard, S. (2006c) 'Is there a school mix effect?', *Educational Review*, 58, 1, 87-94.

Gorard, S. (2006d) 'Value-added is of little value', *Journal of Educational Policy*, 21, 2, 233-41.

Gorard, S. (2006e) 'Does policy matter in education?', *International Journal of Research & Method in Education*, 29, 1, 5-21.

Gorard, S. (2007a) 'The dubious benefits of multi-level modelling', *International Journal of Research & Method in Education*, 30, 2, 221-36.

Gorard, S. (2007b) 'What *does* an index of school segregation measure? A commentary on Allen and Vignoles', *Oxford Review of Education*, 33, 5, 669-77.

Gorard, S. (2007c) 'The true impact of school diversity', *International Journal for Education Law and Policy*, 2, 1-2, 35-40.

Gorard, S. (2008a) 'The value-added of primary schools: What is it really measuring?', *Educational Review*, 60, 2, 179-85.

Gorard, S. (2008b) 'Who is missing from higher education?', *Cambridge Journal of Education*, 38, 3, 421-37.

Gorard, S. (2008c) 'Research impact is not always a good thing: A reconsideration of rates of "social mobility" in Britain', *British Journal of Sociology of Education*, 29, 3, 317-24.

Gorard, S. (2009a) 'Does the index of segregation matter? The composition of secondary schools in England since 1996', *British Educational Research Journal*, 35, 4, 639-52.

Gorard, S. (2009b) 'What are academies the answer to?', *Journal of Education Policy*, 24, 1, 1-13.

Gorard, S. (2010a) 'All evidence is equal: The flaw in statistical reasoning', *Oxford Review of Education*, 36, 1, 63-77.

Gorard, S. (2010b) 'Measuring is more than assigning numbers, in G. Walford, E. Tucker and M. Viswanathan (eds) *Sage handbook of measurement*, Los Angeles: Sage, pp 389-408.

Gorard, S. (2010c) 'Research design, as independent of methods', in C. Teddlie and A. Tashakkori (eds) *Handbook of mixed methods*, Los Angeles, CA: Sage, pp 237-52.

Gorard, S. (2010d) 'Serious doubts about school effectiveness', *British Educational Research Journal*, 36, 5, 735-66.

Gorard, S. (2010e) 'School experience as a potential determinant of post-compulsory participation', *Evaluation and Research in Education*, 23, 1, 3-17.

Gorard, S. (2010f) 'Education *can* compensate for society – a bit', *British Journal of Educational Studies*, 58, 1, 47-65.

Gorard, S. (2011a) 'Measuring segregation – Beware of the cautionary tale by Johnston and Jones', *Environment and Planning A*, 43, 1, 3-7.

Gorard, S. (2011b) 'Now you see it, now you don't: School effectiveness as conjuring?', *Research in Education*, 86, 39-45.

Gorard, S. (2011c) 'The potential determinants of young people's sense of justice: An international study', *British Journal of Sociology of Education*, 32, 1, 35-52.

Gorard, S. (2012a) 'Who is eligible for free school meals? Characterising FSM as a measure of disadvantage in England', *British Educational Research Journal*, 38, 6, 1003-17.

Gorard, S. (2012b) 'The increasing availability of official datasets: Methods, opportunities, and limitations for studies of education', *British Journal of Educational Studies*, 60, 1, 77-92.

Gorard, S. (2012c) 'Querying the causal role of attitudes in educational attainment', *ISRN Education*, 2012, Article ID 501589, doi:10.5402/2012/501589.

Gorard, S. (2012d) 'Experiencing fairness at school: An international study in five countries', *International Journal of Educational Research*, 3, 3, 127-37.

Gorard, S. (2013a) *Research design: Robust approaches for the social sciences*, London: Sage.

Gorard, S. (2013b) 'The possible advantages of the mean absolute deviation "effect" size', *Social Research Update*, 65, Winter, 1-4.

Gorard, S. (2013c) 'The propagation of errors in experimental data analysis: A comparison of pre- and post-test designs', *International Journal of Research & Method in Education*, 36, 4, 372-85.

Gorard, S. (2013d) 'An argument concerning overcoming inequalities in higher education', in N. Murray and C. Klinger (eds) *Aspirations, access and attainment in widening participation: International perspectives and an agenda for change*, London: Routledge, Chapter 11.

Gorard, S. (2013e) 'What difference do teachers make? A consideration of the wider outcomes of schooling', *Irish Educational Studies*, 32, 1, 69-82.

Gorard, S. (2014a) 'The widespread abuse of statistics by researchers: What is the problem and what is the ethical way forward?', *Psychology of Education Review*, 38, 1, 3-10.

Gorard, S. (2014b) 'The link between academies in England, pupil outcomes and local patterns of socio-economic segregation between schools', *Research Papers in Education*, 29, 3, 268-84.

Gorard, S. (2015a) 'Rethinking "quantitative" methods and the development of new researchers', *Review of Education*, 3, 1, 72-96.

Gorard, S. (2015b) 'Introducing the mean absolute deviation "effect" size', *International Journal of Research & Method in Education*, 38, 2, 105-14.

Gorard, S. (2015c) 'The easy way to help kids born in summer keep up at school', *New Scientist*, 17 October, p 29.

Gorard, S. (2015d) 'The complex determinants of school intake characteristics, England 1989 to 2014', *Cambridge Journal of Education*, 46, 1, 131-46.

Gorard, S. (2015e) 'The uncertain future of comprehensive schooling in England', *European Educational Research Journal*, 14, 3-4, 257-68.

Gorard, S. (2016a) 'Challenging perceptions of a north–south regional divide in school performance in England', BERA Annual Conference, Leeds, September.

Gorard, S. (2016b) 'A cautionary note on measuring the pupil premium attainment gap in England', *British Journal of Education, Society and Behavioural Sciences*, 14, 2, doi:10.9734/BJESBS/2016/23618.

Gorard, S. (2016c) 'Does the use of contextual admissions help universities to widen participation?', *Research Fortnight* (www.researchprofessional.com/0/rr/he/views/2016/1/The-problem-with-contextual-admissions.html).

Gorard, S. (2017a) 'An introduction to the importance of research design', in D. Wyse, N. Selwyn, E. Smith and L. Suter (eds) *The BERA/Sage handbook of educational research*, London: Sage, pp 203-12.

Gorard, S. (2017b) 'Multiple linear regression', in R. Coe, L. Hedges and M. Waring (eds) *Research methodologies and methods in education* (2nd edn), London: Sage, pp 317-25.

Gorard, S. (2017c) 'Significance testing is still wrong, and damages real lives: A brief reply to Spreckelsen and van der Horst, and Nicholson and McCusker', *Sociological Research Online*, 22, 2 (www.socresonline.org.uk/22/2/11.html).

Gorard, S. (2017d) 'How *should* numeric data be analysed?', in D. Wyse, N. Selwyn, E. Smith and L. Suter (eds) *The BERA/Sage handbook of educational research*, London: Sage, pp 753-68.

Gorard, S. (2017e) 'How prepared do newly-qualified teachers feel? Differences between routes and settings', *Journal of Education for Teaching*, 43, 1, 3-19.

Gorard, S. and Cheng, S.C. (2011) 'Pupil clustering in English secondary schools: One pattern or several?', *International Journal of Research & Method in Education*, 34, 3, 327-39.

Gorard, S. and Cook, T. (2007) 'Where does good evidence come from?', *International Journal of Research & Method in Education*, 30, 3, 307-23.

Gorard, S. and Fitz, J. (1998a) 'The more things change ... the missing impact of marketisation', *British Journal of Sociology of Education*, 19, 3, 365-76.

Gorard, S. and Fitz, J. (1998b) 'Under starters orders: The established market, the Cardiff study and the Smithfield project', *International Studies in Sociology of Education*, 8, 3, 299-314.

Gorard, S. and Fitz, J. (2000a) 'Investigating the determinants of segregation between schools', *Research Papers in Education*, 15, 2, 115-32.

Gorard, S. and Fitz, J. (2000b) 'Markets and stratification: A view from England and Wales', *Educational Policy*, 14, 3, 405-28.

Gorard, S. and Fitz, J. (2006) 'What counts as evidence in the school choice debate?', *British Educational Research Journal*, 32, 6, 797-816.

Gorard, S. and Rees, G. (2002) *Creating a learning society*, Bristol: Policy Press.

Gorard, S. and See, B.H. (2011) 'How can we enhance enjoyment of secondary school? The student view', *British Educational Research Journal*, 37, 4, 671-90.

Gorard, S. and See, B.H. (2008) 'Is science a middle-class phenomenon? The SES determinants of 16-19 participation', *Research in Post-Compulsory Education*, 13, 2, 217-26.

Gorard, S. and See, B.H. (2009) 'The impact of SES on participation and attainment in science', *Studies in Science Education*, 45, 1, 93-129.

Gorard, S. and See, B.H. (2013) *Overcoming disadvantage in education*, London: Routledge.

Gorard, S. and Selwyn, N. (1999) 'Switching on the Learning Society? Questioning the role of technology in widening participation in lifelong learning', *Journal of Education Policy*, 14, 5, 523-34.

Gorard, S. and Selwyn, N. (2005a) 'Towards a le@rning society?', *British Journal of Sociology of Education*, 26, 1, 71-89.

Gorard, S. and Selwyn, N. (2005b) 'What makes a lifelong learner?', *Teachers College Record*, 107, 6, 1193-216.

Gorard, S. and Siddiqui, N. (2018a) 'There *is* only research: The liberating impact of just doing research', *International Journal of Multiple Research Approaches*, 10, 1, 1-15.

Gorard, S. and Siddiqui, N. (2018b) 'Grammar schools in England: A new analysis of social segregation and academic outcomes', *British Journal of Sociology of Education*, https://doi.org/10.1080/01425692.2018.1443432

Gorard, S. and Smith, E. (2004) 'An international comparison of equity in education systems?', *Comparative Education*, 40, 1, 16-28.

Gorard, S. and Smith, E. (2006) 'Combining numbers with narratives', *Evaluation and Research in Education*, 19, 2, 59-62.

Gorard, S. and Smith, E. (2007) 'Do barriers get in the way? A review of the determinants of post-16 participation', *Research in Post-Compulsory Education*, 12, 2, 141-58.

Gorard, S. and Smith, E. (2008) 'The impact of school experiences on students' sense of justice: an international study of student voice', *Orbis Scholae*, 2, 2, 87-105

Gorard, S. and Smith, E. (2010) *Equity in education: An international comparison of pupil perspectives*, London: Palgrave.

Gorard, S. and Taylor, C. (2001a) 'Specialist schools in England: Track record and future prospect', *School Leadership and Management*, 21, 4, 365-81.

Gorard, S. and Taylor, C. (2001b) *Student funding and hardship in Wales: A statistical summary, Report to the National Assembly Investigation Group on student hardship*, Cardiff: National Assembly for Wales.

Gorard, S. and Taylor, C. (2002a) 'What is segregation? A comparison of measures in terms of strong and weak compositional invariance', *Sociology*, 36, 4, 875-95.

Gorard, S. and Taylor, C. (2002b) 'Market forces and standards in education: A preliminary consideration', *British Journal of Sociology of Education*, 23, 1, 5-18.

Gorard, S., with Taylor, C. (2004) *Combining methods in educational and social research*, London: Open University Press.

Gorard, S. et al (1999a): Gorard, S., Rees, G. and Fevre, R. (1999) 'Patterns of participation in lifelong learning: Do families make a difference?', *British Educational Research Journal*, 25, 4, 517-32.

Gorard, S. et al (1999b): Gorard, S., Salisbury, J. and Rees, G. (1999) 'Reappraising the apparent underachievement of boys at school', *Gender and Education*, 11, 4, 441-54.

Gorard, S. et al (1999c): Gorard, S., Fevre, R. and Rees, G. (1999) 'The apparent decline of informal learning', *Oxford Review of Education*, 25, 4, 437-54.

Gorard, S. et al (2000): Gorard, S., Selwyn, N. and Williams, S. (2000) 'Could try harder! Problems facing technological solutions to non-participation in adult learning', *British Educational Research Journal*, 26, 4, 507-21.

Gorard, S. et al (2001): Gorard, S., Rees, G. and Salisbury, J. (2001) 'The differential attainment of boys and girls at school: Investigating the patterns and their determinants', *British Educational Research Journal*, 27, 2, 125-39.

Gorard, S. et al (2002a): Gorard, S., Rees, G. and Selwyn, N. (2002) 'The "conveyor belt effect": A re-assessment of the impact of National Targets for Lifelong Learning', *Oxford Review of Education*, 28, 1, 75-89.

Gorard, S. et al (2002ba): Gorard, S., Selwyn, N. and Rees, G. (2002) 'Privileging the visible: Examining the National Targets for Education and Training', *British Educational Research Journal*, 28, 3, 309-25.

Gorard, S. et al (2003a): Gorard, S., Taylor, C. and Fitz, J. (2003) *Schools, markets and choice policies*, London: RoutledgeFalmer.

Gorard, S. et al (2003b): Gorard, S., Selwyn, N. and Madden, L. (2003) 'Logged on to learning? Assessing the impact of technology on participation in lifelong learning', *International Journal of Lifelong Education*, 22, 3, 281-96.

Gorard, S. et al (2004a): Gorard, S., Roberts, K. and Taylor, C. (2004) 'What kind of creature is a design experiment?', *British Educational Research Journal*, 30, 4, 575-90.

Gorard, S. et al (2004b): Gorard, S., Rushforth, K. and Taylor, C. (2004) 'Is there a shortage of quantitative work in education research?', *Oxford Review of Education*, 30, 3, 371-95.

Gorard, S. et al (2006): Gorard, S., See, B.H., Smith, E. and White, P. (2006) *Teacher supply: The key issues*, London: Continuum.

Gorard, S. et al (2007a): Gorard, S. with Adnett, N., May, H., Slack, K., Smith, E. and Thomas, L. (2007) *Overcoming barriers to HE*, Stoke-on-Trent: Trentham Books.

Gorard, S. et al (2007b): Gorard, S., See, B.H., Smith. E. and White, P. (2007) 'What can we do to strengthen the teaching workforce?', *International Journal of Lifelong Education*, 26, 4, 419-37.

Gorard, S. et al (2011): Gorard, S., See, B.H. and Davies, P. (2011) *Do attitudes and aspirations matter in education? A review of the research evidence*, Saarbrucken: Lambert Academic Publishing.

Gorard, S. et al (2013a): Gorard, S., Hordosy, R. and See, B.H. (2013) 'Narrowing the determinants of segregation between schools 1996-2011', *Journal of School Choice*, 7, 2, 182-95.

Gorard, S. et al (2013b): Gorard, S., Hordosy, R. and Siddiqui, N. (2013) 'How stable are "school effects" assessed by a value-added technique?', *International Education Studies*, 6, 1, 1-9.

Gorard, S. et al (2015): Gorard, S., Siddiqui, N. and See, B.H. (2015) 'How effective is a summer school for catch-up attainment in English and maths?', *International Journal of Educational Research*, 73, 1-11.

Gorard, S. et al (2016a): Gorard, S., See, B.H. and Morris, R. (2016) *The most effective approaches to teaching in primary schools*, Saarbrucken: Lambert Academic Publishing.

Gorard, S. et al (2016b): Gorard, S., Siddiqui, N. and See, B.H. (2016) 'An evaluation of Fresh Start as a catch-up intervention: And whether teachers can conduct trials', *Educational Studies*, 42, 1, 98-113.

Gorard, S. et al (2017a): Gorard, S., See, B.H. and Siddiqui, N. (2017) *The trials of evidence-based education*, London: Routledge.

Gorard, S. et al (2017b): Gorard, S., Siddiqui, N. and Boliver, V. (2017) 'An analysis of school-based contextual indicators for possible use in widening participation', *Higher Education Studies*, 7, 2, 101-18.

Gorard, S. et al (2017c): Gorard, S., See, B.H. and Siddiqui, N. (2017) 'What works and what fails? Evidence from seven popular literacy catch-up schemes for the transition to secondary school in England', *Research Papers in Education*, 32, 5 (http://dx.doi.org/10.1080/0267 1522.2016.1225811).

Gorard, S. et al (2017d): Gorard, S., Siddiqui, N. and See, B.H. (2017) 'Can "Philosophy for Children" improve primary school attainment?', *Journal of Philosophy of Education* (http://onlinelibrary.wiley.com/doi/10.1111/1467-9752.12227/abstract).

Gorard, S. et al (2017e): Gorard, S., Boliver, V., Siddiqui, N. and Banerjee, P. (2017) 'Which are the most suitable contextual indicators for use in widening participation to HE?', *Research Papers in Education* (http://dx.doi.org/10.1080/02671522.2017.1402083).

Gordon, D., Iwamoto, D., Ward, N., Potts, R. and Boyd, E. (2009) 'Mentoring urban Black middle school male students: Implications for academic achievement', *Journal of Negro Education*, 78, 3, 277-89.

Gottfredson, L. (2004) 'Intelligence: Is it the epidemiologists' elusive "fundamental cause" of social class differences in health?', *Journal of Personality and Social Psychology*, 86, 174-99.

Gottfried, M. (2014) 'Does classmate ability influence students' social skills?', *School Effectiveness and School Improvement*, doi:10.1080/09243453.2014.988731.

Gray, J., Goldstein, H. and Thomas, S. (2001) 'Predicting the future: the role of past performance in determining trends in institutional effectiveness at A level', *British Educational Research Journal*, 27, 4, 391-405

Greenbank, P. (2006) 'Institutional admissions policies in higher education', *International Journal of Educational Management*, 20, 4, 249-60.

Haahr, J., with Nielsen, T., Hansen, E. and Jakobsen, S. (2005) *Explaining pupil performance: Evidence from the international PISA, TIMSS and PIRLS surveys*, Taastrup, Denmark: Danish Technological Institute (www.danishtechnology.dk).

Halliday, J. (2017) 'George Osborne: North-south divide in schools needs urgent attention', The Guardian, 3 February (www.theguardian.com/society/2017/feb/03/george-osborne-england-north-south-divide-schools-needs-urgent-attention-education-gap).

Halsey, A. and Gardner, L. (1953) 'Selection for secondary education and achievement in four grammar schools', *The British Journal of Sociology*, 4, 1, 60-75.

Hand, A., Gambles, J. and Cooper, E. (1994) *Individual commitment to learning. Individuals' decision-making about lifelong learning*, Employment Department Research Series 42, London: HMSO.

Harris, R. (2012) 'Geographies of transition and the separation of lower and higher attaining students in the move from primary to secondary school in London', *Transactions*, doi:10.1111/j.1475-5661.2012.519.x.

Harris, R. and Ratcliffe, M. (2005) 'Socio-scientific issues and the quality of exploratory talk – What can be learned from schools involved in a "collapsed day" project?', *The Curriculum Journal*, 16, 4, 439-53.

Harrison, N. (2011) 'Have the changes introduced by the 2004 Higher Education Act made higher education admissions in England wider and fairer?', *Journal of Education Policy*, 26, 3.

Harrison, N. and McCraig, C. (2015) 'An ecological fallacy in higher education policy', *Journal of Further and Higher Education*, 39, 6, 793-816.

Harrison, N. and Hatt, S. (2009) 'Knowing the "unknowns"', *Journal of Further and Higher Education*, 33, 4, 347-57.

Hattie, J. (2008) *Visible learning*, London: Routledge.

Hattie, J. and Timperley, H. (2007) 'The power of feedback', *Review of Educational Research*, 77, 1, 81-112.

Hayenga, A. and Corpus, J. (2010) 'Profiles of intrinsic and extrinsic motivations: A person-centered approach to motivation and achievement in middle school', *Motivation and Emotion*, 34, 4, 371-83.

Heck, R. and Moriyama, K. (2010) 'Examining relationships among elementary schools' contexts, leadership, instructional practices, and added-year outcomes', *School Effectiveness and School Improvement*, 21, 4, 377-408.

HEFCE (Higher Education Funding Council for England) (2008) *Strategically important and vulnerable subjects, Final report of the 2008 Advisory Group*, Bristol: HEFCE (www.hefce.ac.uk/data/year/2008/Strategically,important,and,vulnerable,subjects,Final,report,of,the,2008,advisory,group,/).

HEFCE (2013) *Non-continuation rates at English HEIs: Trends for entrants 2005-06 to 2010-11*, Bristol: HEFCE (www.hefce.ac.uk/pubs/year/2013/201307/).

Henderson, B. (2008) 'The importance of districts', *School Effectiveness and School Improvement*, 19, 3, 261-74.

Henry, J. and Thornton, K. (2001) 'Shortage puts GCSE maths in jeopardy', *Times Educational Supplement*, 5 October.

Herrnstein, R.J. and Murray, C. (1994) *The Bell Curve: Intelligence and class structure in American life*, New York: Free Press.

Herts, R. (1990) 'The impact of parental involvement on reading achievement in a desegregated elementary school environment', Unpublished EdD dissertation, Arkansas, AR: University of Arkansas.

Heywood, P., Stephani, A. and Garner, P. (2017) 'The Cochrane Collaboration: Institutional analysis of a knowledge commons', *Evidence & Policy: A Journal of Research, Debate and Practice* (https://doi.org/10.1332/174426417X15057479217899).

Honig, M., Venkateswaran, N. and McNeil, P. (2017) 'Research use as learning', *American Educational Research Journal*, 54, 5, 936-71.

Hoover, E. (1941) 'Interstate redistribution of population 1850-1940', *Journal of Economic History*, 1, 199-205.

Horne, M. (2001) *Classroom assistance: Why teachers must transform teaching*, London: Demos.

Hoskins, B., Janmaat, J., Han, C. and Muijs, D. (2014) 'Inequalities in the education system and the reproduction of socioeconomic disparities in voting in England, Denmark and Germany', *Compare*, doi:10.1080/03057925.2014.912796.

Hoskins, S., Newstead, S. and Dennis, I. (1997) 'Degree performance as a function of age, gender, prior qualifications and discipline studies', *Assessment and Evaluation in Higher Education*, 22, 317-28.

House of Commons (1997) *Teacher recruitment: What can be done?, Education and Employment Committee First Report, Vol II*, London: The Stationery Office.

House of Commons (2000) *Sixth report of the Education and Employment Committee, Minutes of Evidence*, 15 March.

House of Commons Library (2017) *Grammar school statistics*, Briefing Paper #1398 (http://researchbriefings.files.parliament.uk/documents/SN01398/SN01398.pdf).

Howson, J. (2001) 'Forsake history but don't leave maths in the lurch', *Times Educational Supplement*, 20 April.

Hoyle, R. and Robinson, J. (2003) 'League tables and school effectiveness: A mathematical model', *Proceedings of the Royal Society of London B*, 270, 113-99.

Hramiak, A. (2001) 'Widening participation and ethnic minority women', Annual SCUTREA Conference Proceedings (http://explore.tandfonline.com/content/ed/rred-thirtieth-anniversary-virtual-special-issue).

Hudson, C. (2005) *Widening participation in higher education art and design: Part 2 Questionnaire report*, Winchester: Council for Higher Education in Art and Design.

Hutchings, M., Greenwood, C., Hollingworth, S., Mansaray, A. and Rose, S. with Minty, S. and Glass, K. (2012) *Evaluation of the City Challenge programme*, Research Report DFE-RR215, London: Department for Education (www.gov.uk/government/uploads/system/uploads/attachment_data/file/184093/DFE-RR215.pdf).

Ingersoll, R. (2001) 'Teacher turnover and teacher shortages: An organisational analysis', *American Educational Research Journal*, 38, 3, 499-534.

Jacob, B. and Wilder, T. (2010) *Wilder educational expectations and attainment*, NBER Working Paper No 15683, Cambridge, MA: National Bureau of Economic Research.

Jacobs, N. (2013) 'Understanding school choice', *Education and Urban Society*, 45, 4, 459-82.

Jenkins, S., Micklewright, J. and Schnepf, S. (2008) 'Social segregation in secondary schools: How does England compare with other countries?', *Oxford Review of Education*, 34, 1, 21-37.

Jerrim, J. and Vignoles, A. (2015) 'University access for disadvantaged children: A comparison across countries', *Higher Education*, 70, 6, 903-21.

Johnson, M. (2001) *Making teacher supply boom-proof*, London: Institute for Public Policy Research.

Johnson, W., McGue, M. and Iacono, W. (2010) 'How parents influence school grades: Hints from a sample of adoptive and biological families', *Learning and Individual Differences*, 17, 3, 201-19.

Jones, G. (1996) *Wales 2010: Three years on*, Cardiff: Institute of Welsh Affairs.

Kalogrides, D. and Loeb, S. (2013) 'Different teachers, different peers', *Educational Researcher*, 42, 6, 304-16.

Kelly, S. and Monczunski, L. (2007) 'Overcoming the volatility in school-level gain scores: A new approach to identifying value-added with cross-sectional data', *Educational Researcher*, 36, 5, 279-87.

Kim, J., Guryan, J., White, T., Quinn, D., Capotosto, L. and Kingston, H. (2016) 'Delayed effects of a low-cost and large-scale summer reading intervention on elementary school children's reading comprehension', *Journal of Research on Educational Effectiveness*, 9, Suppl 1.

Kintrea, K., St Clair, R. and Houston, M. (2011) *The influence of parents, places and poverty on educational attitudes and aspirations*, York: Joseph Rowntree Foundation.

Kirkman, E., Sanders, M., Emanuel, N. and Larkin, C. (2016) 'Does social action help boost the skills young people need to succeed in adult life?', The Behavioural Insights Team, 15 January (www.behaviouralinsights.co.uk/education-and-skills/does-social-action-help-develop-the-skills-young-people-need-to-succeed-in-adult-life/).

Kluger, A. and DeNisi, A. (1998) 'Feedback interventions: Towards the understanding of a double-edge sword', *Current Directions in Psychological Science*, 7, 67-72.

Knight, D. and Strunk, K. (2016) 'Who bears the costs of district funding cuts', *Educational Researcher*, 45, 7, 395-406.

Kyriacou, C., Benmansour, N., Coulthard, M., Hultgren, A. and Stephens, P. (2002) 'Images of teaching: An international comparison', in A. Ross (ed) *Emerging issues in teacher supply and retention: Proceedings of the Second Conference of the Teacher Supply and Retention Project*, University of North London, London: Institute for Policy Studies in Education, pp 77-82.

Kyriakides, L. (2008) 'Testing the validity of the comprehensive model of educational effectiveness: A step towards the development of a dynamic model of effectiveness', *School Effectiveness and School Improvement*, 19, 4, 429-46.

Lamprianou, I. (2009) 'Comparability of examination standards between subjects: An international perspective', *Oxford Review of Education*, 35, 2, 205-26.

Lang, L., Schoen, R., LaVenia, M. and Oberlin, M. (2014) 'Mathematics formative assessment system – Common core state standards: A randomized field trial in kindergarten and first grade', Society for Research on Educational Effectiveness, SREE Spring Conference, 6-8 March, Washington, DC (http://files.eric.ed.gov/fulltext/ED562773.pdf).

Lee, C. (2003) 'Why we need to re-think race and ethnicity in educational research', *Educational Researcher*, 32, 5, 3-5.

Lee, J. (2006) 'Free courses failed to reel in adult learners', *Times Educational Supplement FE Focus*, 23 June, p 1.

Lee, M. and Madyun, N. (2008) 'School racial composition and academic achievement: The case of Hmong LEP pupils in the USA', *Educational Studies*, 34,4, 319-31.

Levačić, R. and Marsh, A. (2007) 'Secondary modern schools: Are their pupils disadvantaged?', *British Educational Research Journal*, 33, 2, 155-78.

Lewis, S. (2017) 'Governing schooling through "what works": The OECD PISA for schools', *Journal of Education Policy*, 32, 3, 281-302.

Liebowitz, D. (2014) 'Does school policy affect housing choices? Evidence from the end of desegregation in Charlotte-Mecklenburg', *American Educational Research Journal*, 51, 4, 671-703.

Lin, K.S., Cheng, Y.Y., Chen, Y.L. and Wu, Y.Y. (2009) 'Longitudinal effects of educational expectations and achievement attributions on adolescents' academic achievement', *Adolescence*, 44, 176, 911-24.

Lloyds Bank (2016) 'Parents willing to pay £53,000 more to live near a top school', 7 September (www.lloydsbankinggroup.com/Media/Press-Releases/2016-press-releases/lloyds-bank/house-prices-near-schools/).

Logan, J., Minca, E. and Adar, S. (2012) 'The geography of inequality: Why separate means unequal in American public schools', *Sociology of Education*, 85, 3, 287-301.

Louis, K., Dretzke, B. and Wahlstrom, K. (2010) 'How does leadership affect student achievement? Results from a national US survey', *School Effectiveness and School Improvement*, 21, 3, 315-36.

Lowell, L. and Salzman, H., (2007) *Into the eye of the storm: Assessing the evidence on science and engineering education, quality, and workforce demand*, Washington, DC: Urban Institute.

Luyten, H., Merrell, C. and Tymms, P. (2017) 'The contribution of schooling to learning gains of pupils in Years 1 to 6', *School Effectiveness and School Improvement*, 28, 3, 374-405.

Lysakowski, R. and Walberg, H. (1982) 'Instructional effects of cues, participation, and corrective feedback: A quantitative synthesis', *American Educational Research Journal*, 19, 559-78.

MacBeath, J. (2012) *Evaluating provision, progress and quality of learning in the Children's University*, Leadership for Learning, Cambridge: Faculty of Education, University of Cambridge (www.childrensuniversity.co.uk/media/13021/cu_evaluation_2012-13_full.pdf).

Manning, A. and Pischke, J. (2006) *Comprehensive versus selective schooling in England in Wales: What do we know?*, IZA Discussion Paper No 2072, Bonn: IZA (https://papers.ssrn.com/sol3/papers.cfm?abstract_id=898567).

Marks, G. (2015) 'The size, stability and consistency of school effects', *School Effectiveness and School Improvement*, 26, 3, 397-414.

Marley, D. (2009) 'A third of schools bore their classes', *Times Educational Supplement*, 9 January, p 12.

Marsh, C. and Blackburn, R. (1992) 'Class differences in access to higher education in Britain', in R. Burrows and C. Marsh (eds) *Consumption and class: Divisions and change*, London: Macmillan, pp 184-211.

Martin, K., Sharp, C. and Mehta, P. (2013) *The impact of the summer schools programme on pupils*, Report to National Foundation for Educational Research (https://www.nfer.ac.uk/publications/ESSP04/ESSP04researchbrief.pdf).

Matsudaira, J. (2008) 'Mandatory summer school and student achievement', *Journal of Econometrics*, 142, 2, 829-50.

McBer, H. (2000) *Research into teacher effectiveness: A model of teacher effectiveness*, Research Report No 216, London: Department for Education and Employment (DfEE).

McCaffrey, D., Sass, T., Lockwood, J. and Mihaly, K. (2009) 'The intertemporal variability of teacher effect estimates', *Education Finance and Policy*, 4, 4, 572-606.

McCoy, S., Banks, J. and Shevlin, M. (2012) 'School matters: How context influences the identification of different types of special educational needs', *Irish Educational Studies*, 31, 2, 119-38.

Melkonian, M. and Areepattamannil, S. (2017) 'The effect of absolute age-position on academic performance: A study of secondary students in the United Arab Emirates', *Educational Studies* (http://dx.doi.org/10.1080/03055698.2017.1382330).

Mendolia, S., Paloyo, A. and Walker, I. (2016) *Heterogeneous effect of high school peers in educational outcomes*, IZA Discussion Paper 9795, Bonn, Germany: IZA (http://ftp.iza.org/dp9795.pdf).

Merrell, C. and Tymms, P. (2005) 'The impact of early interventions and pre-school experience on the cognitive development of young children in England', Presentation at American Educational Research Association Annual Conference, Montreal, April.

Metcalf, H. (2005) 'Paying for university: The impact of increasing costs on student employment, debt and satisfaction', *National Institute Economic Review*, 191, January, 106-17.

Mickelson, R. and Nkomo, M. (2012) 'Integrated schooling, life course outcomes, and social cohesion in multiethnic democratic societies', *Review of Research in Education*, 36, 1, 197-238.

Miles, K. (2010) 'Mastery learning and academic achievement', *Dissertation Abstracts International Section A, Humanities and Social Sciences*.

Moore, J., Mountford-Zimdars, A. and Wiggans, J. (2013) *Contextualised admissions: Examining the evidence*, Cheltenham: Supporting Professionalism in Admissions Programme.

Morgan, P. and Farkas, G. (2016) 'Are we helping all the children that we are supposed to be helping?', *Educational Researcher*, 45, 3, 226-8.

Muller, M. and Hofmann, V. (2016) 'Does being assigned to a low school track negatively affect psychological adjustment?', *School Effectiveness and School Improvement*, 27, 2, 95-115.

Mwetundila, P. (2001) 'Gender and other student level factors influencing the science achievement of 13-14 year old Australian', MA (Ed) Thesis, Flinders University of South Australia.

NACETT (National Advisory Council for Education and Training Targets) (1994) *Review of the National Targets for Education and Training: Proposals for consultation*, London: NACETT.

NAO (National Audit Office) (2002) *Widening participation in higher education in England*, London: The Stationery Office.

Nelson, F. (2016) 'The best state schools have pulled ahead of private schools. Why is that so hard to accept?', *The Spectator*, 28 February (http://blogs.spectator.co.uk/2016/02/the-best-state-schools-have-pulled-ahead-of-private-schools-why-is-that-so-hard-to-accept/).

Neve, T., Feraz, H. and Nata, G. (2017) 'Social inequality in access to higher education: Grade inflation in private schools and the ineffectiveness of compensatory education', *International Studies in Sociology of Education*, 26, 2, 190-210.

Newton, P. (1997) 'Measuring comparability of standards across subjects: Why our statistical techniques do not make the grade', *British Educational Research Journal*, 23, 4, 433-49.

Ni, Y. (2012) 'The sorting effect of charter schools on student composition in traditional public schools', *Educational Policy*, 26, 2, 215-42.

NIACE (National Institute for Adult and Continuing Education) (2003) *Adults Learning Survey – 2003*, Leicester: NIACE.

NSF (National Science Foundation) (2008) *Science and engineering indicators* (www.nsf.gov/statistics/seind08/c2/c2s2.htm).

Nuttall, D., Goldstein, H., Presser, R. and Rasbash, H. (1989) 'Differential school effectiveness', *International Journal of Educational Research*, 13, 7, 769-76.

OECD (Organisation for Economic Co-operation and Development) (2014) *Education at a Glance 2014: OECD indicators*, Paris: OECD Publishing (www.oecd-ilibrary.org/education/education-at-a-glance-2014_eag-2014-en).

OFFA (Office for Fair Access) (2015) *Strategic plan: 2015-2020*, Bristol: OFFA.

Ofsted (2007) *Ofsted TellUs2 survey summary and technical manual* (www.ttrb.ac.uk/viewArticle2.aspx?contentId=14193).

Osborne, J. and Collins, S. (2000) *Students' and parents' views of the school science curriculum*, London: Kings' College London.

Osborne, J. and Dillon, J. (2008) *Science education in Europe: Critical reflections. A report to the Nuffield Foundation*, London: Nuffield Foundation.

Owens, A., Reardon, S. and Jencks, C. (2016) 'Income segregation between schools', *American Educational Research Journal*, 54, 3, 1159-97.

Palardy, G. (2013) 'High school socioeconomic segregation and student attainment', *American Educational Research Journal*, 50, 4, 714-54.

Parker, P., Jerrim, J., Schoon, I. and Marsh, H. (2016) 'A multination study of socioeconomic inequality in expectations for progression to higher education', *American Educational Research Journal*, 53, 1, 6-32.

Parr, A. and Bonitz, V. (2015) 'Role of family background, student behaviors, and school-related beliefs in predicting high school dropout', *The Journal of Educational Research*, 108, 6, 504-14.

Parsons, S., Green, F., Ploubidis, G., Sullivan, A. and Wiggins, R. (2017) 'The influence of primary schooling on children's learning', *British Educational Research Journal*, 43, 5, 823-47.

Payne, J. (1998) *Routes at sixteen: Trends and choices in the nineties*, DfES Research Brief No 55, London: Department for Education and Skills.

Pells, R. (2017) '"Staggeringly high" numbers of teachers threatening to quit the classroom', *The Independent*, 28 May (www.independent. co.uk/news/education/education-news/staggeringly-high-teachers-quit-classroom-recruitment-crisis-retention-schools-funding-education-a7760551.html).

Perry, T. (2016) 'English value-added measures: Examining the limitations of school performance measurement', *British Educational Research Journal* (http://onlinelibrary.wiley.com/doi/10.1002/berj.3247/full).

Pettigrew, A., Hendry, C. and Sparrow, P. (1989) *Training in Britain. A study of funding, activity and attitudes. Employers perspectives on human resources*, London: HMSO.

Phelan, J., Choi, K., Vendlinkski, T., Baker, E. and Herman, J. (2011) 'Differential improvement in student understanding of mathematical principles following formative assessment intervention', *Journal of Educational Research*, 104, 5, 330-9.

Pring, R. (2009) 'Education cannot compensate for society: Reflections on the Nuffield Review of 14-19 Education and Training', *Forum*, 51, 2, 197-204.

Pugh, G. and Mangan, J. (2003) 'What's in a trend? A comment on Gray, Goldstein and Thomas (2001)', *British Educational Research Journal*, 29, 1, 77-82.

Pumfrey, P. (2008) 'Moving towards inclusion? The first-degree results of students with and without disabilities in higher education in the UK: 1998-2005', *Journal European Journal of Special Needs Education*, 23, 1, 31.

Raffe, D., Croxford, L., Iannelli, C., Shapira, M. and Howieson, C. (2006) *Social-class inequalities in education in England and Scotland*, Special Briefing 40, Edinburgh: Centre for Educational Sociology (www.ces.ed.ac.uk/PDF%20Files/Brief040.pdf).

Rees, G., Fevre, R., Furlong, J. and Gorard, S. (1997) 'History, place and the learning society: Towards a sociology of lifetime learning', *Journal of Education Policy*, 12, 6, 485-97.

Reid, I. and Caudwell, J. (1997) 'Why did secondary PGCE students choose teaching as a career?', *Research in Education*, 58, 46-58.

Reynolds, A., Temple, J., Ou, S.-R., Arteaga, I. and White, B. (2011) 'School-based early childhood education and age-28 well-being: Effects by timing, dosage and subgroups', *Science*, 333, 6040, 360-4.

Riccio, J., Dechausay, N., Greenberg, D., Miller, C., Rucks, Z. and Verma, N. (2010) *Toward reduced poverty across generations: Early findings from New York City's conditional cash transfer program*, New York: MDRC.

Ritchie, S. and Tucker-Drob, E. (2017) 'How much does education improve intelligence?', *PsyArXiv Preprints* (https://psyarxiv.com/kymhp).

Roew, E. and Lubienski, C. (2017) 'Shopping for schools or shopping for peers', *Journal of Education Policy*, 32, 3, 340-56.

Rutt, S. and Styles, B. (2013) *Analysis of academy school performance in the 2011 and 2012 GCSEs*, Slough: NFER.

Rutter, M., Maughan, B., Mortimore, P. and Ouston, J. (1979) *Fifteen thousand hours: Secondary schools and their effects on children*, London: Open Books.

Salisbury, J., Rees, G. and Gorard, S. (1999) 'Accounting for the differential attainment of boys and girls at school', *School Leadership and Management*, 19, 4, 403-26.

Salway, S., Allmark, P., Barley, R., Higinbottom, G., Gerrish, K. and Ellison, G. (2010) 'Researching ethnic inequalities', *Social Research Update*, 58, 1-4.

Sanders, W. (2000) 'Value-added assessment from pupil achievement data', *Journal of Personnel Evaluation in Education*, 14, 4, 329-39.

Sanders, W. and Horn. S. (1998) 'Research findings from the Tennessee Value-Added Assessment System (TVAAS) database', *Journal of Personnel Evaluation in Education*, 12, 3, 247-56.

Sanders, W. and Rivers, J. (1996) *Cumulative and residual effects of teachers on future pupil academic achievement*, Knoxville, NT: University of Tennessee, Value-added Research and Assessment Center.

San-Segundo, M. and Valiente, A. (2003) 'Family background and returns to schooling in Spain', *Education Economics*, 11, 1, 39-52.

Santry, C. (2017) 'Teacher shortage crisis deepens, new DfE figures show', *Times Educational Supplement*, 22 June (www.tes.com/news/school-news/breaking-news/teacher-shortage-crisis-deepens-new-dfe-figures-show).

Sargant, N. and Aldridge, F. (2002) *Adult learning and social division: A persistent pattern, Volume 1*, Leicester: NIACE.

Schmidt, W., Burroughs, N., Zoido, P. and Houang, R. (2015) 'The role of schooling in perpetuating educational inequality: An international perspective', *Educational Researcher*, 44, 7, 371-86.

Schoolsnet (2001) 'Paradox lost', *Educational Journal*, 56, 1.

School Teachers' Review Body (2001) *Tenth report*, London: The Stationery Office.

School Teachers' Review Body (2002) *Eleventh report*, London: The Stationery Office.

Schwinger, M., Steinmayr, R. and Spinath, B. (2009) 'How do motivational regulation strategies affect achievement? Mediated by effort management and moderated by intelligence', *Learning and Individual Differences*, 19, 4, 621-27.

Scott, J. (2004) 'Family, gender, and educational attainment in Britain: A longitudinal study', *Journal of Comparative Family Studies*, 35, 4, 569-89.

Scott, S. (2016) 'Higher teacher leaving rate in a decade – And 6 other things we learned about the school workforce', *Schools Week*, 30 June.

Searle, J. and Tymms, P. (2007) 'The impact of headteachers on the performance and attitudes of pupils', in J. O'Shaughnessy (ed) *The leadership effect: Can headteachers make a difference?*, London: Policy Exchange, pp 18-42.

See, B.H. and Gorard, S. (2015a) 'The role of parents in young people's education – A causal study', *Oxford Review of Education*, 41, 3, 346-66.

See, B.H. and Gorard, S. (2015b) 'Does intervening to enhance parental involvement in education lead to better academic results for children? An extended review', *Journal of Children's Services*, 10, 3, 252-64.

See, B.H., Gorard, S. and Siddiqui, N. (2016) 'Teachers' use of research evidence in practice: a pilot study of the use of feedback to enhance learning', *Educational Research*, 58, 1, 56-72.

See, B.H., Gorard, S. and Siddiqui, N. (2017a) 'Impact of participation in uniformed group activities at school on adolescence' self-confidence and teamwork', *International Journal of Educational Research*, 85C, 109-20.

See, B.H., Torgerson, C. and Gorard, S. (2012) 'Promoting post-16 participation of ethnic minority students from disadvantaged backgrounds: A systematic review of the most promising interventions', *Research in Post-Compulsory Education*, 17, 4, 409-22.

See, B.H., Morris, R., Gorard, S. and Griffiths, N. (2017b) *UK Space Agency Principia Education Programme report: The reach and spread of its projects*, Report to the UK Space Agency.

Selwyn, N. and Gorard, S. (2002) *The information age: Technology, learning and social exclusion in Wales*, Cardiff: University of Wales Press.

Selwyn, N. and Gorard, S. (2003) 'Reality bytes: Examining the rhetoric of widening educational participation via ICT', *British Journal of Educational Technology*, 34, 2, 169-81.

Selwyn, N. and Gorard, S. (2004) 'Exploring the role of ICT in facilitating adult informal learning', *Education, Communication and Information*, 4, 2/3, 293-310.

Selwyn, N. and Gorard, S. (2016) 'Students' use of Wikipedia as an academic resource', *The Internet and Higher Education*, 28, January, 28-34.

Selwyn, N., Gorard, S. and Furlong, J. (2006) 'Adults' use of computers and the internet for self-education', *Studies in the Education of Adults*, 38, 2, 141-59.

Selwyn, N., Gorard, S. and Williams, S. (2001) 'Digital divide or digital opportunity? The role of technology in overcoming social exclusion in US education', *Educational Policy*, 15, 2, 258-77.

Selwyn, N., Gorard, S., Furlong, J. and Madden, L. (2003) 'Older adults' use of ICT in everyday life', *Ageing and Society*, 23, 5, 561-82.

Selzam, S., Krapohl, E., von Stumm, S., Rimfield, K., Kovas, T., Dale, P., et al (2016) 'Predicting educational achievement from DNA', *Molecular Psychiatry*, 22, 2, 267-72.

Shankler, A. (1992) 'Choosing teachers and choosing to teach', in E. Boe and D. Gilford (eds) *Teacher supply, demand and quality*, Washington, DC: National Academy Press, pp 12-18.

Shepherd, J. and Rogers, S. (2012) 'Church schools shun poorest students', *The Guardian*, 5 March.

Siddiqui, N. and Gorard, S. (2017) 'Comparing government and private schools in Pakistan: The way forward for universal education', *International Journal of Educational Research*, 82, 159-69.

Siddiqui, N., Gorard, S. and See, B.H. (2015) 'Accelerated reader as a literacy catch-up intervention during the primary to secondary school transition phase', *Educational Review*, 68, 2, 139-54.

Siddiqui, N., Gorard, S. and See, B.H. (2017a) *Children's University and Youth Social Action*, Evaluation Report and Executive Summary, London: Education Endowment Foundation.

Siddiqui, S., Gorard, S. and See, B.H. (2017b) 'Can programmes like Philosophy for Children help schools to look beyond academic attainment?', *Educational Review* (http://dx.doi.org/10.1080/00131 911.2017.1400948).

Skaalvik, E. and Skaalvik, S. (2009) 'Self-concept and self-efficacy in mathematics: Relation with mathematics motivation and achievement', *Journal of Education Research*, 3, 3, 255-78.

Slater, J. (2000) 'We've seen it all before: The current teacher crisis is nothing new', *Times Educational Supplement*, 8 September, p 24.

Sloane, F. and Gorard, S. (2003) 'Exploring methodological aspects of design experiments', *Educational Researcher*, 32, 1, 29-31, 35-7.

Smith, E. and Gorard, S. (2005) '"They don't give us our marks": The role of formative feedback in student progress', *Assessment in Education*, 12, 1, 21-38.

Smith, E. and Gorard, S. (2006) 'Pupils' views of equity in education', *Compare*, 36, 1, 41-56.

Smith, E. and Gorard, S. (2007a) 'Who succeeds in teacher training?', *Research Papers in Education*, 22, 4, 465-82.

Smith, E. and Gorard, S. (2007b) 'Improving teacher quality: lessons from America's No Child Left Behind', *Cambridge Journal of Education*, 37, 2, 191-206.

Smith, E. and Gorard, S. (2011) 'Is there a shortage of scientists? A re-analysis of supply for the UK', *British Journal of Educational Studies*, 59, 2, 159-77.

Smith, E. and Gorard, S. (2012) '"Teachers are kind to those who have good marks": A study of Japanese young people's views of fairness and equity in schools', *Compare*, 42, 1, 27-46.

Smithers, A. and Robinson, P. (2000) *Coping with teacher shortages*, Liverpool: University of Liverpool, Centre for Education and Employment Research.

Smithers, R. (2001) 'Teacher job crisis on eve of new school year', *The Guardian*, 30 August, p 1.

SRA (Social Research Association) (2003) *Ethics guidelines* (http://the-sra.org.uk/research-ethics/ethics-guidelines)

Southby, K. and South, J. (2016) *Volunteering, inequalities and barriers to volunteering: A rapid evidence review*, Leeds: Leeds Beckett University (http://eprints.leedsbeckett.ac.uk/3434/1/Barriers%20to%20volunteering%20-%20final%2021st%20November%202016.pdf).

SPA (Social Policy Association) (2016) 'How is contextualised admissions used?' (www.spa.ac.uk/resources/how-contextualised-admissions-used).

Speight, N. (2010) 'The relationship between self-efficacy, resilience and academic achievement among African-American urban adolescent students', *Dissertation Abstracts International, B: Sciences and Engineering*, 70, 12, 7840-

St Clair, R. and Benjamin, A. (2011) 'Performing desires: The dilemma of aspirations and educational attainment', *British Educational Research Journal*, 37, 3, 501-17.

Sullivan, A., Parsons, S., Wiggins, R., Heath, A. and Green, F. (2014) 'Social origins, school type and higher education destinations', *Oxford Review of Education*, 40, 6, 739-63.

Symonds, J. and Gorard, S. (2010) 'The death of mixed methods? Or the rebirth of research as craft', *Evaluation and Research in Education*, 23, 2, 121-36.

Tang, W. (2004) 'Investigating the factors influencing educational attainment across ethnic and gender groups: Structural analysis of NELS:88-2000 database', *Dissertation Abstracts International Section A, Humanities and Social Sciences*.

Taningco, M. and Pachon, H. (2008) *Computer use, parental expectations, and Latino academic achievement*, Los Angeles: Tomas Rivera Policy Institute, University of Southern California.

Tannock, S. (2008) 'The problem of education-based discrimination', *British Journal of Sociology of Education*, 29, 5, 439-49.

Taylor, C. and Gorard, S. (2001) 'Participation of Welsh students in higher education 1995/6 to 1998/99', *Welsh Journal of Education*, 10, 2, 55-71.

Taylor, C. and Gorard, S. (2005) *Participation in higher education: Wales, Report for independent study into devolution of the student support system: The Rees Review*, Cardiff: National Assembly for Wales.

Taylor, C., Fitz, J. and Gorard, S. (2005) 'Diversity, specialisation and equity in education', *Oxford Review of Education*, 31, 1, 47-69.

Taylor, C., Gorard, S. and Fitz, J. (2003) 'The modifiable areal unit problem: Segregation between school and levels of analysis', *International Journal of Social Research Methodology*, 16, 1, 41-60.

Televantou, I., Marsh, H., Kyriakides, L., Nagengast, B., Fletcher, J. and Malmberg, L. (2015) 'Phantom effects in school composition research', *School Effectiveness and School Improvement*, 26, 1, 75-101.

Terzian, M. and Moore, K. (2009) *What works for summer learning programs for low-income children and youth?*, Washington, DC: Child Trends (https://www.researchgate.net/publication/242573051_WHAT_WORKS_FOR_SUMMER_LEARNING_PROGRAMS_FOR_LOW-INCOME_CHILDREN_AND_YOUTH_Preliminary_Lessons_from_Experimental_Evaluations_of_Social_Interventions_1).

Tomlinson, S. (2012) 'The irresistible rise of the SEN industry', *Oxford Review of Education*, 38, 3, 267-86.

Triventi, M. (2011) 'Stratification in higher education and its relationship with social inequality: A comparative study of 11 European countries', *European Sociological Review*, 29, 3, 489-502.

Turkheimer, E., Haley, A., Waldron, M., D'Onofrio, B. and Gottesman, I. (2003) 'Socioeconomic status modifies heritability of IQ of young children', *Psychological Science*, 14, 6, 623-8.

Tuttle, C., Teh, B.-R., Nichols-Barrer, I., Gill, B. and Gleason, P. (2010) *Student characteristics and achievement in 22 KIPP middle schools: Final report*, Washington, DC: Mathematica Policy Research, Inc.

Tymms, P. (2003) *School composition effects*, Durham: School of Education, Durham University, January.

Tymms, P., Coe, R. and Merrell, C. (2005) *Standards in English schools: Changes since 1997 and the impact of government policies and initiatives*, Report for the *Sunday Times* (www.times-archive.co.uk/onlinespecials/english_in_schools.html).

Universities Scotland (2016) *Futures not backgrounds*, Edinburgh: Universities Scotland (www.universities-scotland.ac.uk/wp-content/uploads/2016/09/10537-%E2%80%A2-Futures-Not-Backgrounds-web.pdf).

Uttl, B., White, C. and Wong Gonzalez, D. (2017) 'Meta-analysis of faculty's teaching effectiveness: Student evaluation of teaching ratings and student learning are not related', *Studies in Educational Evaluation*, 54, 22-42.

van Dorn, R., Bowen, G. and Blau, J. (2006) 'The impact of community diversity and consolidated inequality on dropping out of high school', *Family Relations*, 55, 105-18.

van Houtte, M. and Stevens, P. (2010) 'School ethnic composition and aspirations of immigrant students in Belgium', *British Educational Research Journal*, 36, 2, 209-37.

Vieluf, S., Hochweber, J., Klieme, E. and Kunter, M. (2015) 'Who has a good relationship with teachers?', *Oxford Review of Education*, doi:120.1080/03054985.2014.992874.

Villiger, C., Niggli, A. and Kutzelmann, S. (2012) 'Does family make a difference? Mid-term effects of a school/home-based intervention program to enhance reading motivation', *Learning and Instruction*, 22, 2, 79-91.

Walford, G. (2004) 'No discrimination on the basis of irrelevant qualifications', *Cambridge Journal of Education*, 34, 3, 353-61.

Wallace, C. (2005) *Science paper: Socioeconomic status and intelligence*, Omaha, NE: Creighton University (www.icherney.com/Teaching/Courses/Intelligence/Science%20Papers/Erin_Wallace.doc).

Ward, F., Thurston, M. and Alford, S. (2009) *RESPECT: A personal development programme for young people at risk of social exclusion. Final report*, Chester: University of Chester.

Welsh Office (1997) *A bright future: Beating the previous best*, Cardiff: Welsh Office.

White, P. and Gorard, S. (2017) 'Against inferential statistics: How and why current statistics teaching gets it wrong', *Statistics Education Research Journal*, 16, 1, 55-65.

White, P., Gorard, S., Fitz, J. and Taylor, C. (2001) 'Regional and local differences in admission arrangements for schools', *Oxford Review of Education*, 27, 3, 317-37.

Whitesell, N., Mitchell, C., Spicer, P. and The Voices of Indian Teens Project Team (2009) 'A longitudinal study of self-esteem, cultural identity, and academic success among American Indian adolescents, cultural diversity & ethnic minority', *Psychology*, 15, 1, 38-50.

Williams, M. and Husk, K. (2012) 'Can we, should we, measure ethnicity?', *International Journal of Social Research Methodology*, 16, 4.

Williams, P. (1979) *Planning teacher demand and supply*, Paris: UNESCO.

Woodfield, R. (2011) 'Age and first destination employment from UK universities: Are mature students disadvantaged?', *Studies in Higher Education*, 36, 4, 409-25.

Woodfield, R. (2017) 'Undergraduate students who are required to withdraw from university: The role of ethnicity', *British Educational Research Journal*, 10.1002/berj.3259.

Yates, J. and James, D. (2013) 'The UK clinical aptitude test and clinical course performance at Nottingham: A prospective cohort study', *BMC Medical Education*, 13, 32.

Yeung, R. and Phuong Nguyen-Hoang, P. (2016) 'Endogenous peer effects: Fact or fiction?', *The Journal of Educational Research*, 109, 1, 37-49.

Index